Dialogue with the Past

AMERICAN ASSOCIATION FOR STATE AND LOCAL HISTORY BOOK SERIES

ABOUT THE SERIES

The American Association for State and Local History Book Series publishes technical and professional information for those who practice and support history and addresses issues critical to the field of state and local history. To submit a proposal or manuscript to the series, please request proposal guidelines from AASLH headquarters: AASLH Book Series, 1717 Church St., Nashville, Tennessee 37203. Telephone: (615) 320-3203. Fax: (615) 327-9013. Web site: www.aaslh.org.

ABOUT THE ORGANIZATION

The American Association for State and Local History (AASLH) is a nonprofit educational organization dedicated to advancing knowledge, understanding, and appreciation of local history in the United States and Canada. In addition to sponsorship of this book series, the association publishes the periodical *History News*, a newsletter, technical leaflets and reports, and other materials; confers prizes and awards in recognition of outstanding achievement in the field; and supports a broad education program and other activities designed to help members work more effectively. To join the organization, contact: Membership Director, AASLH, 1717 Church St., Nashville, Tennessee 37203.

Dialogue with the Past

Engaging Students & Meeting Standards through Oral History

GLENN WHITMAN

ALTAMIRA

P R E S S

A Division of

ROWMAN & LITTLEFIELD PUBLISHERS, INC.

Walnut Creek • Lanham • New York • Toronto • Oxford

AltaMira Press
A division of Rowman & Littlefield Publishers, Inc.
1630 North Main Street, #367
Walnut Creek, CA 94596
www.altamirapress.com

Rowman & Littlefield Publishers, Inc.
A wholly owned subsidary of The Rowman & Littlefield Publishing Group, Inc.
4501 Forbes Boulevard, Suite 200
Lanham, MD 20706

PO Box 317
Oxford
OX2 9RU, UK

British Library Cataloguing in Publication Information Available

Library of Congress Cataloging-in-Publication Data
Whitman, Glenn, 1969–
   Dialogue with the past : engaging students and meeting standards through oral history / Glenn Whitman.
      p. cm. — (American Association for State and Local History book series)
   Includes bibliographical references and index.
   ISBN 0-7591-0648-7 (alk. paper) — ISBN 0-7591-0649-5 (pbk. : alk. paper)
   1. Oral history—Study and teaching (Secondary) I. Title. II. Series.

   D16.14.W48 2004
   907'.1'2—dc22   2004004643

Printed in the United States of America

♾™ The paper used in this publication meets the minimum requirements of American National Standard for Information Sciences—Permanence of Paper for Printed Library Materials, ANSI/NISO Z39.48-1992.

To Debra and Grace Whitman

The oral history project is a rare breed in terms of combining education with interaction to the most productive degree. Not only did it teach us about history, but it taught the larger message of respect and responsibility that comes with historical knowledge. With this project, I learned that we were historians, and that I could actually take a part in what had previously been a cold and aloof school subject. History was no longer this large and daunting entity that had nothing to do with me and which I read in a large, boring textbook; it was living and I was part of its preservation. With this realization, I came to regard our class as potential contributors to a larger cause; we could be Studs Terkel, too. It was our job to accurately and thoroughly relay a story, and to do this required great amounts of responsibility and reflection. To get this feeling, I think it is essential that the teacher treat students with respect. This project can't simply be something a teacher assigns to students to keep them busy. If done correctly, it becomes a life lesson. This happens when you respect students as fellow historians, as this is the role they are fulfilling with this project. Impress upon them that this project is not just another paper; it is someone else's life. If you believe your students are a contributing force to history, so will they. The only "negative" thing I took away from the project was a daunting and scary sense of the vast unrecorded narrative out there. This project made me want to take my little tape recorder and sit down for an hour or two with everyone I met; people became not just people but potential storybooks of enlightenment. The project also, at least for me, made me think about larger issues such as time and mortality. Oral historians are constantly working a race against time to get the stories people harbor before they disappear.

—Drew Saylor, St. Andrew's Episcopal School student who in 1999 interviewed Mindy Farber, a member of the first class of women to integrate Johns Hopkins University in 1970.

Contents

Foreword

HIGH SCHOOL STUDENTS AND MIDDLE SCHOOL STUDENTS not only can *learn* history but also can *do* history. Indeed, they often do history better than they learn it. That's what Glenn Whitman has learned from years of experience in getting his students to do oral history with everyone from their grandmothers to high officials in the federal government.

Teachers are ready to get their students into a *Dialogue with the Past*. That's what I have learned from several years of experience running workshops across America based on ideas in *Lies My Teacher Told Me*. I have met thousands of teachers who encourage their students to go beyond the textbook, and oral history is one of the best ways to do this.

Students are ready to do oral history. Every spring I am a judge for National History Day, and I meet youngsters excited about their projects. The best of them rely on interviews students did themselves. One year our team gave its highest rating to a young man who had chosen to study Jackie Robinson. From his small hometown in South Carolina, he had conducted telephone interviews with Mrs. Robinson, two members of the Brooklyn Dodgers front office (by my memory), and two of Robinson's teammates. He had read at least two biographies of Robinson, of course, and enough other history to place him in context. He knew about the nadir of race relations and knew, therefore, that Robinson was not the first African American in the major leagues, but the first *in the twentieth century*. The young man had done fine work, and his project took second place in his division.

Many of Glenn Whitman's students found their oral history projects to be life-altering experiences. They describe new rapport with relatives, new depths of understanding about topics in the past such as the role of women or World War II, and a new passion for history or for school in general. While doing oral history, they learn precisely the skills—library research, preparation, interviewing, note taking, evaluation of sources, critical thinking, writing, editing, presenting—that they will need in careers, as citizens, and in life itself.

Does Whitman's location near Washington, D.C., make it easier for his students to find interesting subjects? Yes, but the Internet and telephone mitigate this problem, as my example from South Carolina shows. Moreover, every community has interesting elders who have lived through important national events and have riveting stories to tell about them. Is oral history only for students at independent schools? No. Whitman interviews teachers who have used it with marvelous results at public schools from the inner city to remote rural areas. Is it only for your better students? No. Whitman reports important improvement in students at all ranges of past performance. Are there pitfalls? Yes, and Whitman tells how to avoid them, in an appealing question-and-answer format that walks teachers through the process ahead of time. Is the whole idea of oral history just pie in the sky in this era of teaching to the test? No. Whitman shows how oral history can dovetail with state-mandated social studies standards and exams.

In short, Whitman not only persuades that oral history is important; he also shows how to teach students to do it, every step of the way, including a collection of valuable appendixes.

But I cannot close without my own pleading on behalf of Whitman's book and the products that will result from it. The benefits described thus far arise from the *process* of oral history and accrue to its practitioners—the students—and sometimes to those interviewed. The *product* too is important, and Glenn Whitman does not neglect it. After your middle school students interview elderly women focusing on the effect of the Great Depression and their response to it, or after one of your sophomores completes a good project on the recent rise of the Republican Party in your formerly Democratic town, get them to make it presentable, grammatical, and organized, and then *bind three copies*—for the author, your school library, and your community library. Now they have created "a book," and only with that last step do they actually create history—a written legacy for the future. And that legacy is important.

As Whitman notes, with every passing year, sources die and events are forgotten, making important topics harder to research via oral history. So I want to end this foreword on a note of special pleading: don't introduce your students to oral history only because it will make your courses more interesting—although it will. Don't do so only because it will be one of the most important learning experiences of their entire K–12 education—although it will. Also do it for me and for the legion of other social scientists and historians who will come upon your students' work ages hence—perhaps after you and they are gone—and will learn important things about your community and how it was to live in what we, from our limited perspective, call "modern times."

James W. Loewen
Catholic University of America
January 2004

Preface

MUCH OF THE WRITING OF *DIALOGUE WITH THE PAST* TOOK place during a yearlong paternity leave from teaching. During that time I had the chance to conduct a very different type of oral history project with our newborn daughter Grace who, thankfully, was a great napper. The decision to break after my first decade as a history teacher was also driven by the encouragement of educators to write an all-encompassing resource to aid them in the integration of oral history into their classrooms or programs. Such a resource, I believed, would also benefit my daughter and future students. By the time Grace begins her high school career, most veterans of World Wars I and II and the Great Depression will be gone, and so will their stories. However, if current students are empowered to conduct oral history interviews with these individuals, their voices will be forever preserved so that my daughter, and future generations, can learn about the past through those who lived it.

I also hope this book inspires educators already in, or planning to become part of, this most important profession to reflect on how we teach. Writing this book represents my belief that educators have a responsibility to share successful projects and ideas with each other. I must also admit that this book was partially written out of regret. Despite my experience teaching students the value of oral history, and how to be oral historians, I failed to follow my own advice and missed the opportunity to interview my grandmother Berdie. With her passing went a vital part of our family's history. This experience shapes my teaching each year as I remind students that depending on the project, the best interviewees might be in their own family.

This book, like any oral history project, is the product of many voices. The students, educators, and all who read drafts, extended advice, and edited various aspects of the book are, in essence, coauthors of this work. I cannot say enough about the student oral historians I worked with on the American Century Project at St. George's School, Blair Academy, and St. Andrew's Episcopal School. Their work has truly been inspirational and educational for me. In the face of extended concern about the historical illiteracy of American students, it is reassuring to know that when challenged to do the work of professional historians, students can make lasting contributions to the nation's "archives of memory."[1]

I am greatly indebted to the many educators at both public and independent institutions who shared their experiences and oral history projects with me. Over the years I have adapted many of their ideas to my work with students, as reflected in the variety of worksheets, class activities, and reproducible materials available throughout this book. While this book seeks to spread the gospel of oral history as an educational and historical methodology, a significant number of exemplary projects are already in place in schools across the country. Many of these projects appear in this book, and they set a high standard for all future oral history projects. The proliferation of the World Wide Web into the classroom allows for access to student work from across the country that is highlighted here. It should be noted, however, that web addresses do change, and materials are sometimes withdrawn from the Internet. What is perhaps unique to this book is its connection to our project's website, www.americancenturyproject.org, a resource for educators, students, and researchers. Over the years this website has been revised though the efforts of a number of my students who dedicated countless hours to this project. A special thanks is extended to Jeremy Brown, who has probably taught me more about website design than I ever taught him about oral history.

Heartfelt thanks needs to go to my colleagues Charlie Malcolm, Ruth Faison, Alex Haight, and Anne Masciuch, who reviewed many of the following pages and have been strong supporters of oral history at St. Andrew's. I am also a great fan of the work editors do to make my work look even better. Particular thanks to my good friend, and great teacher in her own right, Laureen Bonin, as well as Beth Whitman and Beth Luey. Financial assistance came early through two much appreciated professional development grants from the St. Andrew's Episcopal School Parents Association. As a first-time author I was fortunate to have the guidance of Susan Walters at AltaMira Press through every revision of this book. She made the challenges associated with writing less daunting.

I am deeply grateful for the immeasurable advice shared by Donald A. Ritchie, whom I first met on a flight home from the Oral History Association's annual meeting in New Orleans in 1997, and who has been a mentor to me ever since. His influence on my thinking about oral history is reflected both directly and indirectly in the pages that follow. Additional thanks are extended to Dr. Barry Lanman, one of the hardest-working oral history educators I know (even in retirement). And, to my best friend and wife, Debra, you are, and always will be, my why. (At least until we're 103.)

In the final analysis, it is my hope that this book furthers the discussion—which began long before I became an educator—about oral history as a historical and educational methodology and its potential benefits for students. As with oral history itself, we can learn a lot from listening to one another.

NOTE

1. This phrase is taken from the book of the same title by Alice M. Hoffman and Howard S. Hoffman, *Archives of Memory: A Soldier Recalls World War II* (Lexington: University Press of Kentucky), 1991.

CHAPTER 1

Introduction: The Case for Oral History in Your Classroom or Program

The oral presentations were most impressive. The students are poised and articulate beyond their years. The extent of research, analysis, conclusion reaching, and development into the final product showed they responded to the challenge in a dynamic manner. I'm sure that they got out of the project more than they put in, and their rewards will be an enriched appreciation for history and their individual subjects. I have always loved history, but there would have been an even greater affection if there had been this kind of project along the way of my studies.

—Korean War veteran Colonel William D. Davis, interview by St. Andrew's Episcopal student David Mushal, 1997

FOR A MOMENT, THINK BACK TO YOUR EXPERIENCE AS A history student.[1] If you were like me, you recall a textbook-centered, lecture-oriented class that did not get past covering World War II. The format of the class possibly resembled the educational philosophy of Thomas Gradgrind, the dictatorial teacher in Charles Dickens's *Hard Times,* who declares to his village schoolroom students, "Now what I want is Facts. Stick to the facts, sir!" This "Gradgrindian" philosophy of education remains alive in classrooms across the country and gains increased attention with the expansion of outcome-based testing and the emphasis on covering, rather than uncovering, material. Therefore, it should not come as a surprise that the first word students often associate with their history classes is "boring."[2] Such characterizations of the history classroom should leave educators perplexed, as few disciplines can match history in the richness of material and utility for living in the present. The textbook-centered, fact-driven, lecture-oriented class that continues to predominate in schools lacks emotion and does not help students connect with a past that seems relevant to their lives. But if the use of a textbook is balanced for students by having them conduct an oral history interview, their outlook on studying the past is altered. One student, after conducting an oral history project

with a veteran of World War II, even discovered that "there was history before I was born." Thus the purpose of this book: to provide an all-inclusive resource to facilitate educators' immediate integration of oral history methods into their classrooms or programs. Students can then make a human connection with the past that they remember longer than the writings of Jefferson and Lincoln.

Oral history is a historical method that uses recorded interviews to preserve firsthand memories, accounts, and interpretations of a person's life, an event, a place, a way of life, or period. These interviews and supporting materials are then preserved and made available to researchers through an archive, library, state or local historical society that have become more accessible through the World Wide Web.[3] Oral history differs from other mediums that rely heavily on interviews with individuals, such as journalism, "because of the purpose for which the materials are collected, their immediate intended use, and plans made for disposition and long-term availability of all original materials. Something cannot be considered oral history if it lacks a structured interview, the thorough research necessary to prepare for the interview, emphasis on depth and detail of information collected, and adherence to strict processing techniques."[4] Oral history is often part of the fieldwork of folklorists; what differentiates the two is the materials each discipline collects. Whereas the oral historian focuses solely on firsthand information, folklorists collect stories, songs, and artifacts that have shaped communities, whether factual or fictional.

The process and product associated with oral history have immeasurable benefits for educators and students. Few projects that I have encountered at the middle and high school level require such a wide range of skills and intelligences. Through each phase of the oral history process, students are developing and refining valuable primary and secondary source research skills as well as their writing, editing, interviewing, active listening and questioning techniques, and their ability to analyze, interpret, and evaluate information.

Moreover, an oral history project requires students to engage with adults. Such interaction helps build intergenerational bridges and foster respect, empathy, and understanding between these two segments of society. These are essential skills not only for an individual's academic success but also for life.[5] Equally important in an oral history project is the final product. The pride and self-confidence students gain from producing materials that give meaning to an individual's life, as well as helping democratize the historical record, alters their outlook on their role as students.

I have led the American Century Project at three different schools with up to seventy-five students in a given year who had a range of abilities and interest in history. What makes this project unique is that it is perpetual and that every student participates in each phase of the oral history process. The project's title is derived from *Life* magazine editor Henry Luce's 1941 declaration of the twentieth century as the "American century." Just seven years after Luce's pronouncement, the first modern oral history archive was established at Columbia University by Allan Nevins, who sought "an organization which [would make] a systematic attempt to obtain from the lips and papers of American who had lived significant lives, a fuller record of their accomplishments." It spawned similar archives in other parts of the United States and the world as the century progressed. The convergence of this time period and the increased acceptance and use of oral history as a historical methodology allowed for a fuller chronicling of this dynamic period that was shaped by the lives and experiences of individuals that reflect America's racial, economic, and class diversity but are not *yet* equally represented in the history of the time. In the end, the American Century Project seeks to balance what Clifford Kuhn identifies as the "master narrative of history" through a permanent oral history archive that is one of the largest among middle and high schools in the country.[6] Since the development of this project, over three hundred oral history interviews have been conducted with individuals who served in each war of the twentieth century, helped end racial segregation, were the first beneficiaries of Title IX, were newly immigrated to America, or became the first woman Supreme Court justice.

The project grew out of my own introduction to oral history while enrolled in a historical methods class as a naive Dickinson college freshman. One of the requirements for that course was to conduct an oral history interview. Little did I realize how much my experience interviewing three Vietnam veterans at the

Carlisle, Pennsylvania, VFW hall would shape my teaching philosophy. The project also reflects the central tenant of my teaching—to empower students with the opportunity to be and think like historians and to understand how history is shaped and reshaped. Students must therefore experience the functions of a historian. An oral history project provides a laboratory in which students further their understanding of how history is recorded. The traditional reading and interpretation of primary and secondary source documents is balanced by a historical source that has continually gained increased acceptance by historians, and is an original source that students can produce themselves and even fills gaps in their learning. For example, a student interviewed former Washington, D.C., mayor Marion Barry on his work during the civil rights movement. In his analysis of the interview's historical value, the student made a convincing claim that his interview "offers more in-depth detail into the Civil Rights Movement and it gives information on motives and the conflicts concerning the events that might not be given in traditional historical texts. An example of how this interview gives a clearer view on the Civil Rights Movement is shown in the account of the 'Birmingham Incident' in our class textbook (John Garraty's, *The Short History of the American Nation*). Though this sets up a foundation for the events that occurred in Birmingham in 1963, it does not even compare to the detail that is given from a man who was behind the scenes and involved in the decisions at this incident."[7] However, by combining these two sources, students gain a broader understanding of civil rights in America (see table 1.1).

Dialogue with the Past demonstrates that there is a place for an oral history project in all types of middle and high school classrooms and home schools; geographical location does not limit the ability to conduct an oral history project. In addition, every community has residents with interesting and important stories to tell. As the Southern Oral History Program's motto highlights, "You don't have to be famous for your life to be history."[8] Moreover, equipment to conduct recorded phone interviews is reasonably priced and allows for limitless possibilities of project topics and potential interviewees (sometimes referred to as the narrator). Oral history is flexible enough to integrate into existing curriculum in a variety of ways and also helps foster interdisciplinary work. Thirty-one different oral history projects appear throughout this book that have been conducted at twenty-eight different public middle and high schools across the country

Table 1.1. Textbook History versus Oral History

Textbook	Interview with Marion Barry
After leading a series of demonstrations in Birmingham, Alabama, in 1963, King was thrown in jail. When local white clergymen urged black leaders to cease their "untimely" protests, which (the clergymen claimed) "incite hatred and violence," King wrote his now-famous "Letter from a Birmingham Jail." . . . The brutal repression of the Birmingham demonstrations brought a flood of recruits and money to the protesters' cause.	Well again, here we are almost nine years after Brown, almost three from the sit-in movement, a number of cities had desegregated because of the movement, Nashville went in 1960, before I left the restaurants and movie theatres were desegregated. In Birmingham it was just awful, they were not about to do anything. When they were ordered to integrate their swimming pools they closed them up. Not only did they close them up, they put concrete over the pool so you could not swim in them again unless you wanted to drill through the concrete. In a lot of incidents in which cities closed pools, black people would jump the fence and swim in them anyway. They would get arrested and start a protest and other things of that type. But Birmingham had a police chief by the name of Bull Connor, he was one mean white person. He was sort of a stereotypical, tobacco spitting, red neck kind of guy. So they started the sit-in movement there, and Dr. King came up with the idea to fill the jails up. And the people who were ready were young people. A lot of adults were scared, they didn't want to take off from work, the young people were fearless. They went to sit-in and got arrested. You've seen the pictures, dogs attacking, biting them. Dr. King got arrested and wrote his famous "Letter from a Birmingham Jail." We all were outraged but excited that young people were doing this. If you look at revolutions around the world many of them are started and acted on by young people. So we were real proud of them. Again, it focused the nation. Can you imagine being in New York City or Chicago watching on your television screen and all of a sudden you see these dogs biting someone on the legs or a policeman hitting a child with a club or a child being sprayed by water hoses? It's so powerful. It was awful but it helped lead to the Civil Rights Act of 1964.

Source: Quoted from John A. Garraty and Mark C. Carnes, *A Short History of the American Nation* (New York: Longman, 2001), 510.

(including three independent schools). These projects have taken place in courses and schools that emphasize place-based education, service learning, and community service and with students who are mainstream, honors, advanced placement, "at-risk," homeschooled, and affected by learning disabilities. Within this collection of schools are programs that cater to the most advanced students as well as those who need alternative education structures. An oral history project is a natural fit into a history or social studies class, and is often associated with the U.S. history survey course. The exemplary projects throughout this book also reflect the efforts of students enrolled in English, foreign language, science, and musical theater courses or programs. Three of the projects allow students to contribute to a national effort: National History Day, the Veterans History Project, and the Sharing History Project. Since a student's learning should not be limited to a classroom, oral history projects also create a unique opportunity for collaboration between schools and state and local museums and libraries. Such collaboration provides important institutional support and helps debunk the four major concerns educators have with implementing an oral history project: it takes too much time, costs too much money, is limited by one's geographic location, and requires specific equipment (each concern is addressed in this book). Such local support and research also helps fulfill a curriculum requirement that most states have about understanding local history. As an example, seventh grade students in Texas study the history of their state from early times to the present. One of the requirements of the Texas Essential Knowledge and Skills for Social Studies (TEKS) for middle school students is: "The student understands how individuals, events, and issues shaped the history of Texas during the 20th century."[9] An understanding of local history is an integral part of nearly every state's curriculum standards at the middle and high school level. Such knowledge can be attained from a variety of sources, including oral histories, and in conjunction with state and local historical societies, museums, and libraries.

The American Century Project has been conducted with the most advanced and the least motivated students, including students for whom English is a second language. At its core, *Dialogue with the Past* is a call to action and a challenge to educators. Take risks in your classrooms or programs to create young oral historians! This book not only celebrates the important contributions students can make to the preservation of history but also models a nationally recognized oral history project that educators can adapt to their own circumstances. This is a unique addition to the growing literature on oral history because it is entirely focused on the pedagogical needs of educators while giving careful consideration to the impact an oral history project has on students.

- This book is based on more than ten years of field-testing project ideas and resources and is written by an educator who has conducted an oral history project each year with his students and can empathize with the challenges educators face (chapter 2).
- It examines oral history as both a historical and educational methodology (chapters 2–3).
- It answers many of the questions educators have about the use of oral history in their classes or programs (chapters 3–6, 8). These are questions that all those who have ever conducted an oral history project wish they had answered from the outset. Such questions include deciding on what is an appropriate project, where and how to fit a project into the curriculum, how to find interviewees, what are some of the legal and ethical considerations, what is the best equipment to use considering the limits to school and program budgets, what should be included in a transcript, what should be done when the project is complete.
- It provides classroom activities, suggested readings, mock interviews, transcript analysis, classroom activities, and oral history source evaluation guidelines that help prepare students for their work as oral historians (chapters 2–5, 8, appendix).
- It includes interviews with educators and students (chapters 6–7) who have been part of an oral history project to show how the project can be adopted and how it affects students.
- It includes a rich collection of excerpted interviews conducted by students (chapter 8). Each interview was selected for its historical significance and explanation of the strengths and weaknesses of student interviewing.

- It provides assessment rubrics and alternative evaluation guidelines for middle and high school projects, such as an oral history interview portfolio, to measure a student's progress and understanding (chapter 9 and appendixes 15–17).
- It demonstrates how an oral history project meets national standards established by the Oral History Association, Bradley Commission on History in Schools (now the National Council for History Education), National Center for History in the Schools, National Council for the Social Studies, and standards of learning from nine different states (chapter 9).
- It is supported by an interactive website—www.americancenturyproject.org—that allows teachers and students to exchange ideas about oral history.
- It addresses the important link between oral history and the use of technology in the classroom, including the use of PowerPoint, website design, and video documentary, as well as current equipment that is affordable to schools on limited budgets.
- It provides educators with all the resources necessary to conduct an oral history project—*in one place*—and the ability for them to return to their classrooms or programs and implement a project immediately with reproducible forms found in the appendix. This is an important incentive to the large percentage of overworked, underpaid teachers in today's classrooms.

The book's audience—current and aspiring educators, students, as well as researchers—will learn how an oral history project reinvigorates the study of history and provides a more meaningful, enduring, and enjoyable classroom experience. (The use of the term "educators" highlights the fact that a student's learning is not limited to the traditional classroom setting. Therefore, the term seeks to include classroom teachers, educational program and homeschool teachers and directors, school administrators, and curriculum specialists. Each of these groups has the ability to reinvigorate the teaching and studying of the past through the integration of an oral history project into a classroom or program.) In addition, educators and public historians who work with students outside the traditional classroom setting, such as state and local historical societies as well as museum education programs, will see the benefits of a student-driven oral history project and the opportunities available to coordinate with schools. The important contributions students can make to preserving the national memory is evidenced by the exchange between Blair Bjellos and Joan Muller for a project that examined nurses in Vietnam.[10]

Joan Muller (interviewee): Why are you focusing on the nurse? I'm just curious.

Blair Bjellos (interviewer): Every year the AP History class does a documentary. This is the first year we've done oral histories so we could make a longer and more thorough [documentary]. My teacher met this man who works at St. Andrews and he has a whole website about doing oral histories. After college he became really interested in oral histories and he has all his history classes do oral histories and they get to choose any topic they want and our teacher chose nurses in Vietnam for our documentary.

JM: That's really impressive and nice. I thought when I came back from Vietnam I'd really like to talk about my experiences and I've never done it, well, probably one other time, but it was informal. This is the most I've done. I thought, wow, it's been thirty years, but I got to do it.

BB: I'm so glad I got to do this.

Although an oral history project is not the answer to all that ails America's classrooms, it provides students with a more authentic opportunity to connect with the past. For educators interested in reinvigorating the teaching and studying of history, an oral history project is flexible enough to be integrated into the curriculum at any grade level, across disciplines, regardless of student ability or geographic location. All we now need are students who want to participate in the preservation of the past. Every classroom has such students.

NOTES

1. Unless intentionally differentiated, the term "history" throughout this book includes social studies.

2. James Loewen, *Lies My History Teacher Told Me* (New York: Touchstone, 1996), 10.

3. For additional definitions of oral history, see Donald A. Ritchie, *Doing Oral History* (London: Oxford University Press, 2003), 19; and Barbara W. Sommer and Mary Kay Quinlan, *The Oral History Manual* (Walnut Creek, Calif.: Alta Mira, 2002), 1. The Oral History Association defines oral history as "past events and ways of life. It is both the oldest type of historical inquiry, predating the written word, and one of the most modern, initiated with tape recorders in the 1940s" (omega.dickinson.edu/organizations/oha).

4. Sommer and Quinlan, *Oral History*, 3. The similarities and differences between journalism and oral history are further examined in Mark Feldstein, "Kissing Cousins: Journalism and Oral History," *Oral History Review*, Winter–Spring 2004, 1–22.

5. Jerrold Hirsch, "Before Columbia: The Federal Writers' Project and American Oral History Research," in *Portrait of America: A Cultural History of the Federal Writer's Project* (Chapel Hill: University of North Carolina Press, 2003), 141. See also Allan Nevins, *The Gateway to History* (Boston: Appleton-Century, 1938).

6. Clifford Kuhn, "In the Trenches: How Civil Rights Were Won," *New York Times*, March 26, 1997, C14.

7. Marion Barry, interview by Nathan Fleming, December 28, 2000. Available at www.americancenturyproject.org and archived at St. Andrew's Episcopal School.

8. The Southern Oral History Program is located at the University of North Carolina, Chapel Hill. Available at www.sohp.org/mission/index.html.

9. "Chapter 113: Texas Essential Knowledge and Skills for Social Studies Subchapter B. Middle School." Texas Education Agency. www.tea.state.tx.us/rules/tac/chapter113/ch113b.html.

10. Joan Muller, interviewed by Blair Bjellos, January 17, 2003. Available at the Connelly School of the Holy Child: www.holychild.org.

CHAPTER 2

The Student Oral Historian

I left the interview [feeling like a] historian, already deciding what I would do differently the next time.

—Student at St. Andrew's Episcopal School

AT THE LLANO GRANDE CENTER FOR RESEARCH AND DEvelopment in rural Texas, students created intergenerational bridges with community elders though oral history interviews. These interviews recorded the social history of their economically depressed but culturally vibrant communities. Middle school science and English students in Norfolk, Virginia, conducted interviews of residents from Tylerton, Smith Island on the Chesapeake Bay. South Kingstown High School students had an unusual English class experience as they examined both the tumultuous events of World War II and 1968 through conversations with fellow Rhode Islanders. In Allegany County, Maryland, identified by teacher Dan Whetzel as "a poor town rich in history," high school students created the largest collection of silk records in the country through an oral history project on the Lonaconing Silk Mill. Public middle school students in Montclair, New Jersey, uncovered their community's history of desegregation through oral history interviews of town residents in a yearlong language arts and social studies project. And Foxfire (www.foxfire.org), the pioneering secondary school project that began in 1966 at the Rabun Gap-Nacoochee High School, an Appalachian community in Georgia, continues to serve as a model for educators seeking to enhance students' language and writing skills by combining oral history and folklore. These are just a few examples of the expansion of oral history across curriculum, grades, and socioeconomic levels.

Each of these projects represents the diverse opportunities available for middle and high school students to engage with the living past. When I began teaching, I integrated my own experience as a student oral historian into a philosophy that provides students the opportunity to be and think like historians. But when I begin each course by asking, "What does a historian do?" I am often amazed by the difficulty students have in answering the question. Considering how history continues to be taught, their reaction is not surprising. My students have to learn that history does not center on memorizing dates and names from textbook readings. History classes should be balanced between providing historical context for understanding contemporary issues, while at the same time serving as a first step in the training of the next generation of historians and history teachers.

Consequently, over the course of a year, my students are assessed on their ability to function as historians. Each class is exposed to a wide range of primary and secondary source documents from which students develop individual interpretations of the past. More significantly, however, I have them do an oral history project. Often, as a result of this project, students feel empowered by the opportunity to "do history," to directly engage with those individuals who made, witnessed, or were part of history, rather than spend the year reading about voiceless men and women in textbooks.

WHAT WE DO: THE AMERICAN CENTURY PROJECT

Classroom oral history projects generally fall into one of two categories: biographical/life review interviews or projects that usually focus on a particular theme, an event, period, topic, or place.[1] Our project is unique in that it is perpetual: each class of students adds to the rich collection of interviews archived in the school library. However, equal emphasis is placed on the oral history process and the final product, two complementary educational goals. The decision to focus on an expansive period—the American or twentieth century—as opposed to a specific event or narrower time frame, which is generally the case for most oral history projects, allows students more flexibility to pursue an area of their interest. As a student once commented, "I think that the Oral History Project was one of the first times that I was ever challenged with the freedom of selecting a topic, actively pursuing that interest, then individually refining the results into a manageable product that could be handed in. Because the project was self-driven from start to end, we had a chance to truly own the project." Moreover, as students research, they become "experts" in their topic. Thus, when we arrive at that point of our study of U.S. history, they are, in essence, coteachers for the course. Although each interview provides only a snapshot of a particular period or event from one individual's perspective, when combined with the collection of interviews generated over the years, a broad and deep history of the American century emerges.

The project is integrated into a U.S. history survey course in which national themes of race, war, culture, and politics have led students to interview some prominent individuals, especially because of our close proximity to the nation's capital. However, more and more students are looking past their initial desire to secure an interview with the most famous person possible by conducting interviews on events and with persons of local interest. This decision often emerges out of a student's realization—and with a small push by this teacher—that they can contribute more to the records of state and local historical institutions as their interviews complement, supplement, or fill in the missing gaps of an institution's collection that might lack orally communicated historical sources.[2] This collection of interviews serves as an important reminder of how individuals shape their community.

The following outline highlights each phase of the American Century Project and illustrates how each part contributes to a historically reliable, valid interview. Throughout the process students are developing all of the skills required of a historian as well as working toward preparing a bound copy of their work for public presentation and an institutional archive.

Oral History Method Training

An integral part of the American Century Project that reinforces itself through each phase of the project is training students to understand the challenges associated with oral history as a historical methodology. Such training actually begins when students discuss their summer reading of Studs Terkel's *My American Century* at the beginning of the school year and continues after reading portions of Donald A. Ritchie's *Doing Oral History* just prior to the project's introduction in early November. Method workshops for interviewee selection, interview preparation, and transcription techniques take place during the course of the project. Students apply their evolving understanding of the oral history process in a mini-interview and transcription that takes place over two nights and is titled "Where

Were You?" It focuses on the days surrounding the assassination of John F. Kennedy.

Interviewee Selection

Students are responsible for selecting an individual of no relation to interview about a particular period or event in American history. This is a formidable, yet enriching task for most students. The objective is to take students out of their comfort zone by requiring them to interview a nonfamily member. Interviewees must be willing to sign a release form that allows access to tapes, transcripts, electronic publications, and additional materials, though restrictions can be attached. Over the years, permission to publish transcripts on the Internet has been an important addition to the release. Without a release, interviews would be inaccessible. (See appendix 7.)

Biography

Students develop a one-page biography (with photograph) that provides a sense of the interviewee's background and a context for understanding the place of the interview in each person's life.

Historical Contextualization

After securing an interviewee, students are responsible for a research paper (approximately 7–10 pages) that examines primary and secondary source documents, creating a context for better understanding the interview. Students are expected to include in their source selection "newspapers of the day" as well as what leading historians say about the period, event, or person the interview covers. Requiring students to conduct in-depth research into their subject allows them to become "experts" on a particular period or event and provides them with a context for developing interview questions. Throughout the project, students are constantly reminded that they can never do enough research in preparation for their interviews. (See appendix 13.)

Interview and Transcription

Each interview is expected to last approximately one hour, which usually equals six hours of transcription— often the most dreaded part of the project for students.[3] Prior to the interview, students use their research to formulate a logically ordered set of questions that are refined during a conference with the teacher. Even with a list of prepared questions, the unpredictability of an oral history interview challenges students to think on their feet by developing follow-up questions for clarification or further exploration. An important skill developed in this phase is listening, which allows for what *Doing Oral History* author Donald A. Ritchie once explained to my students was one of the most important follow-up questions: "I didn't know that, can you tell me more?" Students are required to transcribe the entire interview as well as to provide an audio/video time indexing log. (See appendixes 11–12.)

Historical Analysis

Students' ability to determine the historical value of their interview is an essential skill in training them to be and think like historians. It also teaches students to analyze the strengths and weaknesses of oral history as a historical methodology. In a three- to five-page paper, students are required to determine where their interview fits into the existing history that they uncovered in their historical contextualization and how it might add or detract from an overall understanding of the American past. Students examine questions as to whether their interview was biased, if it shed new light on a particular period or event, and whether or not it comple-

ments or contradicts the research they collected prior to conducting their interview. Students are also expected to examine their own biases and consider how their place in time might foster certain questions and responses. They begin the analysis of their interview by completing the Written Document Analysis Worksheets from the National Archives and Records Administration (www.archives.gov). (See appendix 14.)

Final Product

Students submit two bound copies of their project as well as their interview tapes. One bound copy is archived while the other is graded and returned. An additional copy is given to the interviewee. The bound copy includes a statement of purpose, biography (with photograph), historical contextualization, transcription, historical analysis, and works consulted page.

Public Presentation

At the end of the project students must present their interview to a general audience that includes their interviewees at the Annual Oral History Coffee House.

Figure 2.1.   Oral History Coffeehouse attendee viewing a student's poster exhibition. (Photo by Ruth Faison, St. Andrew's Episcopal School)

This event celebrates the work of the student oral historians and the lives of those they interviewed. Over the years, students have transformed their interviews into poster exhibits, one-act plays, PowerPoint presentations, and even an interpretive dance, which are shared with the community during the Annual Oral History Coffee House.[4] With written permission, their interviews are also posted on the project website, www.americancenturyproject.org—making them accessible to a worldwide audience.

ORAL HISTORY AS AN EDUCATIONAL METHODOLOGY

When I began teaching, my mentor gave me a "learning pyramid" that significantly influenced my interest in empowering students with their own learning (figure 2.2).[5] Since most aspects of an oral history project—in particular the interview—fall toward the base of this pyramid, students are remembering more when they are actively involved in the learning process.

An oral history project also allows students to experience each of the five interdependent "dimensions of learning," identified as confidence and independence, skills and strategies, knowledge and understanding, use of prior and emerging experience, and reflection.[6]

In addition, an oral history project is a more authentic assessment of a student's work as a historian. According to Grant Wiggins, of the Center on Learning, Assessment, and School Structure (CLASS), "Assessment ought to be educative in the basic sense that students are entitled to direct testing that educates them about the purpose of schooling and the nature of adult work. Authentic tasks thus supply greater incentives for students to persist with day-in and day-out learning and insight into the reasons for specific lessons. An assessment task, problem, or project is authentic if it:

(1) Is realistic;
(2) Requires judgment and innovation;
(3) Asks the student to 'do' the subject;
(4) Replicates or simulates the contexts in which adults are 'tested' in the workplace, in civil life, and in personal life;
(5) Assesses the student's ability to efficiently and effectively use a repertoire of knowledge and skills to negotiate a complex task;
(6) Allows appropriate opportunities to rehearse, practice, consult resources, and get feedback on and refine performances and products."[7]

An oral history project certainly meets all of Wiggins's criteria while at the same time satisfying national and

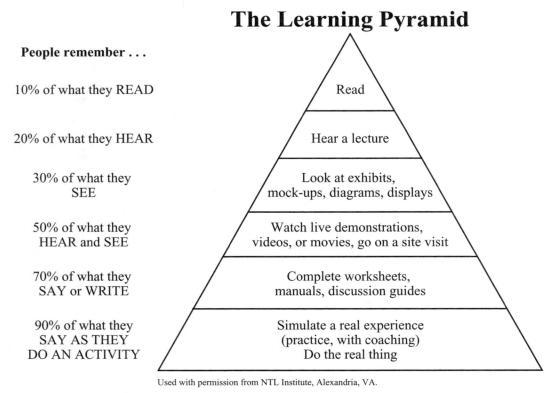

The Learning Pyramid

People remember . . .

10% of what they READ — Read

20% of what they HEAR — Hear a lecture

30% of what they SEE — Look at exhibits, mock-ups, diagrams, displays

50% of what they HEAR and SEE — Watch live demonstrations, videos, or movies, go on a site visit

70% of what they SAY or WRITE — Complete worksheets, manuals, discussion guides

90% of what they SAY AS THEY DO AN ACTIVITY — Simulate a real experience (practice, with coaching) Do the real thing

Used with permission from NTL Institute, Alexandria, VA.

Figure 2.2.   The Learning Pyramid

Living History Lessons

By BARBARA RUBEN
Special to The Washington Post

PHOTOS BY MARK FINKENSTAEDT FOR THE WASHINGTON POST

From D-Day to Duvalier's Haiti, from communism in Stalinist Russia to communes in Arlington, students at a Potomac school are listening to the voices of the 20th century rather than reciting musty facts from a history textbook. Through an extensive school-based oral history project, students at St. Andrews Episcopal School have interviewed immigrants and White House luminaries, Holocaust survivors and hippies.

Daniel Kleinman, 17, a junior from Bethesda, talked with Jody Powell about his years as a White House press secretary for his advanced placement U.S. history class.

It was fascinating to hear Powell's interpretation of Jimmy Carter's presidency, said Kleinman, adding that Powell had a remarkable view of the period, from the press at the Camp David accords to the hostage situation in Iran.

Kleinman, who is considering a career as a journalist, said, "This gave me a whole different perspective on the press than I'd get from a reporter."

For Whitney Cummings, the oral history

See HISTORY, Page 10, Col. 1

Laura Barringer, above left, wanted to know more about school desegregation, so she interviewed Elizabeth Campbell, 96, who was active in desegregation efforts in Arlington. At right, Kate Zeller reads from her interview with a Cuban immigrant. The St. Andrews history students showed off their work to fellow students, parents and their interview subjects during an open house, below.

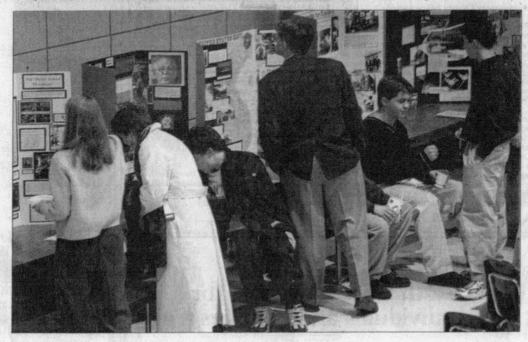

Figure 2.3. *Washington Post* article following the annual Oral History Coffee House.

state standards of learning that are discussed in detail in chapter 9. As Alistair Ross points out in "Children Becoming Historians," "the best way to acquire the skills and attitudes that historians have is to practice them in real inquiry. Oral history presents a rich field for such investigation, and one that is immediately and excitingly available to the young child."[8]

What is essential about my students' authentic work as oral historians is the extensive reading in professional works of oral history our project involves; the requirement I place on my students to do biographical and historical background research in preparation for their interviews; the fact that the interviews are often with strangers; and the public presentation of their work to parents and the community at the annual "coffee house," as well as postings on our website.

Our school's location near the nation's capital also offers unique opportunities. I continually marvel at some of the prominent interviewees students have independently secured over the years—former chairman of the Joint Chiefs of Staff General John Shalikashvili, civil rights activists Amiri Baraka and Roger Wilkins, New Jersey Governor Christine Todd Whitman, and Supreme Court Justice Sandra Day O'Connor. The complexity of an individual's life has also led to people being interviewed twice on different experiences. Senator Birch Evans Bayh was interviewed about his role in Watergate as well as his experience in the U.S. Senate. However, more often than not, students conduct interviews with less prominent individuals whose stories would otherwise have been lost to historians. I am particularly impressed by what students have learned from people like Josephine (Joey) Thompson, who sought therapy for polio in Warm Springs, Georgia, with President Franklin Delano Roosevelt, or Blanche Shafer's perspective on women working in factories during World War II. Bob Rast, a Vietnam veteran, spoke for the first time about his experiences in Southeast Asia to a sixteen-year-old high school student. A failure to conduct these latter interviews would be a loss to our collective memory.

As a teacher in an independent school near Washington, I can give my students experiences that are not available to all teachers. But nearly all of the activities and learning opportunities described here are easily transferable. Three facets of this project that make it accessible to courses across all disciplines are the flexibility of when it can be introduced into the curriculum, the wide range of skills and multiple intelligences that must be deployed to effectively complete it, and the various topics available for students to explore.[9]

Some colleagues have been reluctant to implement this project because of a concern that coverage of the core curriculum for the AP exam or other standardized tests will be compromised. However, this project allows students to probe deeper into a content area of their choosing while at the same time using many of the skills that are evaluated on such assessments. Students see this project as an extension of their preparation for standardized tests and not as a separate entity of the course. Not only is the project flexible enough to integrate into a curriculum, but it requires students to use many skills of a historian: extensive primary and secondary source research and evaluation, interviewing, writing and rewriting, historical interpretation, and analysis. Few projects require such a variety of skills because of a perception that a multiskill project is an unrealistic expectation for amateur student historians. This, however, is an underestimation of students when they are fully engaged and invested in such a project, as well as the valuable history that can be produced when even unseasoned student historians are schooled in the methodology of oral history. In the end, "there is a real-world component [in an oral history project] because the community is involved; that creates the intrinsic motivation necessary for a [student] to want to acquire the academic skills required to produce that product."[10]

NOT FOR ADVANCED STUDENTS ALONE

Oral history projects need not be limited to advanced or honors students, or students who live in an area overflowing with prominent interview subjects. As an example, those students who chose not to enroll in AP U.S. History at St. Andrew's Episcopal School conducted an oral history project that focused on immigration for their course, The United States in the Twentieth-Century World. As outlined by course instructor Charles Malcolm, these interviews allowed students to compare a variety of immigration experiences that broadened their collective understanding of the diverse histories, culture, and values immigrants bring to the United States. Each year, students interview immigrants from Vietnam, China, Eastern Europe, Central America, and a host of other places that highlight America's complex role in the twentieth-century world and provide a source of comparison to earlier periods of immigration to America. While these two projects focus on a particular period (the American century) or theme (immigration), life, event, and family oral histories can be integrated across all disciplines and grade levels.

Further evidence of an oral history project engendering a sense of intellectual curiosity and empowerment among a range of students in different circumstances is evident in two projects conducted in Dubuque, Iowa, and New York City. Students at Central Alternative High School, located in what teacher John Adelman calls "a big small town," conducted three projects: Tribute to Victory: Dubuque in World War II, The Tuskegee Airman, and The Little Rock 9. In the last two projects, the students took the initiative and raised funds to have members of each group travel to Dubuque for an educational seminar. Project interviews are conducted in person, by phone, or through an e-mail questionnaire. Tensions between Arab and black students at the School for International Studies, a middle school located in Brooklyn, New York, led to an after-school project, Telling Lives, in which students conducted interviews with individuals in this mostly Arab-dominated section of New York following the events of September 11, 2001. Each of these projects reflects the flexibility associated with integrating an oral history project in schools with a range of a student abilities and interests, regardless of geographic location.

THE DEMOCRATIZATION OF HISTORY

In a C-SPAN production of historians commenting on the question, Why study history? Arthur Schlesinger Jr. commented, "Because it is fun." But fun for whom? Despite the rigors of this oral history project, many of my students declared it was fun, "an underestimated and often neglected educational tool,"[11] because they were charged with the same responsibility as professional historians, making, as Carl Becker declared over a half century ago, "Every-man his own historian."[12] Moreover, students present their work in a form that is accessible to a large audience. Student oral history interviews enlarges the scope of our understanding of particular events or periods by making the historical record more human and inclusive through interviews with under-represented or marginalized groups of people. Student oral historians often generate original responses from their interviewees because of the unique teacher–student relationship that emerges between project participants. Everyone who is interviewed serves as a teacher for the course. In many ways, students are also fulfilling a civic responsibility by making people feel that their history is worth something.

The important work of student oral historians is highlighted in a letter to a Vietnam veteran from his son after he received a copy of the final project:

I got the packet today . . . I can't tell you how much I enjoyed reading it, and how much it touched me. These are questions I've always wanted to ask you, and about you, and the war that I always wanted to know about, and hear you talk about. I guess it's like [the son's wife] said, "It's easier to talk to a stranger than to talk to someone who is close to you." I know you've talked to me a little about it, but never this in depth or that much about your feelings. I want you to know that after reading this, even more so now, that I thank God that my father is alive and that my children have a real grandfather instead of just a memory to hear about from me.

At the end of each interview, students are required to analyze the historical value of their project. "The unique perspective of an interviewee," one student commented, "is a wealth of knowledge which can help to recreate a sense of the past." Another student concluded at the end of her interview that "oral history is one of the most interesting ways to learn about the past. It is historically valuable because, in a sense, it is a window into the past." A window that, when opened, empowers students to participate in the preservation of history through a project with the potential to be deeply meaningful to students, interviewees, their immediate friends and family, educators and most of all, the generations to come.

NOTES

Much of this chapter originally appeared as "Teaching Students How to Be Historians: An Oral History Project for the Secondary School Classroom," *History Teacher,* Fall 2000, 469–81.

1. All the materials that support this project can be found at www.americancenturyproject.org and may be used with proper acknowledgment.
2. Barbara Allen and William Lynwood Montell, *From Memory to History: Using Oral Sources in Local Historical Research* (Nashville, Tenn.: American Association for State and Local History, 1981), 3, 15.
3. Thus far, all interviews conducted as part of the American Century Project were done using analog and digital voice recording equipment.
4. Excerpted video clips from the 2001 and 2003 Oral History Coffee House can be seen at the project's website—www.americancenturyproject.org—under Oral History Coffee House.
5. Learning pyramid used with permission from the National Training Laboratories Institute for Applied Behavioral Sciences, Alexandria, Va., www.ntl.org.
6. Learning Record Online, "The Five Dimensions," www.cwrl.utexas.edu/~syverson/olr/dimensions.html.
7. Grant Wiggins, *Educative Assessment: Designing Assessments to Inform and Improve Student Performance* (San Francisco: Jossey-Bass, 1998), 22–24.

8. Alistair Ross, quoted in Robert Perks, ed., *The Oral History Reader* (New York: Routledge, 1998), 446–47.

9. This term refers to the eight multiple intelligences defined by Howard Gardner that are examined more closely in how they are used in an oral history project in chapter 9, "Meeting Standards." See Howard Gardner, *Multiple Intelligences: The Theory in Practice* (New York: Basic, 1993); Thomas Armstrong, *Multiple Intelligences in the Classroom* (Arlington, Va.: Association for Supervision and Curriculum Development, 1994); and Armstrong, Project Summit: Schools Using Multiple Intelligence Theory, www.pz.harvard.edu/sumit/MISUMIT.HTM.

10. Barbara Combs and Christy Stevens with Linda Koch, eds., *Considering Assessment and Evaluation: A Foxfire Teacher Reader* (Mountain City, Ga.: Foxfire Fund, 1999), 109. See also Combs and Stevens, *From Thinking to Doing: Constructing a Framework to Teach Mandates through Experience-Based Learning, Considering Reflection, and Considering Imagination and Creativity*. Both are available at www.foxfire.org.

11. Judy H. Gulledge and Christine A. Capaci, *Pennywinkle: Oral Histories from Tylerton, Smith Island in the Chesapeake Bay* (Norfolk, Va.: Letto Gooch, 1999), ii.

12. Carl Becker, "Everyman His Own Historian," *American Historical Review*, January 1932, 221–36.

CHAPTER 3

Getting Started

Oral history has transformed my classroom. Students have discovered skills they never knew they had. My students learn to do research and to ask penetrating questions. They learn to listen, to transcribe, to edit, and to lay out a publication. They learn composition skills and some familiarity with tone, form, and audience. They are able to meet new people with ease and to make their way with confidence in communities, libraries, and other settings far from Bell Gardens. They gain recognition within the community, and they learn to respect the diversity of Bell Gardens as well as the story of their heritage as it is woven into the community history.[1]

—Michael Brooks, teacher, Suva Intermediate
School, Bell Gardens, California

WHENEVER I PRESENT THE AMERICAN CENTURY PROJECT to educators, three questions predominate: (1) In what ways can I integrate oral history into an already full curriculum? (2) How do you have time to do it in light of the demand to cover material for state and national standards of learning and advanced placement exams? (3) What is the most important information educators and students need to conduct a successful oral history project? My response to each question is the same: Courage.

Educators must have the courage to realize that students learn best by uncovering and creating material on their own, rather than simply covering it. Susan Moon is a teacher of English and Spanish at Lamar County High School in Barnesville, Georgia, where she has been actively involved in implementing the Foxfire method of teaching since 1990. She refers to Aunt Addie Norton, an interviewee in one of the Foxfire books, who says, "I tell you one thing, if you learn it by yourself, if you have to get down and dig for it, it never leaves you. It stays there as long as you live, because you had to dig it out of the mud before you learned what it was."[2] A student who studies the "problem without a name" of the 1950s will connect better with the history by interviewing a cross-section

of women from the period than by attending a lecture on the topic or reading a textbook or the rich collection of written materials. This said, in no way can oral history stand alone; in fact, oral history complements the more traditional, written sources and allows students to gain a broader perspective from which they can make their best interpretations of a period.

The courage needed for this project is not limited to the classroom teacher or administrator who sees the value in what might be considered a nontraditional educational methodology. Students are also being forced to think and act in new ways and are challenged to sometimes ask difficult questions of their interviewees. One of the more contentious aspects of the project we do is the requirement for students to interview a nonfamily member, which forces them out of their comfort zone while helping them develop vital interpersonal skills with adults. Finally, researchers and scholars must have the courage to accept the work of student oral historians. This is particularly important considering the goal of the Veterans Oral History Project: "To collect the memories, accounts, and documents of war veterans and of those who served in support of them during World War I, World War II, and the Korean, Vietnam, and Persian Gulf wars, and to preserve their stories of experience and service for future generations."[3]

The only possible means for preserving the experiences of 19 million American war veterans, of whom approximately 1,500 die each day, is to enlist the service of students who can help preserve the memories of America's servicemen and women or individuals who served in support of veterans.

READY-MADE ORAL HISTORY RESOURCES

Those reluctant to make the extensive commitment in time and energy required of a classroom oral history project can use various entry points for integrating "ready-made" oral history sources into the curriculum. Such sources provide another perspective for evaluating the past and are often more engaging because "there is something innate in the human mind that makes the narrative form an especially attractive medium in which to contain, transmit, and remember important information."[4] Even before the course officially begins, I introduce oral history to my students through a required summer reading of Studs Terkel, *My American Century*. This book exposes students to excerpts from almost the entire collection of oral histories by America's most prominent oral historian, though Terkel is a self-proclaimed "guerrilla journalist." When we return to class in the fall and begin our study of the twentieth century, students often use Terkel's interviews to support their interpretations of events such as the Great Depression, World War II, or civil rights in America. Such application of Terkel's work to a broader understanding of the American century reaffirms what a graduate school professor once said to me: "Good history requires a good story." In essence, that's what oral history is, a story that helps students in their search for "more reality, for direct experience and for first-person testimony."[5]

Terkel's work also serves two other functions. First, despite his reputation as America's leading oral historian, he identifies the errors that he, and most oral historians, encounter at some point in their career such as "pressing the wrong button on a tape recorder that led to his losing (erased or failed to record) Michael Redgrave, Peter Hall, Martha Graham, Jacques Tati and almost succeeded in making Bertrand Russell disappear."[6] In many ways this humanizes the process for students because they will make the same mistakes as leading oral historians. Second, having students read and interpret professional oral histories such as Terkel's provides them with a standard of excellence in the field and a model for their own work. Terkel's work spawned a very useful activity created by Professor Joyce Grant of Michigan State University. "Using Primary Sources to Learn of the Life of Studs Terkel, His Interviews, and Individual Stories of WWII Veterans" is a unique way to explore the life and work of Terkel (www.studsterkel .org/Using%20Primary%20Sources.doc), as is Beth Collins, "Using Oral History in the Classroom," in which students evaluate one of Terkel's interviews as a primary source (www.studsterkel.org/education.php). Two additional sources that I have found to be excellent introductions to oral history for students are Wheeler and Becker, "A Generation in War and Turmoil: The Agony of Vietnam," in *Discovering the American Past* and Davidson and Lytle, "The Bottom Rail," in *After the Fact: The Art of Historical Detection*.[7]

Additional ready-made oral history sources that I have integrated into my classes include the slave narratives collected by the Federal Writers' Project during the 1930s, which were organized into a book and tape/CD collection entitled *Remembering Slavery: African Americans Talk about Their Personal Experiences of Slavery and Emancipation*.[8] While the written narratives in *Remembering Slavery* have proven particularly engaging to my students, the recorded interviews bring them closer to the realities of slavery and emancipation through the voices of those interviewed. The use of both written transcripts and audio recordings serves as a reminder that the written transcript and recorded interview are two very different historical sources and generate different historical interpretations. This is again reinforced by oral historian Alessandro Portelli, who argued "the tone and volume range and the rhythm of popular speech carry implicit meaning and social connotations which are not reproducible in writing . . . The same statement may have quite contradictory meanings, according to the speaker's intonation, which cannot be represented objectively in the transcript, but only approximately described in the transcribers' own words."[9] One of the ironies about using oral history in the classroom is that it is often used as a written document; thus the orality is removed from oral history. The duality of the slave narratives highlights this divergence between the written transcript and recorded interview despite both being the product of the same interview. In the end, "listening to the recording connects us to the speaker both affectively and cognitively, facilitating empathy and deepening our understanding."[10]

Brett Harvey, *The Fifties: A Women's Oral History*, provides an engaging alternative perspective of this period and is a favorite of students. Moreover, the continual integration of technology into the classroom through the World Wide Web offers students access to a rich set of interviews previously accessible only through library research, such as the Rutgers University World War II Oral History Archives (http://fas-history.rutgers.edu/oralhistory/orlhom.htm) and the May 4, 1970 collection, Inquire, Learn and Reflect, at Kent State University (www.library.kent.edu/exhibits/4may95/index.html). The Whole World Was Watching: An Oral History of 1968 (www.stg.brown .edu/projects/1968) is not only valuable for the content available through each interview from this tumultuous year in American history, but also because it serves as an exemplary model for a student-driven oral history project.

Ready-made resources can be integrated into your course or program in a variety of ways. I often have students use such sources, whether they be from written text or a video, for comparative purposes. For example, when we study the Vietnam War, I often ask the students, "Who is missing from the political decisions reflected in the documents we read?" When they mention the voice of the soldier, I will then provide excerpts of books such as Mark Baker, *NAM: The Vietnam War in the Words of the Men and Women Who Fought,* and view a portion of *Vietnam: A Television History,* which includes interviews with politicians and soldiers from both sides of the war. I will also use Wallace Terry, *Bloods: An Oral History of the Vietnam War by Black Veterans,* and Ron Steinman, *Women in Vietnam: The Oral History.* Each of these sources reminds students that Vietnam was not just a white man's war. An additional benefit of expanding a student's knowledge about the war through oral history sources is the chance to examine how history is written—historically by those in power—and how oral history can democratize the historical record. As Barbara Sommer and Mary Kay Quinlan point out, "Exploring many sides of an issue throughout multiple first-hand individual accounts offers the opportunity to uncover layers of meaning embedded in the stories and insights into how people understand and interpret the past and their place in it."[11]

What follows is an annotated listing of additional ready-made resources that educators have found particularly useful. It includes selections from a shorter list by Cynthia Stokes Brown found in *Like It Was: A Complete Guide to Writing Oral History,* which I encountered when I began using oral history with my students. Books marked with an asterisk represent sources that are particularly good for middle school students. When looking at such sources, I often have students complete an oral history source evaluation that forces them to think about the reliability and usability of this historical methodology (see worksheet 3.1). Students use this worksheet to examine their own work in preparation for the historical analysis component of their project.

Fiction

- Atwood, Margaret. *The Handmaid's Tale.* New York: Anchor, 1998.

  "This is a science-fiction novel based on the supposed tape-recorded accounts found in the belongings of a woman who died under the tyranny of a society taken over by fundamentalist Christians, a theocracy in which certain groups of women are forced to be child bearers."[12]

- Dos Passos, John. *U.S.A.: The 42nd Parallel/1919/The Big Money.* New York: Library of America, 1996.

  A one-volume edition of this trilogy that includes interviews "to capture the texture and background noises of early 20th century life."

- Gaines, Ernest J. *The Autobiography of Miss Jane Pittman.* New York: Dial, 1971; Gaines, *A Gathering of Old Men.* New York: Vintage, 1992.

  Each of these books provides a glimpse into issues of race. *The Autobiography of Miss Jane Pittman* presents the tape-recorded recollections of a 110-year-old black woman who lived from slavery to the civil rights movement. *A Gathering of Old Men* examines racial tensions following the death of a Louisiana farmer by a black man as told from fifteen different points of view.

- Smith, Lee. *Oral History.* New York: Ballantine, 1996.

  A story of a college student who returns to her childhood home of Hoot Owl Holler, armed with a tape recorder, to collect the remarkable story of one Appalachian family.

Nonfiction

- Astor, Gerald. *June 6, 1944: The Voice of D-Day.* New York: Dell, 2002.

  "Author, journalist, and veteran Astor has assembled an exciting collection of personal recollections from the men who, in their late teens and early twenties, made history on June 6, 1944, when they invaded occupied France, Hitler's vaunted 'fortress Europe,' to wrest the continent from Nazi domination. The voices of 70 men recount the exhilaration, fear, and valor they felt during the greatest land, sea, and air battle of World War II."[13]

- Brazeau, Peter. *Parts of a World: Wallace Stevens Remembered.* New York: Random House, 1983.

  "This excellent oral biography, based on interviews with friends, relatives, and colleagues, was written long after the death of its subject, the American poet Wallace Stevens."[14]

- Chafe, William Henry, et al., eds. *Remembering Jim Crow: African Americans Tell About Life in the Segregated South.* New York: New Press, 2001.

  Using 25 of the 1,200 interviews collected as part of Duke University's Behind the Veil Project (http://cds.aas.duke.edu/btv/index.html), *Remembering Jim Crow* is a powerful chronicle of African American life in the Jim Crow South as told by those who survived this period in American history. The book is accompanied by a recording of each interview.

Worksheet 3.1. Oral History Source Evaluation

Evaluator's name: _____

(1) Title of the source or project:

(2) Type of oral history source (Check one and provide bibliographical information):

Book   _____

Article   _____

Video documentary   _____

Website   html address _____

(3) Format of oral history source:

Edited transcript   _____

Verbatim transcript   _____

Audio and video   _____

Transcript and audio   _____

Other _____

(4) Who is the author or creator of the oral history source?

Student(s)   K–8   _____   Museum/historical society   _____

Student(s)   8–12   _____   Professional historian/independent scholar _____

College/university   _____   Other: _____

(5) Describe source (purpose, goals, and objectives)?

_____

_____

(6) Who conducted the interview and what are his or her qualifications?

_____

_____

(7) What does the source offer that you can't find elsewhere?

_____

_____

(8) In what ways does this source further your historical understanding?

_____

_____

(9) What has been left unanswered by this source and where can those answers be found?

_____

_____

(10) How does this source relate to other documents and sources?

_____

_____

Source Rating: Rate and than explain why or why not this is a valuable historical source.

            1   2   3   4   5   6   7   8   9   10

Not valuable   Valuable   Extremely valuable

- Charhadi, Driss Ben Hamed. *A Life Full of Holes.* New York: Grove, 1982.

  An oral autobiography of an illiterate Moroccan as told to the writer Paul Bowles. "Bowles's book stirred such interest among Peace Corps Volunteers because it dramatized in a plain and moving manner the pain and humiliation of poverty. Bowles, who spoke the local dialect of Arabic, had struck up a conversation with Charhadi, who had a gift for storytelling. He gradually coaxed out the sad story of the man's life and tape-recorded it over a number of sessions. Then he translated it, edited the narrative, and published it in English. The book attracted attention, came out in a French version, and sold well. Happily—and this is what impressed the Volunteers—Bowles divided the proceeds from the book with Charhadi, who was able to buy a house, get married, and thus escape poverty."[15]

- Curry, Jack. *Woodstock: The Summer of Our Lives.* New York: Grove, 1989.

  Chronicles the stories of nineteen individuals associated with the 1969 Woodstock concert on the twentieth anniversary of the event.

- Dann, John C. *The Revolution Remembered: Eyewitness Accounts of the War for Independence.* Chicago: University of Chicago Press, 1999.

  A look at the Revolutionary War through oral history interviews with seventy-nine veterans collected during pension claim interviews following the war.

- Delany, Sarah Louise, Elizabeth A. Delany, and Amy Hill Hearth. *Having Our Say: The Delany Sisters' First 100 Years.* New York: Dell, 1996.

  A story of two sisters who witnessed the racial challenges faced by black Americans throughout the twentieth century as told to Amy Hill Hearth.

- Duberman, Martin. *Stonewall.* New York: Plume, 1994.

  An important look at an overlooked event and a marginalized group represented by six gay and lesbian individuals who participated in the Stonewall riots that took place between June 27 and July 2, 1969 following a police raid on a Greenwich Village, New York, gay bar.

- Gluck, Sherna Berger. *Rosie the Riveter Revisited: Women, the War, and Social Change.* New York: New American Library Trade, 1988.

  Hear the stories of ten black, white, and Latina women, interviewed as part of an oral history project, as they recount their experiences of helping the war effort and also how their lives were changed because of it.

- Hampton, Henry, and Steve Fayer. *Voices of Freedom: An Oral History of the Civil Rights Movement from the 1950s Through the 1980s.* New York: Bantam, 1991.

  Uses nearly 1,000 interviews with both prominent and lesser-known blacks and whites who struggled with events from the murder of Emmett Till through the continued challenge of racial inequality in the 1980s.

- Hoffman, Alice M., and Howard S. Hoffman. *Archives of Memory: A Soldier Recalls World War II.* Lexington: University Press of Kentucky, 1991.

  This is a unique look at one man's war experience, who happens to be an experimental psychologist, as he's interviewed by his historian wife. This is much more than an oral history of World War II, as it compares and contrasts a man's memory over a ten-year period with other forms of historical evidence. This book is an important read for those interested in the function of memory in the work of oral historians.

- Kenan, Randall. *Walking on Water: Black American Lives at the Turn of the Twenty-First Century.* New York: Vintage, 2000.

  Kenan, who cites Studs Terkel as an influence, collected over two hundred interviews that examine what it means to be black in this country in a book that is part oral history and part travelogue.

- Knox, Donald. *Pusan to Chosin: An Oral History.* New York: Harvest, 1987; Knox, Donald, and Alfred Coppel. *The Korean War: Uncertain Victory: An Oral History.* New York: Harcourt, 1998.

  These books offer important insight into the experiences of those individuals who served the United States in what is commonly referred to as the "forgotten war."

- Lewin, Rhoda G., ed. *Witnesses to the Holocaust: An Oral History.* Twayne's Oral History Series, no. 2. New York: Twayne, 1991.

  A collection of interviews from all sides of the Holocaust that includes a teacher's guide to activities.

- Louv, Richard. *Fly Fishing for Sharks.* New York: Fireside, 2001.

  A travelogue that takes the reader to America's great fishing holes where the author engages in some inspirational dialogue with America's fishermen and women. You don't have to like fishing to like this book!

- Perdue, Theda. *Nations Remembered: An Oral History of the Five Civilized Tribes, 1865–1907.* Westport, Conn.: Greenwood, 1980.

This volume, one of the less known of the oral histories collected under the Federal Writers' Project, sheds important light on one of the most marginalized groups in U.S. history and the recording of that history. An excellent resource to demonstrate, as the author points out, how oral history helps democratize the historical record.[16]

• Rocklin, Joanne. *Strudel Stories*. New York: Yearling, 2000.

This is a collection of stories and the history of one family that are recounted as family members bake a strudel.

• Simmons, Leo W., Don C. Talayesva, and Robert V. Hine. *Sun Chief: The Autobiography of a Hopi Indian*. New Haven: Yale University Press, 1963.

The story of Hopi Indian Don Talayesva, who is caught between the culture of Native Americans and whites as told by Dr. Simmons.

• Spiegelman, Art. *Maus: A Survivor's Tale*. Random House, 1986; and *Maus: My Father Bleeds History/Here My Troubles Began*. New York: Pantheon, 1997.

In this two-volume set, Art Spiegelman presents his interviews with his father, Vladek, a Holocaust survivor, in comic book form. Each volume takes you though the story of Vladek's life in Poland before the war and than during his struggle to survive the Nazi "final solution" for the Jews.

• Terkel, Studs. *Working: People Talk About What They Do and How They Feel About What They Do*. New York: New Press, 1997. Adapted for the stage by Stephen Schwartz and Nina Faso. Ayers, Rick, and Studs Terkel. *Studs Terkel's Working: A Teacher's Guide*. New York: New Press, 2001.

A unique way to integrate oral history into the classroom and provide an excellent model for adapting oral history interviews into a theatrical performance. A teacher's guide is also available that provides examples for how to use Terkel's work into the classroom as well as for conducting oral history interviews. *Working* was first performed in 1978. *The Good War* by Terkel has also been adapted for the stage.

• Tillage, Leon. *Leon's Story*. New York: Sunburst, 2000.

A school custodian tells his story of growing up in a segregated South to a group of middle school students that was recorded by a child's parent. Most appropriate for younger students.

• X, Malcolm. *The Autobiography of Malcom X*. New York: Ballantine, 1977.

This autobiography of the slain civil rights leader was partially developed through interviews Alex Haley conducted with the author.

Video

• *Nobody's Business*. Directed by Alan Berliner. Milestonefilms, 1996. Videocassette. 60 minutes.

A spirited look at one son's successful attempt—with some challenges—to conduct a life history interview of his often reluctant father.

• Garvey, Helen. *Rebels with a Cause: The Hopes, Rebellions, and Repression of the 1960s As Told by Members of SDS (Students for a Democratic Society)*. Directed by Helen Garvey. Zeitgeist Video, 2000. Videocassette. 110 minutes.

A unique look at the 1960s through twenty-eight interviews with SDS activists, including Tom Hayden, Elizabeth Stanley, and Junius Williams.

• *One Survivor Remembers: Gerda Weissmann Klein*. Directed by Kary Antholis. Direct Cinema Limited, 1996. Videocassette. 39 minutes.

This Oscar-winning documentary demonstrates the emotional aspect of telling stories, in this case a child's survival of the Holocaust, and lends itself to discussions about memory and how to conduct interviews that deal with emotional topics.

• Hirsch, Lee. *Amandala! A Revolution in Four-Part Harmony*. Directed by Lee Hirsch. Artisan (Fox Video), 2003. DVD.

Chronicles the fall of apartheid through the memories of those who helped make it happen and the sounds that inspired a revolution.

• *Unchained Memories: Readings from the Slave Narratives*. Directed by Ed Bell and Thomas Lennon. HBO Video, February 2003. Videocassette.

Provides dramatic readings of some of the 2,000 oral history interviews conducted with former slaves through the Federal Writers' Project between 1936 and 1938.

Websites

• American Life Histories: Manuscripts from the Federal Writers' Project, 1936–1940. memory.loc.gov/ammem/wpaintro/wpahome.html.

Includes Voices from the Thirties: An Introduction to the WPA Life Histories, a collection of life history interviews with more than 10,000 men and women from a variety of regions, occupations, and ethnic groups.

• Smithsonian Institution's Archives of American Art Oral History Program. artarchives.si.edu.

This collection of nearly two hundred interviews highlights the interdisciplinarity of oral history. Interviews include those that were part of the New Deal and the Arts Oral History Program conducted in the 1960s.

- Voices from the Days of Slavery: Former Slaves Tell Their Story (transcripts and audio); Born in Slavery: Narratives from the Federal Writers' Project, 1936–1938. Library of Congress, American Memory Collection. memory.loc.gov/ammem/vfshtml/vfshome.html.

How-to Resources for Educators

While many educators recognize the benefits of an oral history project, they often have little experience with oral history as a historical methodology prior to implementing their first project. Over the past decade a considerable number of how-to oral history books and websites have become available that are particularly useful. In addition to printed resources, oral history workshops have emerged to help guide educators through the process. A list of workshops and sponsoring organizations can be found in the "Sources and Resources" in the appendix to this volume.

- H-Oralhist. www2.h-net.msu.edu/~oralhist.

  H-Oralhist is a discussion list maintained by H-Net, Humanities, and Social Sciences Online in affiliation with the Oral History Association. It provides all levels of oral history practitioners an excellent opportunity to exchange ideas and ask questions.
- Moyer, Judith. Step-by-Step Guide to Oral History. www.dohistory.org/on_your_own/toolkit/oralHistory.html.

  An excellent how-to resource that introduces an individual to all aspects of oral history research.
- The One Minute Guide to Oral History. Regional Oral History Office, University of California at Berkley. bancroft.berkeley.edu/ROHO.

  A quick reference guide for any educator; includes information about the summer institute as well as access to various oral history projects such as the University History Series, which focuses on the free speech movement, the Suffragists Oral History Project, the Earl Warren Oral History Project, and Health Care, Science, and Technology, which focuses on the medical responses to AIDS in San Francisco between 1981 and 1984.
- Oral History Workshop on the Web. Institute for Oral History. Baylor University. www3.baylor.edu/Oral_History/Workshop.htm.

Provides an introduction to oral history for beginners as well as a transcribing style guide. Also includes numerous articles on various topics related to oral history as well as access to the institute's collection.

- Ritchie, Donald A. *Doing Oral History.* London: Oxford University Press, 2003.

  This continues to be the most comprehensive resource for anyone interested in oral history. It was revised in 2003 to reflect changes in the field, especially in regard to technology. It is written in a question-and-answer format and covers topics from the history of oral history, archiving oral history projects, and digital technology and the Internet.
- Shopes, Linda. "Making Sense of Oral History." *History Matters.* historymatters.gmu.edu/mse/oral.

  This article examines oral history as a historical methodology by someone who has spent more than twenty-five years as an oral history practitioner. The articles cover topics from What is oral history? to examining issues related to oral history online.
- Sommer, Barbara W., and Mary Kay Quinlan. *The Oral History Manual.* Walnut Grove, Calif.: AltaMira, 2002.

  A useful, succinct guide through all the steps of an oral history project. An appendix includes reproducible forms that can be immediately integrated into a class or program.
- Stokes Brown, Cynthia. *Like It Was: A Complete Guide to Writing Oral History.* New York: Teachers and Writers Collaborative, 1988.

  A guide written by a teacher that shows how to transform oral history interviews into various writing assignments such as articles, biographies, narratives, and poetry. This guide is best used as a compendium to *Ready from Within: Septima Clark and the Civil Rights Movement* (WildTrees, 1986), which the author feels "provides a model of how the transcription of oral interviews can be shaped into literary forms." *Like It Was* also provides an annotated list of resources that use oral history as sources for biography, history, politics, and fiction. As the author states, "the result is a fascinating profusion of literary forms, highly inventive and unconventional."

ORAL HISTORY AS A HISTORICAL METHODOLOGY

Ready-made oral history sources force students to further evaluate the question, What is history? This question became particularly relevant following the publication of the collection of experiences of former

Frank and Ernest

Figure 3.1. Frank and Ernest by Bob Thaves. (Used with permission. www.frankandernest.com)

slaves through the Federal Writers' Project that brought attention to the question, Who is missing or silenced in our history? As a class, we attack these questions by reading two essays prior to my introducing oral history to the students. I have found Edward Hallet Carr, "The Historian and His Facts," in *What Is History?* (1932), and Arthur Schlesinger Jr., "History as a Weapon," in *The Disuniting of America: Reflections on a Multicultural Society* (1998), particularly useful and accessible, especially to high school students. This exercise addresses one of the biggest challenges for the student oral historian and is an important precursor to an oral history project because of the emotional and personal attachment students often make with their interviewees and their stories. Such an attachment challenges the students' ability to be objective when considering how to place their interview into a broader historical context. Throughout our study of history, I remind students to always question their sources, including their own oral history interviews.

What is oral history? and What is its historical value? are essential questions when using this historical methodology. My students are reminded that not too long ago most historians would not use oral history because they questioned its validity. Even though oral history is the oldest form of historical reporting and can be traced back to the Zhou dynasty in China and Thucydides' interviews with participants in the Peloponnesian Wars, it is still challenged for its reliability.[17] When we begin our project, I have students read a 1992 *Wall Street Journal* article entitled "Little Big Horn from the Indian Point of View" that highlights the controversy surrounding oral history. Students examine the debate caused by the book *Soldiers Falling into Camp*, which was written by Native Americans and draws on the Native American oral tradition

to revise the events of General Custer's defeat in 1876. Because this book relies heavily on oral history, it was initially prohibited from being sold at the Little Bighorn National Monument as a "fictionalized" treatment.[18] The students quickly learn that oral history must be evaluated in light of its strengths and weaknesses; each interview is only a small snapshot of particular period or event. One interview does not tell the whole story, nor do multiple interviews on a particular subject because they are interpreting the past using one historical method. Among professional oral historians there is also considerable debate as to which source, the tape or transcript, is oral history. When oral history is combined with more traditional sources, a more compelling and complete history is created. For educators, and even the casual historian, this balance of the historical record is evidenced in documentaries such as Ken Burns's *Jazz* and *Baseball*, as well as the *Eyes on the Prize* series, which intertwine various types of historical sources, including oral history interviews.

From their first introduction to oral history, students begin realizing problems associated with it and, like all historians, understand that oral history needs to be validated by other forms of historical reporting. As President Calvin Coolidge once declared about residents in his hometown of Plymouth, Vermont, they "remember some of the most interesting things that never happened."[19] Bias, glorification, and sometimes outright fabrication must be verified through more traditional research of primary and secondary sources, as well as multiple interviews related to the same subject. Despite such challenges, "the memories of direct participants are sources far too rich for historical researchers to ignore. Interviewers must be aware of the peculiarities of memory, adept in their methods of dealing with it—[through thorough research]—conscious of its limitations, and open to its treasures."[20]

In the widely read "The Death of Luigi Trastulli: Memory and the Event," Alessandro Portelli makes an interesting point: "Historical inaccuracies in oral history do not make an interview useless. 'Wrong' tales, like the many versions of Trastulli's death, are so very valuable. They allow us to recognize the interests of the tellers, and the dreams and desires beneath them."[21] However, it requires the diligent historian to separate fact from fiction.

Not only do I make students aware of the historical and interpretive challenges they will face when they read oral history, but at various points in their actual project students are forced to examine the conflict between memory and history and are reminded that all historical sources should be treated with equal skepticism. Such skepticism should also be turned on themselves as interviewers. A challenge that most student oral historians face is making an emotional attachment to their interview which affects their ability to remain historically objective.[22] This is supported by Ronald Grele, who points out a particular problem oral historians have: "losing their perspective by assuming that because someone says something it automatically contains a truth beyond those of established historians who have written in the past."[23] It is important to remember that since, at its core, oral history is a dialogue, both the interviewer and interviewee bring their own biases and "unconscious preconceptions" that either explicitly or implicitly impact the objectivity of the interview.[24] The biggest challenge most students have to being objective is presentism, interpreting the past from a current position in time and/or biases.

In "What Is Oral History?" Linda Shopes argues that "historians must exercise critical judgment when using interviews—just because someone says something is true, however colorfully or convinc-

ingly they say it, doesn't mean it is true. Just because someone 'was there' doesn't mean they fully understand 'what happened.'"[25] Shopes reinforces this point by using the example of how the "assassination of John F. Kennedy not only reshaped Americans' subsequent views of him but even changed how they remembered their earlier perceptions. Although Kennedy was elected with just 49.7% of the vote in the fall of 1960, almost two-thirds of all Americans remembered voting for him when they were asked about it in the aftermath of his assassination."[26]

This challenge highlights the need for students to have thoroughly researched their topic in preparation for the interview. In the end, students determine that their oral history projects are what Edward Hallet Carr once referred to as a "dialogue between the historian and his facts."[27] Students quickly seem to understand the contributions their work can make to their overall understanding of American history. However, they also begin to realize, as Samirah Raheem pointed out in her 1997 interview of Amiri Baraka on the 1967 Newark rebellion, "this interview reflects the opinion and experience of one man."

An excellent case study—which is accessible to students—on the challenges posed by oral history sources emerges in the debate surrounding *Born in Slavery: Slave Narratives from the Federal Writers' Project, 1936–1938*, which can be found at lcweb2.loc.gov/ammem/snhtml. "An Introduction to the Slave Narratives," by Norman Yetman, includes sections on "The Limitations of the Slave Narrative Collection: Problems of Memory" and "Should the Slave Narrative Collection Be Used?" that allow students to debate the utility of this historical collection. Additional required reading on this topic is C. Vann Woodward, "History from Slave Sources," in the *American Historical Review*. Woodward identifies some of the problems associated with the slave narratives. "Given the mixture of sources and interpreters, interviewers and interviewees, the times and their 'etiquette,' the slave narratives can be mined for evidence to prove almost anything."[28] But what is most important about Woodward's assessment, and for training the student oral historian, is the essential understanding that oral history sources "have their peculiarities, as all historical sources do, but they are not all that different from the norm. The norm for historical sources is a mess, a confusing mess, and the task of the historian is to make sense of it."[29]

In the end, the use of oral history resources compiled by others constitutes passive oral history. At the very least, such sources represent what the founder of the Consortium of Oral History Educators, Dr. Barry A. Lanman, identifies as "an opportunity to learn from the actual history-makers themselves instead of from textbooks."[30] Ready-made oral history sources also allow students to think about the reliability of this historical methodology—an important precursor to any oral history project. In the end, while "passive" oral history is often engaging, it falls short of altering the traditional manner in which students learn. However, deploying students in active oral history—in which they conduct the work of an oral historian—empowers them to become producers of historical records rather than passive absorbers of historical information.

NOTES

1. Michael Brooks, "Long, Long Ago: Recipe for a Middle School Oral History Program," *OAH Magazine of History*, Spring 1997, 32.
2. "Voices of Experience: Oral History in the Classroom," *Magazine of History*, Spring 1997, 31.
3. For more information about the Veterans Oral History Project, see www.loc.gov/folklife/vets.
4. David Kennedy, "The Art of the Tale: Story-Telling and History Teaching," *History Teacher*, May 1998, 318.
5. Alessandro Portelli, *The Death of Luigi Trastulli and Other Stories: Form and Meaning in Oral History* (New York: State University Press of New York, 1991), vii.
6. Studs Terkel, *My American Century* (New York: New Press, 1997), 489.
7. William Bruce Wheeler and Susan D. Becker, *Discovering the Past: A Look at the Evidence*, 5th ed. (New York: Houghton Mifflin, 2002), 2:253–89; James West Davidson and Mark H. Lytle, *After the Fact: A Look at the Evidence* (New York: McGraw-Hill, 1992), 148–77.
8. See also Julius Lester, *To Be a Slave* (New York: Puffin, 2000); Paul D. Escott, *Slavery Remembered: A Record of Twentieth-Century Slave Narratives* (Chapel Hill: University of North Carolina Press, 1979).
9. Portelli, *The Death of Luigi Trastull*, 47.
10. Bret Eynon, "Oral History and the New Century," in "Reflections on Oral History in the New Millennium," *Oral History Review*, Summer–Fall 1999, 2.
11. Barbara W. Sommer and Mary Kay Quinlan, *The Oral History Manual* (Walnut Creek, Calif.: AltaMira, 2002), 1.
12. Cynthia Stokes Brown, *Like It Was: A Complete Guide to Writing Oral History* (New York: Teachers and Writers Collaborative, 1988), 112. Brown's book provides an extensive list of annotated oral history resources within different forms of writing publications.
13. Thomas G. Anton, review of *June 6, 1944: The Voice of D-Day*, by Gerald Astor, *Library Journal on the Web*, 1994.
14. Brown, *Like It Was*, 111.
15. David Espey, *A Writer Writes: Remembering Paul Bowles (Morocco 1962–1964)*, www.peacecorpswriters.org/pages/2002/0201/prntvrs201/pv201wrwr.html.
16. See also Joseph Medicine Crow and Herman J. Viola, *From the Heart of the Crow Country: The Crow Indians' Own Stories* (Lincoln, Neb.: Bison, 2000). Joseph Medicine Crow was the oral historian of the tribe.
17. Thucydides explains his research methodology as well as his use of oral history in the opening pages of *The History of the Peloponnesian Wars*. See also Robert P. Grathwol, Donita M. Moorhus, and Douglas J. Wilson, *Oral History and Postwar German–American Relations* (Washington, D.C.: German Historical Institute, 1997), 9.
18. Marj Charlier, "Little Big Horn From the Indian Point of View," *Wall Street Journal*, September 15, 1992, 16.
19. Donald A. Ritchie, *Doing Oral History* (London: Oxford University Press, 2003), 34.
20. Ritchie, *Doing Oral History*, 14. See also "Memory and History: Essays on Recalling and Interpreting Experience" from the Institute of Oral History at Baylor University, www3.baylor.edu/Oral_History/Workshop.htm.
21. Portelli, *Death of Luigi Trastulli*, 2. See also Daniel James, *Dona Maria's Story: Life History, Memory, and Political Identity (Latin America Otherwise)* (Durham, N.C.: Duke University Press, 2001).
22. Valerie Yow, "Do I Like Them Too Much? Effects of the Oral History Interview on the Interviewer and Vice-Versa," *Oral History Review*, Summer 1997, 55–79.
23. Ronald J. Grele, *Envelopes of Sound: The Art of Oral History*, 2d ed. (New York: Praeger, 1991), 201.
24. Arthur Schlesinger Jr., *The Disuniting of America* (New York: Norton, 1998), 54.
25. Linda Shopes, "Making Sense of Oral History," History Matters: The U.S. Survey on the Web, 5–6, historymatters.gmu.edu/mse/oral.
26. Shopes, 6.
27. Edward Hallet Carr, *What Is History?* (New York: Vintage, 1961), 35.

28. C. Vann Woodward, "History from Slave Sources," *American Historical Review*, April 1974, 475. See also Jerrold Hirsch, *Portrait of America: A Cultural History of the Federal Writers' Project* (Chapel Hill: University of North Carolina Press, 2003).

29. Woodward, "History," 475.

30. Quoted in Jeff Carter, "History and Technology: Using Today's Tools to Help Students Access, Analyze, and Make History," *Cable in the Classroom,* November 2002, 13.

CHAPTER 4

Creating an Oral History Project

If you have a person you have a story.

—Teacher Mike Lewis, Allegany High
School, Allegany County Maryland

IN MY OWN EXPERIENCE AND IN CONDUCTING RESEARCH for this book, I discovered that four factors contribute to a successful student-driven oral history project. First, you need innovative educators who are willing to empower students with their own learning. As Larry E. Hudson Jr. and Ellen Durrigan Santora point out in "Oral History: An Inclusive Highway to the Past," this means that "the teacher should not be 'merely the-one-who teaches, but one who is himself taught in dialogue with the students, who in turn while being taught also teaches.' This is not a beverage easily consumed by all teachers."[1] Second, you need students who are willing to think and work in new ways. This does not mean that only the brightest or mainstream students are best suited to be oral historians. In fact, an oral history project has been particularly useful for engaging the least motivated students and improving the language skills of students who use English as a second language. Not surprisingly, when an oral history project is presented to students they are often hesitant about this opportunity. However, as student testimonials attest, this experience is often the highlight of their academic studies despite the enormous amount of time and number of challenges they face. Third, you need interviewees who are willing to share their stories and become a teacher for your course or program. This means that students, as in the case of two interviews, might have to mow the lawn or help fix the roof of a potential interviewee in order to secure their participation in an oral history project. Students might also be challenged in convincing their interviewees that their lives are worth something and that their stories need to be preserved. This is particularly evident in an exchange between Alan Berliner as he interviewed his father Oscar for the film, *Nobody's Business*, which I show to my students when discussing some of the challenges of interviewing. (See appendix for viewing guide.)

Alan Berliner: Tell me about this picture.

Oscar Berliner: I am just posing for a picture to be taken.

AB: There's no story behind the picture?

OB: You want me to make up stories. Alan, before we go on any further, I am just an ordinary guy whose lived an ordinary life. I was in the army, I got married, I raised a family, I worked hard and had my own business. That's nothing to make a picture about.

AB: Somebody in the audience right now might be saying, Why am I watching this film about this guy?

OB: I agree. I don't know what the hell you're doing. My life is nothing, no different than billions of other people. Who the hell would care about Oscar Berliner, who the hell am I?

AB: Everyone has a life that has something special.[2]

Fourth, there is immeasurable value to having the support of a school community that appreciates alternative educational methodologies. This is the most challenging requirement considering the proliferation of standardized testing and the territorial nature of educators who might be jealous of the extensive amount of time students apportion to their work as oral historians.

Finally, there is one factor that does not adversely impact a student-driven oral history project: geographic location. Whether your school or program is located in a geographically isolated area or one overflowing with potential interviewees, every community has a story to tell. Moreover, recorded telephone interviews allow students to connect with individuals outside their communities and can broaden the scope and reach of any oral history project. When I first introduce the American Century Project to my students, I begin by asking them to generate a list of the first ten names that they connect to American history. Inevitably, the list includes Washington, Jefferson, Lincoln, and Martin Luther King Jr.

When I conducted this activity at a Washington-area all-girls school, amazingly, their list of Americans initially did not include any women. This list says a lot about how history is written and taught, and it highlights the value of an oral history project. "Who is missing from this list?" is one of the most important questions when creating an oral history project and preparing students to be oral historians. We can democratize the manner in which history is presented by uncovering the voices of marginalized groups who have traditionally received little or no mention in traditional school texts.

By definition, an oral history project is a "series of individual interviews recorded one at a time with a number of narrators focusing on one subject, topic, or event."[3] When considering the type of project appropriate for their class, I often ask educators to think backwards and first determine what they hope to accomplish by this project, what they want students to learn in terms of the oral history process, and what they expect the final product to look like. In addition, educators need to consider how much time they want to commit to such a project. This said, an oral history project is flexible enough to fit into any type of educational situation.

SHARING AUTHORITY: ORAL HISTORY AS A COLLABORATIVE PROCESS

One of the unique aspects of a student-driven oral history project is the role each major participant—educator, student interviewer, and interviewee—plays in the project. Each brings a certain amount of authority to the project, which is essential to ensuring the quality and utility of the final product. While the teachers often introduce and guide students through each phase of an oral history project, in many ways they hand off or relinquish authority for the making of history to the student and interviewee.[4] This is a sig-

nificant alteration to the traditional one-directional flow of teaching students. This idea reminds us that by its nature oral history is a shared experience in the dialogue that takes place between interviewer and interviewee and how this dialogue is shaped by the experience or authority each brings to the interview. The interviewee's responses result from the questions posed by the interviewer that were formed from extensive preinterview research. The interviewee's experience, which is greatly shaped by his or her memory, is what forms the substance of the interview. As Ronald Grele points out in his book, *Envelopes of Sound: The Art of Oral History*, "it is this dialectic between the telling of the story and the inquisitive and critical mind, whether of the 'professional' historian or of the interested neighbor, which gives oral history its real dimension."[5]

Figure 4.1. St. Andrew's Episcopal student Emily Taylor with her photography teacher, Ivona Kaz-Jepsen, who was interviewed on her experiences as a displaced person from Lithuania following World War II.

TYPES OF PROJECTS: LOOK IN YOUR BACKYARD

A limitless number of project types and potential interviewees is available for an oral history project. As you look to create the most appropriate project for your class or educational program, first consider your own backyard. Often the best project types and interviewees are those that we encounter every day at home, in school and around the community. I am often amazed by the surprised look on the faces of students when they find out that their science teacher served in Vietnam or their music teacher marched with Martin Luther King Jr. from Selma to Montgomery. Students can also build intergenerational bridges while preserving their family's history through an oral history project. A family history project is especially well suited to middle school students because of the rapport they have already established with relatives. My History is America's History, sponsored by the National Endowment for the Humanities, provides educators and students a guide to preserving their family story. Not surprisingly, whenever I introduce a family oral history project, the first response from students is that "nothing has ever happened in my family." I immediately counter this shortsightedness by explaining an interview I conducted with my father where I found out that he once delivered toupee tape to John Wayne and also met President Harry Truman. Without this interview, these stories would have been lost to my family.

Backyard oral history projects can also lead students to preserve the history of a school or a "Main Street" where students interview local businessmen and businesswomen as well as residents of a particular town. Students can also preserve the history of a neighborhood, organization, business, town politics, and the local environment with those individuals who witnessed or participated in a town's evolution. A few sources that I have found particularly useful when examining local history and are put out in conjunction with the American Association for State and Local History include *Nearby History,* by David E. Kyvig and Myron A. Marty; *Using Local History in the Classroom,* by Fay Metcalf; and *From Memory to History: Using Oral Sources in Local Historical Research,* by Barbara Allen and William Montell. The American Association for State and Local History's website, www.aaslh.org, provides easy access to their collection of publications and serves as a helpful resource for local history projects.

FINDING THE RIGHT PROJECT FOR YOUR CLASS OR PROGRAM

This book was created to allow educators to integrate oral history into their classrooms or programs more easily, without having to reinvent the wheel. The proliferation of oral history into the classroom or as part of educational programs has created some exemplary projects that teachers and educators can use as models. The question always arises as to whether some projects are better suited to certain age levels. While subjects such as the Holocaust, war, and racism pose certain emotional and psychological challenges, teachers must determine the ability of their students to handle such topics as well as vulgar language and racial epithets. What follows is an annotated list of projects that are national in scope and/or being conducted at the middle and high school levels.

National Oral History Projects

- National History Day. An effective way to integrate an oral history project into the classroom is part of National History Day, which "is a year-long education program that engages students in grades 6–12 in the process of discovery and interpretation of historical topics that change each year." More than half of all National History Day projects now include some form of oral history. www.nationalhistoryday.org.

- Sharing History Project. In conjunction with the HBO documentary *Unchained Memories: Readings from the Slave Narratives,* which first aired in February 2003, the Sharing History Project encourages students to document their own lives and the lives of their communities through photography and oral history. www.hbo.com/docs/programs/unchained_memories/sharing_history.html.

- StoryCorps: An Oral History of America. This is a "national project to instruct and inspire people to record each other's stories in sound" modeled after the 1930s WPA recordings. Students can preserve the stories of relatives either by going to one of the StoryBooths found in various parts of the country or using one of the StoryKits, a recording package that allows individuals to conduct broadcast-quality interviews anywhere. Visit the project's website at storycorps.net. It should be noted that this manner of collecting oral histories of uncelebrated Americans that will be deposited in the American Folklife Center at the Library of Congress has raised concern that the popularization of the oral history process threatens the professionalization of this historical method.

- Veterans History Project. Sponsored by the American Folklife Center at the Library of Congress, this project seeks to preserve the reminiscences of those who served abroad or supported the war at home during World War I, World War II, Korea, Vietnam, and the Persian Gulf War through partnerships with schools, youth organizations, libraries, museums, and veterans organizations. The importance of this project is highlighted by the fact that approximately 1,500 veterans die each day. www.loc.gov/folklife/vets.

Middle School Projects
- Got Roots? Takes teachers and students through every phase of an oral history project, providing lesson plans, student handouts, assignments, and assessment rubrics. wneo.org/oralhist/Ric/ricgotroots overview.htm.
- *Keeping the Struggle Alive: Studying Desegregation in Our Town.* Renaissance Middle School students in Montclair, New Jersey, probed deeper into their community's history of desegregation in a language arts–social studies project that combines oral history interviews with more traditional sources. This project is published as a book under the same name.[6]
- The Langston Hughes Middle School Project. "Every year students conduct interviews with a selection of Reston residents, all of whom had lived in the Reston community for at least fifteen years. The students are required to tape and transcribe the interviews. The transcripts include a physical description of the interviewee, background information, the interview setting and the interview itself. The Reston Reflections Oral History Archive gives a unique perspective on the development and history of the Reston community." www.gmu.edu/library/special collections/pcaoral.html.
- Long, Long Ago Oral History Project. Each year fifth, sixth, seventh, and eighth grade students at Suva Intermediate School, Bell Gardens, California, have volunteered after school to preserve and publish the stories of their communities in a magazine based on residents, ranging from World War I veterans to movie stars such as Walter Mattau. The project's coordinator, Michael Brooks, was the first recipient of the Oral History Association's Precollegiate Teaching Award in 1995.[7]
- *Pennywinkle: Oral Histories from Tylerton, Smith Island in the Chesapeake Bay.* This book is the end-product of a project at Northside Middle School in Norfolk, Virginia, in which students conducted interviews of island residents as part of their work in English and science class.

High School Projects
- The Rocky Gap High School Oral History and Technology Project is place-based education. "It is grounded past, present, and future in this place, Bland County, Virginia. The history, the culture, the technology, the writing skills, and the organizational and managerial lessons are all rooted in this place, in these mountains." www.bland.k12.va.us/bland/rocky/gap.html.
- Telling Their Stories: Oral History Archives Project is an elective history course at the Urban School of San Francisco, where students conducted digital video-taped interviews with six Holocaust survivors from the Bay Area. The project website, www.tellingstories.org, includes over twenty hours of full-text and video and will be expanded as other twentieth-century topics are explored. This is a model program for the collaboration between school and community as well as in the use of technology in the classroom. As one of the program coordinators, Howard Levin, said, it is "authentic doing" for Urban's students.
- Visions: The Soul & Spirit of South Baton Rouge Churches; and Pictures in My Mind: An Oral History of South Baton Rouge Community Business and the Business Community. A collaboration between the Williams Center for Oral History at Louisiana State University and a summer program conducted at McKinley High School resulted in two local oral histories. www.lib.lsu.edu/special/williams.
- We Made Do: Recalling the Great Depression (Mooresville High School, Moorsville, Indiana). www.mcsc.k12.in.us/mhs/social/madedo.
- What Did You Do in the War, Grandma? (www.stg.brown.edu/projects/WWII_Women/tocCS.html); and The Whole World Was Watching: 1968 (www.stg.brown.edu/projects/1968/). South Kingston Rhode Island English students chronicled the home front during World War II and the watershed year of the 1960s with interviews of fellow Rhode Islanders. An additional project, The Family in the Fifties: Hope, Fear, and Rock 'n' Roll is described in an article by Linda Wood, project director, in the *OAH Magazine of History,* Spring 1997, 36–38 which is also available online.

Table 4.1 provides additional project ideas and demonstrates the interdisciplinary nature of oral

Table 4.1. Oral History Projects across Disciplines

Subject	Project Types
History	• Create a museum display for National History Day or a community presentation that combines oral history interviews with more traditional sources. • Interview local heroes in the community. • Create a video documentary or website that incorporates interviews. • Create an exhibit at the local VFW hall, soldiers home, or VA hospital.
Science	• Interview residents about environmental issues (e.g., Three Mile Island, Love Canal, or Centralia, Pennsylvania). • Interview local farmers or miners about their work and its relationship to the land.
English	• Write an autobiography or poetry based on interviews. • Develop a literary magazine in the tradition of *Foxfire*.[1] • Study the art of writing by conducting life history interviews with writers.
Math	• Geometry class can interview local architects or an engineer about building and project design.
Health/Physical Education	• Compare teenage life today with that of fifty years ago. • Conduct interviews with members of a championship team.
Foreign Language	• Conduct an interview in a foreign language. • Use interviews to understand different cultures.
Art/Music	• Create a one-act play. • Create artwork that reflects aspects of an interview.
Geography	• Study why people live where they do. • Examine the racial segregation of a town or city.
Technology	• Create an online aural essay that combines voice excerpts from interviews, matched with text from the transcript, with images and additional primary and second sources, including the interview transcript.[2]
Community Service	• Create a neighborhood mural based on interviews with community residents. • Preserve your school's history through oral history interviews. • Examine how the local area has changed through interviews with community residents. • Conduct life history interviews at a nursing home and then exhibit the stories for the residents.

Notes:
1. Eliot Wigginton, ed., *The Foxfire Book: Hog Dressing, Log Cabin Building, Mountain Crafts and Foods, Planting by the Signs, Snake Lore, Hunting Tales, Faith Healing, Moon* (Garden City, N.Y.: Anchor/Doubleday, 1972). For the complete list of Foxfire books, go to www.foxfire.org.
2. See Charles Hardy III and Alessandro Portelli's aural essay, "I Can Almost See the Lights of Home: A Field Trip to Harlan County, Kentucky," *Journal for MultiMedia History* 2 (1999), www.albany.edu/jmmh/vol2no1/lightsportelli.html.

history. Each of these suggestions can easily be part of the curriculum of more than one class.

QUESTIONS EDUCATORS FREQUENTLY ASK

As you consider the most appropriate project for your class or program, here are some questions frequently posed by educators who are considering the benefits as well as the pitfalls associated with an oral history project.

What Types of Oral History Projects Are Possible with Students?

Oral history projects generally fall into the following two categories:

- **Biographical/life review projects** have students preserve the life experiences of the interviewee. This creates a challenge due to the broad research that is required in a project that attempts to cover a person's life.
- **Thematic oral history projects** focus on a specific topic or event that can be international, national, or local in scope. Inevitably, a thematic oral history

project will also include a review of some portions of the interviewee's life relevant to the topic. One of the benefits of such a project is the opportunity for students to compare experiences of each of the interviewees by creating a list of questions each interviewee will be asked. For example, when doing projects on World War II, my students always ask whether their interviewee agrees with Studs Terkel, who called World War II the "good war," and if they feel they were part of what Tom Brokaw calls the "greatest generation." Questions relating to where an interviewee was when Pearl Harbor was attacked and their feelings about the use of the atomic bomb all lend themselves to seeing the various views of the same event and bring students closer to a more objective history.

Is An Oral History Project Appropriate for Students with Learning Disabilities, Students Who Speak English As a Second Language, or At-Risk Students?

Oral history is the great equalizer—throughout this book you will find exemplary projects for each of these student populations. These projects demonstrate how an oral history project can help develop the language and writing skills of nonnative speakers, as well as engage students who have difficulties connecting with their academic work. Teachers who work with such students often convey how their students felt empowered as oral historians, increasing confidence in themselves as students and as individuals. This was evident in a series of collaborative projects—supported by school board members—for at-risk students that were part of a special education program. The projects were coordinated by Shadows-on-the-Teche, a National Trust plantation home, and New Iberia Senior High School (New Iberia, Louisiana) teacher Toby Daspit, who cotaught a course entitled African-American Studies: Oral Traditions of the African American Community in Iberia Parish with Jamie Credle and Pat Kahle from Shadows.[8] Irma Olmedo's article, "Junior Historians: Doing Oral History with ESL and Bilingual Students,"[9] further highlights the benefits of using this educational methodology with all types of students as does a joint project conducted by ESL students at Bell Multicultural High School and the Latino Community Heritage Center in Washington, D.C.

How Should the Work Be Distributed among the Students?

After deciding on the appropriate project, you then have to decide on how to distribute the work among students. Individuals working alone get to experience all aspects of a designated project, but considering the collaborative nature of oral history, working with a partner or teams can yield additional opportunities as well as help in the division of labor. Moreover, working with partners helps students who are less confident working alone. This is particularly true with middle school students.

What Is the Biggest Difference between Conducting an Oral History Project with Middle School and High School Students?

The rather simplistic answer is that there is a need for more structure when conducting a project with middle school students. However, for many middle and high school students, an oral history project is a new educational experience and requires very deliberate instruction and continual coaching and feedback.

When Is the Best Time to Conduct an Oral History Project?

There are various entry points for an oral history project into the curriculum. While some advanced

THE AMERICAN CENTURY PROJECT TIMELINE

Early November: Project introduced and materials distributed

First week of December: Interview selection and *preinterview worksheet*.[1] Research should begin as soon as an interviewee is secured and cleared with the teacher.

Third week of December: *Historical contextualization* due.[2] Initial fifteen interview questions due and student/teacher conferences.

Most interviews take place over the December holiday break, although students need to remain flexible to accommodate the interviewee's schedule.

Second week of January: Interview transcription due.[3]

Third week of January: *Biography*,[4] revised *historical contextualization*,[5] and *analysis* due.[6]

First week of February: Final draft and disk (copy of the project sent to interviewee as a courtesy as well as an opportunity to evaluate the transcription before web posting).

Third week of February: Museum exhibition due.

Last week of February: Oral History Coffee House.

Notes:
1. http://www.americancenturyproject.org/in_classroom/pre_interview.htm
2. http://www.americancenturyproject.org/in_classroom/hist_contextual.htm
3. http://www.americancenturyproject.org/in_classroom/transcribing_editing.htm
4. http://www.americancenturyproject.org/in_classroom/biography.htm
5. http://www.americancenturyproject.org/in_classroom/hist_contextual.htm
6. http://www.americancenturyproject.org/in_classroom/analysis.htm

placement course teachers choose to conduct a project following the completion of their exams in early May, a project connects better to a course when it is integrated into the curriculum in a context that adds breadth and depth to the project. For example, when middle or upper school students are studying the colonial American family, a family oral history project provides an opportunity to compare sixteenth-century and twenty-first-century life. In the context of studying a war, an artistic period, or a scientific idea, an oral history project serves as an important source for furthering one's understanding of the material. As the project timeline suggests, I also take advantage of extended breaks from school (Thanksgiving and the December holidays) that give students more time to

Table 4.2. Advanced Placement United States History Syllabus Trimester II, Week III

Continue working on historical contextualization. See me throughout the week with questions and/or concerns and drafts. Remember the goal of the historical contextualization: Become an expert in your subject. Also, begin preparing your preliminary interview questions. You must meet with me prior to leaving for break and conducting your interview.

Monday, December 10
Class I: The Road to Pearl Harbor (Why did Japan bomb Pearl?)

Assignment I. For Wednesday. Actively read and index in Zinn's *A People's History of the United States*, chapter 16, "A People's War." Be prepared to respond to the following question: Considering that Terkel called World War II the "good war," do you think Zinn would agree with this analysis?

Tuesday, December 11
Class II: Mobilizing for war ("War Socialism"). Why did the Allies and the United States decide to "beat Hitler first"?

Assignment II. See Monday's assignment.

Wednesday, December 12
Class III: In-class workshop: Preparing for the oral history interview and transcription. View *Nobody's Business* and complete viewing guide (see appendix). Role-play common interview mistakes.

Assignment III. (1) Examine and interpret documents of World War II. (2) Complete historical contextualization paper due Monday or before. (3) Continue developing preliminary interview questions *(you must see me for a one-on-one meeting before we leave for break)*.

Friday, December 14
Class IV: The war in the Pacific and the decision to drop the A-bomb on Hiroshima and Nagasaki: V-J Day.

Assignment IV. (1) Complete historical contextualization paper due Monday. (2) Continue developing preliminary interview questions *(you must see me for a one-on-one meeting before we leave for break)*.

Oral History Project Due Date Reminders:
- Monday, December 17 (or before): Historical contextualization paper due
- Wednesday, December 19: Initial fifteen questions due
- Wednesday/Thursday, December 19–20: Teacher–student conferences
- December 21–January 10: Conduct and transcribe interview

work independently and set up interviews without the daily grind of school life. In the end, academic study should not take place in a vacuum. Have students study an area and then encounter it on both a direct level and relevant basis through an oral history project. The integration of an oral history project into traditional coverage of course material is demonstrated by a weekly syllabus (see table 4.2). When students begin the American Century Project, they are formally studying World War I. When the project ends, they will have just completed an examination of the 1960s. In order to cover traditional course content as well as prepare students to be oral historians, I conduct mini-workshops during class periods on topics such as interviewee selection, asking the right questions, and understanding the equipment.

How Long Should an Oral History Project Last?

A project's length largely depends on how much time a teacher wants to commit to this work. A project can last a day, a semester, or an entire year. When studying the assassination of John F. Kennedy, I have students record their parents' response to two questions for homework: (1) Where were they when Kennedy was shot? (2) What do they remember thinking about this event? Students return to class the next day and compare their responses. The American Century Project lasts nearly four months; it is distributed in early November and culminates at the end of February. One of the major reasons for this time frame is to utilize the long Thanksgiving and winter holidays for two very different reasons. First, ideas for interviewees are often generated from family dinners. Second, the extended breaks give students, as well as interviewees, some flexibility and additional time for conducting their work. True, such demands do take away from family time, but I was pleasantly surprised—I might say shocked—when one set of parents approached me early in the school year to ask if their son would have time to travel to Florida over the New Year with them without disrupting his work on the oral history project.

Does Every Project Have to Be Transcribed in Full?

In order to create the most complete historical record, each interview should be transcribed as close to the actual responses as possible. This said, limits on the amount of time that can be given to a project, as well as what the final project is expected to look like, might allow for an incomplete transcript. Most projects that are done in less than a month do not include a complete transcription. Oral history interviews that are used as the basis for writing an edited autobiography usually utilize excerpts from an interview and not the whole transcript. Instead of transcribing, it is helpful—especially if you are considering establishing an archive—to have students complete an interview time indexing log (see appendix 12) that provides a brief summary of each five-minute portion of an interview.

What Are Some Alternatives to Transcribing the Interview?

Depending on the teacher, the course, the desired outcome, and the amount of time that is being committed to an oral history project, there are a variety of alternatives to the full transcription: (1) an interview portfolio (see appendix 17), (2) time indexing (see audio/video recording log in appendix 12), (3) research paper that combines interview excerpts with more traditional sources, (4) a project journal or reflection paper, (5) museum exhibit, (6) interview summary.

However, the uniqueness and value of an oral history interview rests in preserving the interview and making it accessible to researchers and historians. This is aided by a complete transcript that is permanently archived along with the recorded interview.

What Is the Difference between the More Traditional, Institutional Archive and Archiving an Oral History Project on the World Wide Web?

While the World Wide Web is a great resource, it is not a permanent archive and is only modified and updated as long as someone or some institution remains committed to it. For example, the website that supports the American Century Project (www.american centuryproject.org) is neither as extensive nor as consistently maintained as the project archive that exists in our school library. Moreover, due to financial and time constraints, the website cannot provide what is truly one of the most valuable and attractive dimensions associated with an oral history interview, the recorded responses of the interviewee. Therefore, it is recommended that classroom or programs create an institutional archive that is connected to your school or program electronic catalog. If your school or program does not have the resources to create an archive

Figure 4.2. A student's museum exhibit that includes interview excerpts as well as selected images being viewed at the annual Oral History Coffee House. (Photo by Ruth Faison, St. Andrew's Episcopal School)

an alternative would be to collaborate with a local library, museum, or historical society that seeks to broaden its collection. You can also register your project with Oral History Online (www.alexanderstreet2.com/oralhist). With an archive in place a project website becomes a great way to promote and share your work with the global community.

What Are Some Common Errors Made by Educators and Students?

- Poor recording equipment yields an inaudible interview.
- Student questioning does not clearly establish the relationship of the interviewee to the event under examination. Were they a witness or active participant in a historical event?
- While preparing an interview outline and a list of questions is an essential part of the oral history project process, students are often reluctant to stray from these materials when new and unsuspected opportunities emerge during the interview.
- Students need time to reflect and share their experiences with their peers. Too often, such reflection time is hard to fit into a class or program.
- Students fail to take advantage of the true value of oral history as the opportunity to get personal with an interviewee.
- Transcripts are not checked for both historical and grammatical accuracy by educators. (See appendix 11 for transcription and editing guidelines.)
- Inconsistent or poor-quality interview recording because of inferior equipment, background noise, or lack of technical training for interviewer.
- The original copy of the interview recording is used for transcribing purposes rather than a backup copy. Transcription places undo wear and tear on the tape that reduces both its quality and longevity. Always create and work from a backup recording!
- Far too many projects are not archived—either in an institutional library or on the Web—for use by the larger community that limits the usability of the students' work.

What Opportunities Exist for Educators to Be Trained in Conducting an Oral History Project?

Oral history is a historical methodology used in a variety of disciplines. Thus, the number of workshops and training programs continually grows. A variety of single-day and multiday workshops are available through organizations such as the Oral History Association, American Association for State and Local History, and the American Folklife Society. Each of these organizations hosts an annual meeting which is very useful and provides a variety of workshops and sessions. The Veterans History Project provides free training for schools and organizations interested in becoming partners in that program. Workshops are also available through regional oral history societies, humanities councils, and oral history offices located at a variety of colleges and universities. (See oral history sources and resources.)

Is a Project Possible to Do with Block Scheduling or in One Semester?

One of the challenges associated with such scheduling is the greater fear that material must be covered faster than in a yearlong course. Under these conditions, oral history projects are rarely conducted. One example of using oral history in a block schedule format (10–12 weeks of classes that meet each day for approximately 90 minutes) is to divide an oral history project into ten to twelve steps and do a portion of the project each week. By making the oral history project, and each of its steps, the primary means of developing essential research, writing, and historical thinking skills, you can cover material while enriching a student's experience.

How Do I Develop Support for an Oral History Project with Administrators and Colleagues?

In light of the issue of national and state curriculum standards, this question takes on increased importance. Chapter 9 provides details on matching curriculum standards to an oral history project, which goes a long way toward convincing school administrators of the value of an oral history project. However, here are some suggestions that are based on your ability to promote and advocate your project.[10]

- Invite administrators to your class or to a student interview. In public schools this could include your school superintendent and members of the board of education. In independent schools this should include members of the board of trustees and headmaster. If you are seeking support from the larger community invite local businesspeople.
- Publicize your work in community newspapers, radio, and television stations.
- Submit your projects for awards that bring recognition to you, your school or program, and the students. Awards geared to elementary, middle, and high school programs are distributed by the Oral History Association, Consortium of Oral History

Educators, Organization of American Historians, as part of National History Day as well as the National Council for History Education, National Council on Public History, and National Council for Social Studies. Awards are also helpful when applying for grant money. As nationally recognized oral history educator Michael Brooks claimed, "Awards generate respect and that respect generates money."[11]

- Include colleagues in the project as potential interviewees or as mentors for the students. One school pairs students with faculty members who help in the writing and editing process.
- Work interdisciplinarily by creating a project with a colleague who teaches another subject.
- Enlist the support of area institutions or organizations such as local college, state, and local historical societies, the library for resources, and, if needed, a site to hold a public presentation or archive project materials.
- Create a project website and then link it to the school's homepage to highlight this unique learning opportunity.

What Are Some Logistical Challenges to a Successful Oral History Project?

A teacher or educator can never underestimate the importance of planning for an oral history project. Even then, as in an oral history interview, you must be prepared for the unexpected. Here are some frequent challenges educators face:

- The need to transport younger students to and from interviews. Elicit the help of parents in this endeavor, which is essential for expanding the support network for your project.
- Having enough equipment. If it is not possible for your school or program to loan equipment to students, most students have at their home various types of recording devices from small, handheld tape recorders often used for business to minidisk recorders. Have students share their equipment. Another way is to collaborate with a department in your school or program. For example, a history department and a foreign language department paired up to purchase some tape recorders and external microphones that could be used for an oral history project as well as for oral components of foreign language classes.

What about the Safety of Students Who Do Interviews away from School?

This is an important concern that can be addressed in a variety of ways. First, educators can help ensure the reliability of interviewees by generating a list of potential interviewees that students must select from. Second, educators or parents can attend interviews. However, the presence of an individual other than the interviewer and interviewee has the potential to create discomfort for the student. Adults who attend an interview should wait in an area away from where the interview is being conducted in order to avoid being a distraction. In those instances where an adult attends an interview they can assist by asking those questions missed by the student either out of nervousness or inexperience. Third, if the interviewee is willing, have students conduct the interview at school which reduces some of the advantages of going to an individual's home where they might be able to weave some personal items, such as photographs or correspondences, into the interview. You can learn a lot about people by being in their surroundings.

What about Interviews That Deal with Emotional or Difficult Subjects or Memories?

Certain interview topics have proven more challenging for students due to the intense emotional and psychological response individuals have with certain memories. Interviews with war veterans, Holocaust survivors, prisoners of war, or survivors of other traumatic events or experiences have challenged students because of the emotional response by the interviewee. I would be reluctant to give such interviews to younger students. While the ability to share their stories can be therapeutic for the interviewee, this is a lot to bear for students often experiencing their first oral history interview and with very little understanding of the psychology of memory. I have prepared my students for potentially emotional interviews by showing them oral history interviews such as *One Survivor Remembers: Gerda Weissmann*. After viewing this video, we discuss what they might do if faced with a situation in which an interviewee begins to cry or needs to stop. In the end, the personal is what makes oral history such a unique historical method. So the instruction I often give to students is to respect the challenges posed by memory and the needs of the interviewee but to be willing to "lean into discomfort." However, always remember to respect an interviewee's right not to answer a question.

How Can I Do an Oral History Project When It Costs So Much Money?

One of the great myths of an oral history project is that its cost makes it prohibitive. In fact, an oral history project can be done with minimal resources such as a tape recorder and a computer for transcription. This said, better equipment also yields higher quality of interviews. Educators have secured money through grants from state and local humanities councils (www.neh.gov/whoweare/index.html), book sales, car washes, or merely by enlisting the support of area businesses who either donate their time and resources or provide services at a reduced fee. Since I require my students to have their projects professionally bound, I also provide them a letter to take with them when they are ready to copy and bind their projects; a discount often ensues. An important source is also a local college or university that can share their expertise on different aspects of your project, from content to technical needs. Fund-raising and writing should be inclusive. Students can develop important skills and have a unique educational experience if they are part of the writing and soliciting process. For example, students in Central Alternative High School raised about $4,000 to bring those involved in the events surrounding the "Little Rock Nine" to Dubuque for a public seminar.

WHAT'S NEXT?

Now that you have been convinced of the merits of oral history as an educational and historical methodology, all that is left is for you to start your own project. In no way am I minimizing the hard work that lies ahead or overlooking those remaining questions related to the wide range of experiences educators bring from their individual classrooms or programs. However, keep in mind the high learning curve for the educator who is leading his or her students through an oral history project and for the student who is actually doing oral history. The mistake would be to let your questions preclude you from missing out on this unique educational opportunity with your students. In the end, have what Charles R. Keller noted as the "essentials to good teaching, 'the courage to exclude' and the 'imagination to include.'"[12]

NOTES

1. Larry E. Hudson Jr. and Ellen Durrigan Santora, "Oral History: An Inclusive Highway to the Past," *History Teacher*, February 2003, 210.
2. Alan Berliner, *Nobody's Business*, directed by Alan Berliner (Milestone Films, 1996). 60 minutes.

3. Barbara W. Sommer and Mary Kay Quinlan, *The Oral History Manual* (Walnut Creek, Calif.: AltaMira, 2002), 122.
4. Michael Frisch, *A Shared Authority: Essays on the Craft and Meaning of Oral and Public History* (Albany: State University of New York Press, 1990). See also *Oral History Review*, Winter-Spring 2003, which includes a special section on shared authority. The editor's introduction identifies this concept as "one of the most influential ideas to impact the practice of oral history in recent years."
5. Ronald J. Grele, *Envelopes of Sound: The Art of Oral History*. 2d ed. (New York: Praeger, 1991), xv. See also Ronald J. Grele, "History and the Languages of History in the Oral History Interview: Who Answers Whose Questions and Why?" in Eva M. McMahan and Kim Lacy Rogers, eds., *Interactive Oral History Interviewing* (Hillsdale, N.J.: Erlbaum, 1994), 1–18.
6. See also Youth of the Rural Organizing and Cultural Center, *Minds Stayed on Freedom: The Civil Rights Struggle in the Rural South: An Oral History* (Boulder: Westview, 1991).
7. Michael Brooks, "Long, Long Ago: Recipe for a Middle School Oral History Program," *OAH Magazine of History*, Spring 1997.
8. "Voices of Experience: Oral History in the Classroom," *OAH Magazine of History*, Spring 1997, 24. Three of the projects conducted by Iberia High School students include "Crossing the Color Line: An Oral Perspective of the Integration of Iberia Parish Schools," "A Journey through the Years: An Oral History of the 1930s and 1940s in Iberia Parish," and "Somewhere in the Neighborhood: African American Communities in Iberia Parish During the Jim Crow Era." "Voices of Experience: Oral History in the Classroom," *OAH Magazine of History*, Spring 1997, 24.
9. Irma M. Olmedo, "Junior Historians: Doing Oral History with ESL and Bilingual Students," *TESOL Journal*, Summer 1993, 7–10, www.ncela.gwu.edu/pubs/tesol/tesoljournal/juniorhi.htm. See also I. M. Olmedo, "Creating Contexts for Studying History with Students Learning English," *Social Studies* 87, no. 1 (1996): 39–43; and Olmedo, "Redefining Culture through the Memories of Elderly Latinas," *Qualitative Inquiry* 5, no. 3 (1999): 353–76.
10. See also Linda Wood, *Oral History Projects in Your Classroom* (Pennsylvania: Oral History Association, 2001), 20, for additional suggestions.
11. Brooks, "Long, Long Ago," 33.
12. Allan E. Yarema, "A Decade of Debate: Improving Content and Interest in History Education," *History Teacher*, May 2002, 391.

CHAPTER 5

Conducting an Oral History Project

For the historian comes to the interview to learn: to sit at the feet of others who, because they are from a different social class, or less educated, or older, know more about something. The reconstruction of history itself becomes a more widely collaborative process in which non-professionals must play a critical part.

—Paul Thompson, *The Voice of the Past: Oral History*[1]

REGARDLESS OF THE TYPE OF PROJECT AND LENGTH, THERE are essential components to all oral history projects. The student oral historian must keep in mind the five Rs when conducting an oral history project: research, rapport, respect, reflection, and restraint. Each of these will be apparent in the steps of an oral history project that follow.

STEPS IN THE ORAL HISTORY PROJECT PROCESS

Research/Historical Contextualization

As James Hoopes points out in *Oral History: An Introduction for Students*, "Every good history course includes work meant to give the experience of *doing* history. This is often a research paper, and it should be the most interesting, stimulating aspect of the course. Too often, though, it is tedious, not because it is hard work, but because the challenge to human sympathy and imagination is neglected."[2] In the case of an oral history project, a traditional research paper is no longer the final product but rather a necessary stepping-stone from which students go into the field and interact with people who were part of, or witness to, history. At the core of a historian's work is the ability to research topics from multiple perspectives in order to insure the fullest possible understanding of a particular period, event, or person. This becomes even more critical when preparing to conduct an oral history interview. State and local historical societies as well as libraries can be very useful to students. They often have sources of local interest that can aid community oral history projects. They also have a larger sense of the community and can lead students to potential interviewees or alternative sources. Students who come into an interview thoroughly versed in the history they are examining undoubtedly have better interview experiences for two reasons. First, a student who researches the topic effectively and thoroughly is better able to gain the trust of his interviewee. This said, research should not be limited to the interview topic. For example, students who interview Vietnam War veterans are also responsible for understanding the larger domestic and foreign contexts in which this war took place.

The goal should be for the student historian to become an "expert" in the subject. An additional way to research is by inviting scholars from a local college or university, museum, library, or historical society to

---

RESEARCH TIPS

- Students should make sure that they examine "newspapers of the day" to get a sense of what was written during the time period the interview covers. Local and national newspapers will provide an important perspective of the event, period, or person.
- Students should also get a sense of what leading historians of a particular period are saying about their topic. For example, when students conduct an interview on the 1950s, I make sure they review the work of David Halberstam or Stephen Ambrose when examining American foreign policy, in particular World War II. Students are also reminded of the inevitable bias that percolates through the work of all historians and must make sure their research is balanced.
- Students should examine oral history interviews conducted on their topic. This will provide exposure to another primary source as well as possible questions for their own project.

LINKING RESEARCH AND INTERVIEW

Throughout your research keep a list of questions that emerge so you can then use them during the interview.

---

speak to a class or group about a project's content, as well as oral history as a historical methodology. It is impossible for historians to do too much research, though there comes a point for every historian to stop researching, a difficult decision for even the most experienced historians.

Second, a thoroughly prepared interviewer will be better able to think on his feet should the interview go toward a new direction. As part of the research, I often make students construct a research time line that matches the history of the period they are examining and the history of their interview. This is particularly helpful for visual learners to see where their interviewee's history fits into the larger events of the time. Table 5.1 is an example from an interview conducted with a Vietnam War conscientious objector.

Another excellent source for research is the interviewee. Students should ask whether their interviewee has materials that would help prepare them for the interview. This is more than an opportunity to broaden research; it also promotes rapport between project participants.

Finding Interviewees

When I was speaking to a group of students about their project on women nurses in the Vietnam War, their biggest concern was how to find an interviewee. Since this discussion took place the weekend before Veterans Day, I suggested that they attend the ceremonies held at the Vietnam Veterans Memorial in downtown Washington, D.C. While this would be a significant challenge for the reticent student, this idea yielded at least two interviewees for the project. VFW halls, nursing homes, newspaper advertisements, postings on listservs, announcements at religious in-

stitutions, personal letters, and word of mouth are also means to find interviewees. One very shy student walked next door, introduced herself and the American Century Project to her neighbor who happened to be a Supreme Court justice, and secured an interview. E-mail has emerged as unique way for students to connect with potential interviews. In the case of one student, his e-mail letter demonstrates the positive results that come when students are empowered with their own learning and pursue their own passions. (See letter, page 41.) The intergenerational bridge that was created between Mike Bryan and Mr. Burke became even more pronounced after Mr. Burke died suddenly after the interview.

It is essential when introducing an oral history project to interviewees that they are made aware of two things that might seem threatening to them: (1) they will be expected to sign a release form, and (2) the interview will be recorded. There are some potential challenges associated with interviewee selection. Despite living in an area overflowing with prominent interviewees, I encourage my students to find individuals whose life and history remain undiscovered. A few factors significantly impact a prominent interview. First, students' research must include reading, in full, any book that has been written about, or by, their interviewee. This became particularly difficult for one student who secured an interview with Congressman John L. Lewis on his involvement in the civil rights movement with only five days to prepare. A precondition for this interview was that the student had to complete *Walking with the Wind: A Memoir of the Movement*, by John Lewis and Michael D'Orso, before the interview. This condition was established because of an experience one student had of asking

Table 5.1. Research Time Line

Period/Event History	Year	Life History
	1948	Born in Long Island, N.Y.
JFK elected	1960	
JFK assassinated	1963	
LBJ reelected	1964	
Gulf of Tonkin Resolution		
	1966	Graduates from Great Neck HS
Tet Offensive	1968	
Nixon elected		
Kent State	1970	Graduates from Bates College
		Drafted, applies for CO status
	1970–72	Alternative military service, Laconia, N.H.
United States withdraws from Vietnam	1974	
Nixon resigns		
	1978	Boston U. M.A. in social work
	1991	Moves to Seattle

Dear Mr. Burke,

I am a junior, taking history at St. Andrew's Episcopal School in Potomac, MD. Our biggest project of the year is the Oral History Project. The purpose of this project is to learn history by listening to the views of a person who directly experienced an historical event or lived through a particular historical period. After gaining this insight, we are to compare this person's point of view with the "history books" discussion of the historical event or time period. I would be extremely excited if you would consider helping me out with this project. By interviewing you, I would learn about baseball in the Negro Leagues, the Baltimore Elite Giants, and your life experience.

For as long as I can remember, my passion has been and is baseball. I have played on numerous teams in every infield position and am currently captain of my school's baseball team. I was very fortunate to be able to go to Cuba with the Baltimore Orioles in 1999 where I made a little of my own history by being the first American to bat on Cuban soil in 40 years. I am an avid collector and have over 2,000 major and minor league autographs. I follow the minor leagues and have gotten to know many players personally. Each summer our family takes a trip through a different part of the United States to see as many major and minor league games as we can cram into the schedule.

If I could combine my love of baseball with my interest in 20th century American history, the beginnings of the Civil Rights Movement and the Negro Leagues, this project would be an incredible learning experience. It would truly be an honor to talk baseball and black history with you.

When I started researching this project on the Internet, I found the nlbpa.com (Negro League Baseball Players Association) site, sent an email, and received a reply from Robert "Bert" Orlitzky. He suggested that I call you and tell you that "Bert said it was ok to call." I will also follow-up this email with some pictures.

The project time line: Project starts before Thanksgiving and ends in February. The amount of time that we could spend together depends on your schedule. I hope that you would have some time to talk in person together and then we could follow-up by phone or email as your schedule permits. My history teacher, Mr. Glenn Whitman, has developed a website that describes the Oral History Project. Please go to the following website: http://www.americancenturyproject.org. On the left hand column click on "Oral History Project."

Thank you for your time and consideration of this request. I look forward to hearing from you.

Yours truly,

Mike Bryan

Figure 5.1. St. Andrew's Episcopal student Mike Bryan with interviewee, Ernest Burke, a former player in the Negro Baseball League. (Photo by Ann Bryan)

interview questions in which the interviewee responded, "Didn't you read my book?"

Two additional challenges emerged during interviews with prominent individuals. First, students have returned from their interviews suggesting that the responses seemed too rehearsed or dull. This was particularly apparent to one student who interviewed a leading figure of the civil rights movement who had been interviewed, by his recollection, nearly one hundred times. A second challenge comes when formulating an interview topic. Because Supreme Court Justice Sandra Day O'Connor was unwilling to speak about her time on the court, the interview focused on events leading to up to her appointment. Similarly, the subjects covered in an interview with former Washington, D.C., mayor Marion Barry ended just as he assumed office. While the students felt they were not getting the "good stuff," what they did uncover is as important to the historical record as that which is better known about these two individuals.

Preinterview Worksheet (See Appendix 6)

When students make initial contact with their interviewee, I have them complete a preinterview worksheet. This form is crucial to a successful interview because it gives focus to the interview topic and thus the research that needs to be conducted in preparation for the interview. It also fosters early dialogue between the major participants in the project.

The Interview Release Form (See Appendixes 7–8)

A good release form protects educator, students, institution, and interviewee. It should establish clear, understandable expectations. The biggest concern of potential interviewees is their belief that by participating in an oral history project they are giving up rights to publish their story on their own. It is therefore essential that the interviewee understands his or her right to use the information shared in the interview even though they are giving copyright to the sponsoring institution for a particular oral history interview. The release form also highlights the professional nature of the project. However, do not allow restrictions by the interviewee to prevent you from conducting the interview. Respect their concerns and see that they are addressed and documented, and if necessary, have the instructor make contact with them. We have had interviews that could only be used for a classroom grade, could not be opened until the death of the interviewee or other designated date, could only be used by researchers with written permission of the interviewee, or could not be put on

our website. It is important to note that the publication of an oral history interview that predates the Web requires a new release to be signed by the interviewee if it is to be put on the site. As history demonstrates, archived interviews will be around a bit longer than the technology with which they were conducted. Therefore, in order for interviews to be usable in the future, a release form should acknowledge "successor technologies." As a habit, I provide each interviewee a courtesy notification when their story is used in the public domain beyond the limits established in the release form. John A. Neuenschwander, *Oral History and the Law* (Carlisle, Pa.: Oral History Association, 2002), addresses many of the issues surrounding a release or donor form and also provides sample forms. As pointed out in the *Oral History Manual*, whatever form you use should include the following:

- Clear identification of the narrator's name
- Clear identification of the project repository
- Intended use of the interview
- A statement that the narrator is transferring "legal title and all literary property rights to the interview including copyright" to the repository
- A place for the interviewee/narrator to sign
- A place for the interviewer to sign[3]
- A place for a parent's signature if interviewer or interviewee is younger than eighteen.

An additional release form is required from the interviewer (see appendix 8).

One legal and ethical challenge that faces oral history projects is the institutional review board (IRB), which was created to protect research subjects.[4] While IRBs can mostly be found at colleges and universities, they lend themselves to important discussions for students on the impact an oral history project can have if not conducted in a manner that is respectful to the interviewee and his or her family. In "Institutional Review Boards Have a Chilling Effect on Oral History," Linda Shopes points out that "the current regulations were designed to protect people from unwittingly subjecting themselves to harmful scientific and medical experiments. Applied to oral history interviews and other forms of nonscientific research, they present numerous, serious difficulties, especially because many IRBs are constituted entirely of medical and behavioral scientists who have little understanding of the principles and protocols of humanistic inquiry."[5] The Oral History Association's evaluation guidelines and the American Historical Association's "Statement on Interviewing for Historical Documentation" "define a set of responsibilities interviewers have to narrators, to the public, to the profession, and to sponsoring institutions" that should be the standard for institutional review of oral history projects.[6] Fortunately for oral historians, beginning in 2003, oral history became excluded from IRB review. A policy statement developed by the Oral History Association and the American Historical Association in consultation with the Office of Human Research Protocol (OHRP) established that "most oral history interviewing projects are not subject to the requirements of the Department of Health and Human Services (HHS) regulations for the protection of human subjects at 45 CFR part 46, subpart A, and can be excluded from institutional review board (IRB) oversight because they do not involve research as defined by the HHS regulations."[7]

Borrowed Materials Receipt (See Appendix 9)

Often interviewees are willing to loan students materials and artifacts as part of the project. When borrowing such materials, both the student and interviewee should itemize what was taken, its intended use, and the expected date of return. If the materials are being permanently donated to a collection, that should be noted as well.

Developing Rapport with Your Interviewee

One of the biggest mistakes students make is failing to establish a good relationship with their interviewees prior to conducting the interview. Students who show up to the interview, push play and record, and say, "Tell me your story" often have a poor interview experience. I encourage students to contact their interviewees as part of their research, asking whether they have any books or memorabilia they could examine. With the proper release form, students can respectfully use such materials in their projects (see appendix 9). In the past, students have taken interviewees to coffee or lunch. When such a personal meeting is not possible, I encourage students to call their interviewee once or twice prior to conducting the interview.

Recording the Interview

Since oral history is about collecting the voice of an individual and preserving it for future use, the equipment you choose will determine the sound quality and usability of an interview beyond the transcript for generations to come. However, considering the cost associated with recording equipment, it should not be surprising that this becomes one of the biggest challenges for educators considering an oral

history project for their classroom or program. At minimum, a cassette "field" recorder and an external microphone: either a lavaliere (clip-on) microphone that is especially helpful for soft-spoken interviewers and interviewees, or an omnidirectional microphone that stands freely on a table and can be placed close to the interviewee should be available for every five students. This equipment should capture a fairly good-quality interview, which, if stored properly will last for many years.

An additional piece of equipment to help ensure good sound quality is headphones, which allow you to hear what is being recorded through the microphone. Making available a consistent set of recording devices, enables you to better control the overall sound quality of the interviews, as opposed to having students use their own equipment. The field recorders should be serviced by a technician each year.

The recorded interview sets oral history apart from all other historical sources. Therefore, consideration of equipment, and thus the consideration of cost, must be at the forefront of the oral history project planning process. In the end, don't let cost or a lack of equipment be a deterrence for giving students the chance to be oral historians. Educators in underfunded schools and programs have valued the interview experience and process so much that they sent their students out, in some cases, with no equipment other than pen and paper.

There are a lot of choices when it comes to recording oral history interviews that can be done using cassette tape recorders, digital audiotape, compact and minidisk recorders, as well as videocassette and digital cameras (see table 5.2). Avoid using microcassette recorders because they have poor sound quality. While most educators continue to use the cassette recorder, which has been the choice of oral historians for the past fifty years, many are also using minidisk because of the enhanced

"I just wish I'd known more about tape recorders when I first started my oral history class. I never thought about having just one or two good machines that kids could share. I got a lot of cheap recorders, and now I have a lot of cheap broken recorders. We had to get new ones every year" (Toby Daspit, New Ibernia High School, African American studies class).

Source: Quoted in Pamela Dean, Toby Daspit, and Petra Munro, Talking Gumbo: A Teacher's Guide to Using Oral History in the Classroom. (Baton Rouge, La.: Williams Center for Oral History, 1998), 25.

Table 5.2. Interview Equipment Pricing

Equipment	Estimated Cost in 2004
Microcassette recorder	$29–75 (Radio Shack)
Recorder (full-size)	$29–65 (Radio Shack)
	From $229 (Marantz)
Minidisk recorder	From $349 (www.sony.com) High Speed Net MD Walkman/Recorder
Video camcorder (VHS)	From $250
Digital video camera/recorder	From $699 (Sony Handycam-Radio Shack)
Video/digital camera tripod	From $40
Omnidirectional microphone and stand	From $10 (Radio Shack)
	$89 for Audio-Technica AT804
	Suggested windscreen $10
Omnidirectional lavalier microphone	From $100
Wireless phone recording controller	From $20 (Radio Shack)
	Packages
Full-size recorder package	From $550 (Marantz recorder, omnidirectional microphone stand, windscreen, and carry case)
Minidisk recorder package	From $500

sound quality in comparison to analog tape at an affordable cost. The cost of equipment deters educators from doing a project. However, funds can be secured from publishing your work and enlisting students in raising money in the local community to help offset project costs. Some companies, such as Bradley Broadcasting (www.bradleybroadcast.com), have recording equipment packages for schools or programs at a reduced cost. Table 5.2 reflects the equipment that my students have used over the years. The UCLA Oral History Program (www.library.ucla.edu/libraries/special/ohp/ohp-mag.htm) and Matrix's Oral History Tutorial (www.historicalvoices.org/oralhistory/audio-tech.html) are excellent resources for exploring op-tions for recording equipment that can be purchased from a wide range of dealers, including Radio Shack (www.radioshack.com), Bradley Broadcasting (bradleybroadcast.com), B&H (bhphotovideo.com), Sweetwater Sound (sweetwater.com) and FULL COMPASS (fullcompass.com). Equipment reviews can also be found at Radio College and AIR (Association of Independents in Radio).

Oral historians use a wide range of equipment. The sound quality of a recorded interview—and thus its appeal to listeners on the World Wide Web, a video or other media production is determined by both the quality of the recording equipment, and how students use it. For low-budget projects and newcomers to the field who do not yet have equipment and want to get started, Charles Hardy III of West Chester University, who has worked extensively on issues of sound quality, believes that minidisk is better than audiocassette. Hardy points out that there are a wide range of usable recorders on the market, and that the key with all of

them is to use an external microphone. Flash recorders for projects with more money are better than minidisk. Since so many people and schools already have home video cams, Hardy also recommends that the "people abandon audio-only recording altogether for digital video with a good mike or mikes, then back up audio on CD or [analog tape]."[8] On the other hand, Donald A. Ritchie reminds us to tread slowly into moving away from the preferred method of oral history recording for the last forty years, analog tape. "Ritchie warns that oral historians may risk early obsolescence by getting too far in advance of any new technology . . . New technology tends to pose vexing questions that encourages us, wisely, to wait until the technology has proven itself."[9]

Voice Recording Equipment

- It is recommended that you use a quality tape such as C-60 (30 minutes per side), which better handles the overwork during the transcription process as it is thicker than the C-90 (45 minutes per side) and C-120 (60 minutes per side) tapes, which stretch and bleed more.[10] Since interviews can last more than one hour, make sure students bring at least two tapes.
- Label each side of the tape prior to conducting the interview.
- A tape recorder with an external omnidirectional microphone because it can be handheld, which is a useful feature.
- If possible, make a copy of the tape after the interview that can be used for the transcription process, while the original recording, called a master, is deposited in an archive.

- Digital minidisk (MD) players are very popular among students and produce better sound quality than analog recorders.
- Telephone interviews are possible through varied types of attachments between the phone and recording equipment. These can be purchased at places like Radio Shack for a minimal fee.
- Bring an extension cord to the interview in case the nearest outlet is further away than expected.
- Have an extra set of batteries available.
- Remember to preserve your recording by locking the plastic tabs on each side of a tape or in the corner of a minidisk. This prevents the copying over of any material (see figure 5.2). Removing the tabs should occur only after the interview is complete.

Video Recording Equipment
- The use of such equipment requires at least two individuals, the interviewer and someone to operate the camera.
- Make sure your video camera is mounted on a tripod.
- Conduct the interview in a location where there is good lighting.
- Whenever possible, use a lavaliere microphone or other external microphone placed close to the interviewee to ensure the best sound quality.

Preparing students to use their equipment gives them a chance to practice with it. Do not overlook this important step in the oral history process, as a failure to practice has led some students to forget that a tape does not have three sides, or how to disengage the voice activation button on many recorders, leading to the loss of some important information. In one case, a student returned home to find out that she did not push both play and record on her tape recorder. Luckily, the interviewee let himself be interviewed again, but both participants agreed that it was not the same quality as the first interview. It is also important that the students check whether their equipment is working during the interview. I suggest that they do this right after they make the initial introduction as well as during a natural break in the interview.

Interview Outline
In preparation for an interview, students should create a logically ordered outline that includes major topics to be covered as well as initial questions. This outline should be based on information gathered during preinterview meetings as well as through research. An outline provides important structure to an interview but should not be a straitjacket; like all good stories, it should be organized with a beginning, a middle, and an end and should include factual as well as personal questions. Students should stray from their outline when new opportunities for securing unanticipated information emerge during the interview. As students develop

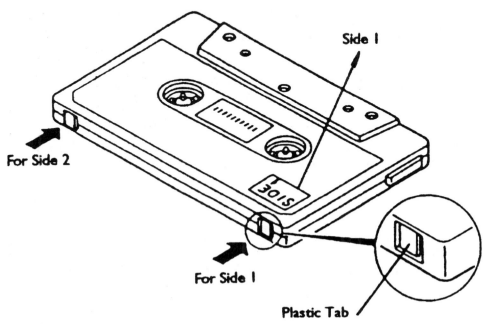

Figure 5.2.   From Stephen E. Everett. *Oral History Techniques and Procedures* **(Washington, D.C., Center of Military History-United States Army, 1992). http://www.army.mil/cmh-pg/books/oral.htm**

questions, they should consider what people one hundred years from now would want to ask their interviewees if they were still alive. I demonstrate the importance of this thought by asking students what questions they would want to ask Thomas Jefferson if he were alive today. Invariably, a student wants to know "what did he mean in the Declaration of Independence by 'All men are created equal'?" In the end, the ultimate benefit of an interview outline is to keep the nervous student focused and organized.

The Interview (Interview Reminders in Appendix 10)

There are a few ways to help soften the unease students will have with what, in many cases, will probably be their first experience conducting an oral history interview. In general, interview questions should be simple, brief, broad, and, where appropriate, bold. The length of an interview should be limited to approximately ninety minutes. An interviewer or interviewee's fatigue has an adverse affect on the quality of the interview. If necessary, take a break or return another day. Have students read and/or listen to professional oral histories such as those of Studs Terkel (www.studsterkel.org) or view Tim Russert on *Meet the Press* or C-SPAN's *Booknotes* (www.booknotes.org) and watch Brian Lamb's distinct, and at times effectively simplistic, interviewing style. Since we archive all our projects, students are required to review the work of students from previous years. Moreover, when the project initially begins, have students from the previous year's class share their experience as oral historians with their peers. Students should also realize that many times their interviewees are as unsure of the oral history process as they are. Finally, over the years, the one mistake students continue to make is failing to get personal with their interviewee. While this is challenging, and thus should take place toward the interview's conclusion, it provides insight that traditional research cannot and separates oral history from all other types of historical sources.

An interview should always begin with an introduction along the lines of the following:

This is _____ and I am interview-
        (student interviewer)

ing _____ on _____
        (interviewee)   (interview topic)

as part of the American Century Project. The inter-

view took place on _____ at _____
                          (date)   (location)

_____.
     (location)

LOCATION, LOCATION, LOCATION

The quality of an interview is often related to where it takes place. Make sure to find a quiet area, with no background noise, for the interview.

Throughout the interview it is important to be an active listener. Students should thus come to an interview with a notepad to jot down questions that emerge during an interviewee's response that can be used for follow-up questions. As Donald A. Ritchie points out, "An interview succeeds when the fully engaged interviewer constantly evaluates his interviewee's responses and changes gears."[11] Interviewers should keep in mind the experience of Thomas Dublin as he reflected on his interviews with coal mining families: "Once, when looking over photographs with Tom and Ella Strohl [whom he had previously interviewed], I expressed surprise at seeing so many pictures taken on hunting trips with his buddies. When I commented that I had not realized how important hunting had been in Tommy's life, he responded good-naturedly, 'Well, you never asked.'"[12] Students should also appear interested in their interviewee's responses by making good eye contact, keeping in mind that this person is sharing his or her life.

I often suggest that students also include one final question along these lines: Is there anything I failed to ask you that you think is important for me to know to understand this topic? If nothing emerges from this

---

PREPARING FOR THE INTERVIEW

- Have students interview one another for twenty minutes each during class.
- Have students watch a mock interview in front of the class between the instructor and another individual and critique its strengths and weaknesses.
- Have students complete and discuss the mock interview worksheet.
- "Interview bloopers" activity. In pairs, have students role-play one common interview no-no. The class has to identify the blooper. The following bloopers can be written out on index cards and given to the pairs who will have up to ten minutes to prepare a skit: asking more than one question, asking a leading question, asking a yes-or-no question, not asking a follow-up question, interrupting, and talking too much.

Source: The interview bloopers activity comes from Pamela Dean, Toby Daspit, and Petra Munro, Talking Gumbo: A Teacher's Guide to Using Oral History in the Classroom (Baton Rouge: Williams Center for Oral History, 1998), 44.

Worksheet 5.1.   Mock Interview

Either in small groups or working alone, identify and correct the errors made by the interviewer in this transcript of the first ten minutes of a mock interview with a Vietnam veteran.

Interview Transcription Interviewer (or Narrator): John Smith Interviewee: G. Whitman Date: 7/15/01 Location: Mr. Smith's house	
G. Whitman: In what year did you go to Vietnam? John Smith: 1968. GW: How long were you there for? JS: One year. GW: What was it like seeing people being killed around you? JS: It was difficult but I would rather not talk about it. GW: Do you think America was justified about fighting a war in Vietnam? JS: Absolutely not. GW: Where were you during the Tet offensive? JS: Well, that's an interesting story. My platoon was actually shifted south toward Saigon just days before the offensive and we were positioned just outside of the American embassy, which as you know was nearly overrun. I saw some amazing stuff that day that I will never forget. GW: Well, that's all the questions I have, thanks for your time.	

Questions to consider:

1. How should an interview be organized (beginning, middle, and end)?

2. What better way could this interview have been started?

3. If you were going to interview someone, what types of questions would elicit the most beneficial responses?

4. Where should emotional, tough questions come in an interview?

5. How might the interview have been better concluded?

question, the interview is over. A thank-you is appropriate followed up with a handwritten note of appreciation.

Finally, make sure the release form is signed prior to leaving the interview. Students should also be encouraged to ask their interviewee if it would be possible to conduct a follow-up interview if they have further questions. This is important because rarely do students, or even professional historians, get it perfect the first time.

Transcribing/Editing the Interview (See Appendix 11)

When it comes to transcribing and editing an oral history interview two questions emerge: (1) Should I transcribe an interview in its entirety? (2) What should be included in the transcription? Depending on the goal of your project, notes or excerpts from an interview might be enough. What is important to remember is the role a transcript plays in the dissemination of information collected in an interview. The transcription serves as a backup to analog tape that in a controlled environment should last twenty years or more and until recently, has been the principal audio format in which interviews were conducted. More importantly, when considering the utility of an oral history interview and project, researchers often first examine the written or typed transcription to determine what they can use in their work before, or even if, they head to the tape or disk. Therefore, I feel strongly that notes and excerpts should be culled from a completely transcribed interview, done by the student. Transcribing machines, with foot pedal, allow individuals to better control the pace of the recording. Such machines cost anywhere from $200 to $500. Professional transcribing services are also available. Despite the advantages of a transcription service, students should transcribe the interview themselves in order to best understand the primary source document they created and to also experience the production of history.

Oral historians disagree about what should be included in a transcript. "Some [oral historians] argue that the transcript should be absolutely verbatim, with no editing except to provide punctuation and to (perhaps) add some information as first names and exact dates, carefully bracketed to indicate that it was added by the interviewer/editor. Others argue that the editor should work with the narrator in checking facts, correcting unclear statements, and adding details so that the final manuscript is the most accurate account of events being discussed that the narrator can produce.

An extreme style of editing rewrites the transcript in perfect English, deleting unpleasant remarks, and even eliminating interviewer questions."[13]

When the transcript is complete, I suggest that the interviewee be given a chance to review it and make any changes that he or she believes are warranted. Such revisions should be noted at the top of the written transcript by stating, "Mr. Whitman reviewed and revised certain portions of this transcript on July 6, 2003." The difference between the original transcript and the revised transcript can be identified by researchers through a review of the recorded interview.

Transcription Time Indexing Log (See Appendix 12)

A transcription log provides a brief summary of the interview at five-minute intervals. This is important for archival purposes and has often been used as a substitute by educators who feel they do not have enough time for their students to transcribe an interview in full. The five-minute intervals should be based on elapsed time and not counter codes that are equipment specific.

Analyzing/Evaluating the Interview (See Appendix 14)

The extent to which an interview transcription contributes to a more complete understanding of history is what will be determined through its historical analysis. Like any other historical source, oral history cannot stand alone and must be examined in light of its strengths and weaknesses and in conjunction with other sources examined in the preinterview research. Keep in mind that history is a complex subject. A student's responsibility now is to determine the historical value of the interview remembering that, according to Donald A. Ritchie, "much of oral history is whether or not you believe your sources." For students, analysis and evaluation of their interview is difficult because of the higher level cognitive thinking that is involved as well as the emotional attachment they make to their interview that tends to distort their ability to be historically objective.

COMPLETING AN ORAL HISTORY PROJECT

An oral history project is not finished until it becomes public and project materials can be accessed by a larger audience. Permanent archiving of oral history interviews therefore needs to be a part of any oral history program and can be aided with the assistance of local historical societies, libraries, museums, or universities (see chapter 10). While a student-driven oral history project goes a long way to preserving the stories that otherwise would have been lost to history, a failure to properly store and create access to interviews limits the valuable contributions students can make to the preservation of the past.

NOTES

1. Paul Thompson, *The Voice of the Past: Oral History*, 3d ed. (London: Oxford University Press, 1988), 12.
2. James Hoopes, *Oral History: An Introduction for Students* (Chapel Hill: University of North Carolina Press, 1979), 20. Hoopes's work demonstrates how oral history research can be combined into a traditional research paper that uses written documents as well oral history interviews.
3. Barbara W. Sommer and Mary Kay Quinlan, *The Oral History Manual* (Walnut Creek, Calif.: AltaMira, 2002), 15.
4. "Recognition of the need for guidelines dealing with human subjects in research emerged following the Nuremberg trials, where the medical experimentation abuses of World War II Nazi doctors came to public attention. This led to the creation of the Nuremberg Code in 1945, the first legal attempt to deal with ethical issues of modern research. As biomedical research efforts expanded the international need for a more specific code of ethics was formulated in the 1964 Declaration of Helsinki." "A Brief History of the IRB," www.fordham.edu/general/Undergraduate/A_Brief_History_of_t7035.html.
5. Linda Shopes, "Institutional Review Boards Have a Chilling Effect on Oral History," *Perspectives Online: The News Magazine of the American Historical Association*, September 2000, www.theaha.org/perspectives/issues/2000/0009/0009vie1.cfm.
6. Shopes, "Institutional Review Boards," 3.
7. Linda Shopes and Donald A. Ritchie, "Oral History Excluded from IRB Review," Oral History Association, omega.dickinson.edu/organizations/oha. This site also includes "Historians and Institutional Review Boards: A Brief Bibliography." See also Donald A. Ritchie and Linda Shopes, "Oral History Excluded from IRB Review," *OHA Newsletter,* Winter 2003, and the Department of Health and Human Services Regulations for the Protection of Human Subjects at 45 CFR, Part 46, Subpart A to Oral History Interviewing.
8. Charles Hardy, August 27, 2003, personal e-mail message (accessed August 28, 2003).
9. "The Changing Current of Oral History," *OHA Newsletter*, Winter 2003, 13. This article was a summary of Donald A. Ritchie's keynote address at the September 2003 meeting of the Association of State and Local History in Providence, Rhode Island. See also Ritchie, *Doing Oral History: A Practical Guide*, 2d ed. (London: Oxford University Press, 2003), 57–60.
10. More information on recording can be found at Edward D. Ives, *The Tape-Recorded Interview*, 2d ed. (Knoxville: University of Tennessee Press, 1995), or by visiting Radio College, www.radiocollege.org; or www.minidisk.org.
11. Ritchie, *Doing Oral History*, 94.
12. Quoted in Linda Shopes, "What Is Oral History?" *History Matters: The U.S. Survey on the Web*, 8, historymatters.gmu.edu/mse/oral.
13. Condensed and adapted from material written by Willa K. Baum in *Transcribing and Editing Oral History* (Nashville, Tenn.: American Association for State and Local History, 1977), 38–39. See also Rebecca Jones, "Blended Voices: Crafting a Narrative from Dual History Interviews," *Oral History Review*, Winter–Spring 2004, 23–42.

 *Listening to Experience: Interviews with Five Oral History Educators*

THE INTEGRATION OF AN ORAL HISTORY PROJECT INTO THE classroom often comes from the initiative of teachers who desire to engender a renewed sense of intellectual curiosity about their subject. What is ironic is that this chapter's title runs contrary to the experience, or lack thereof, that most teachers initially bring to the earliest projects they conducted with students. What emerges is a unique collaboration between teacher and student that, for some oral history educators such as Delia Perez, "shifted the way I approach teaching as both my students and I learned that students can teach teachers, and for me that it is acceptable to learn along with students. In the end, sharing power with the students made for a more respectful and better learning environment."

What follows are interviews with teachers from across the country who have integrated an oral history project into their classroom. These interviews were conducted either by phone or in person and reflect the possibilities associated with the process and final product of an oral history project.

THE EDUCATORS

Gerry Albarelli first conducted an oral history project in 1985 with students in Providence, Rhode Island. He has been a freelance interviewer with Columbia's Oral History Research Office for twelve years and is the author of *Teacha! Stories from a Yeshiva*. In response to September 11, 2001, he began conducting an after-school project called Telling Lives with middle school students at the School for International Studies in the Cobble Hill section of Brooklyn and at MS-131 in Chinatown.

Francisco Guajardo is a lecturer at the University of Texas Pan-American in the College of Education's Educational Leadership Program. He taught for twelve years at Edcouch-Elsa High School, where he also directs the Llano Grande Research Center. Edcouch-Elsa is located in the southernmost part of Texas, fifteen miles north of the Rio Grande River.

Delia Perez is a former Edcouch-Elsa student who returned to teach at the school. In 1997 she conducted her first oral history project with her world history class.

Judy Gulledge is the instructional resource coordinator at Gramby High School in Norfolk, Virginia. In 1998, along with colleague Christine Capaci, she conducted an interdisciplinary oral history project with eighth grade science and English students at Northside Middle School in Norfolk. Along with their students they turned the interviews of residents of Smith and Tangier Islands on the Chesapeake Bay into a book, *Pennywinkle: Oral Histories from Tylerton, Smith Island in the Chesapeake Bay.*

Dan Whetzel has taught for twenty-five years and is currently at Allegany High School, in Cumberland, Maryland, a school in the second poorest county in the state. In his elective social studies seminar, Dan, along with colleagues Mike Lewis and Brian White, has conducted six oral history projects that became published books: *The Lanaconing Silk Mill: 1907–1957; Reflections of the Silver Screen: A History of Allegany County Movie Theatres; Surviving the Great Depression: A History of Allegany County During the 1930s; Allegany County Veterans of World War II: Through Their Service; Work and Wait: Allegany County, The Home-Front Years, 1941–1945;* and *Primetime: A History of Allegany County during the 1950s.*

Linda Wood is the former head of the New England Association of Oral Historians and library media specialist at South Kingston High School in Rhode Island, where she led teachers in numerous oral history projects including What Did You Do in the War Grandma?, The Family in the Fifties: Hope, Fear and Rock-n-Roll, and 1968: The Whole World Was Watching. She is also the author of *Oral History in Your Classroom* (Oral History Association, 2002) and recipient of the OHA Precollegiate Teaching Award in 1999.

Glenn Whitman: When did you first begin using oral history with students?

Gerry Albarelli: In 1985, I began doing it in a very rough way. I had just finished the creative writing graduate program at Brown and got a job teaching gifted, poor lower school kids in Providence, and I took those kids around in my car and had them interview people in nursing homes and where they could find them and made a little publication in which they illustrated the stories they collected. In 1991, when I was working at the yeshiva, I had the kids tell me stories from home and collected those stories and again made a magazine. Many of those stories were passed down from the Holocaust. At the same time, I was working at the Harvey Milk High School, which is a high school for gay and lesbian students in New York, where I was teaching writing and video production. We ended up making a documentary and the kids wanted to make a documentary about themselves. So they interviewed one another and interviewed people out in the Village on the streets where their favorite question was, "What do you think about a high school for gay and lesbian students?" Another thing that I did in terms of the connections that I see between oral history and fiction, right now I am teaching a creative writing course at Eugene Lang College, where I have students read stories and then have people come in who I think could have stepped out of one of these short stories to be interviewed. For instance, we had a guest who grew up in the Brownsville section which he describes as a "Yiddish household" in Brooklyn in the 1920s and we had been reading that kind of fiction—Yiddish-inflected fiction, including Grace Paley—and he just spoke after being asked three questions during a class interview.

Francisco Guajardo: In a formal sense, I began to use oral history with my students probably in 1992; it was very much an experimental process for me. I should say that there is a whole lot of history and context that informs that. I was born in Mexico, lived there the first few years of my life, and then came with my family to Texas. My learning as a kid really happened around the dinner table, sitting around the porch, having conversations with my parents, with my aunts and uncles, with neighbors and it was all done through a very much folk, oral way, so that it is stories for me that informed my learning. Through story I figured it was, for me, very natural and intuitive, that I would become a teacher through story. My whole pedagogical approach is really fundamentally based on story and of course that means so much and that implies so much. It implies a whole lot as we are developing a pedagogical movement that is rooted in story and for Mexican people in this country, which is my context, it is a very powerful learning tool because everyone understands story, everyone has heard stories, everybody has learned from them and everybody has a story. It is the one thing nobody can take away from you and that you unequivocally own. It feels right for a lot of peo-

ple. I am a huge book advocate and book supporter; on the other hand, as we were doing an oral history with the father of educational anthropology, George Spindler, who has been teaching at Stanford University for fifty years, we brought him down to south Texas and Spindler said, "I don't know where we went wrong thinking that wisdom comes from books, wisdom comes from people." If we would only understand that I think we can cut across a lot of the [b.s.] in education. But we don't get it; books tend to be esoteric and so insulting by implication for kids to check their vigor and passion at the door. I didn't understand this intellectually but I understood this instinctively. So when you ask me when did you begin oral history I say my learning began when I was a kid listening to the stories, for me it is part of the reason that I went into teaching because I understood the power of story in teaching and learning. Oral history was a strategy and we used the strategy because I might have seen something about Foxfire. In 1996–1997 as we became more frustrated we went after some money, we hit an Annenberg Rural Challenge grant where we could buy fancy toys and travel where we found people, not just of color or on the margins, but other people who valued stories, everybody does, but not too many people ever formalize it. So in 1997 we formally began that oral history project of the Llano Grande Center using the oral histories not just for instruction or schooling but for community development, economic development initiatives, creating PhDs. The oral history process has been at the center of the community revitalization effort.

Dan Whetzel: Perhaps twenty years ago, but it was integrated into world history and I chose to do it in the medieval Europe unit. The reason I did it there was because of family coats of arms. I have the students design their own coats of arms based on interviews they conducted with their parents and grandparents about their family history. From that, I thought that I would offer this as an extra credit project, interview your parents and grandparents and write a report on the history. It was a rather loosely organized effort to start. The most recent projects date from 1999 [silk mill project] which was our publishing date though we worked on that book for two years. That was an extracurricular or after school—whenever—type of program, and there was four very capable students. I can't say there was a plan. We didn't start out to write a book. Mike Lewis lives in Lonaconing where the mill was located and he said, "You got to come up and see this." One day we started to talk and believed we should do something. The owner of the mill said, "Everybody says that but nothing ever happens." We asked students to work and do the research. We had interviews, but at that point we didn't know what to do. So I called a friend of mine who was in publishing and he offered to help us make a booklet. After the Silk Mill book was published, a colleague of mine was hired by the board and we worked really well together. We made a decision to integrate the oral history program into the Social Studies Seminar, which is a semester class. We had twelve students that agreed to sign up for the course knowing they would be working on an oral history project. That book was the *Theatres of Allegany County*. Again, we were kind of floundering because we never did the class before. I could name six or eight theaters that I remembered and the more we got into it the longer the list grew. I think we ended up with twenty something theaters. Every little town had a theater. Don't you know that when the book came out, the next day we get a phone call at school from this older gentleman who was very upset saying, "How can you call this a book on the theaters of Allegany County when you don't have the Gem Theater in there?" Sure enough there was a theater but it didn't even make the talkies; it closed in 1925. We are now faced with a problem of popularity. The books are anticipated by the local citizens; we have over forty students signed up for this course. We are now negotiating with the principal. It is not a traditional class at all, we are more the facilitators. The kids know more about each particular subject than we do as teachers. The students really become experts on a particular topic. While this is a semester course, in reality we work on the book all year long.

Linda Wood: My first oral history project was at Chariho Regional High School, during the bicentennial year where I was filling in for a librarian but had very little to do. Being that it was the bicentennial year, I invented something to do. I had read Eliot Wigginton's Foxfire books and I was quite into doing your own thing, making your own bread, soap, raising pigs which we did at home. So I thought that this was really cool and I would do an oral history project. At the same time my husband, who was a newspaper reporter, had done a series of articles on the new Rhode Island Committee for the Humanities, and he said, "You should go talk to Tom Roberts who was the executive director and see if you can get funding for an oral history project." I met with him and in those days, at least in Rhode Island, a humanities project had to have a public interest aspect to it and it had to be for

adults. So I had to write the application to use the students to present a public policy issue to adults. The Humanities Committee told me that I should talk to Jim Findlay, a history professor, at the University of Rhode Island because he had done oral history. He came to the high school and worked with the students and me, and taught us what oral history was. The first project was called "Yankee Ingenuity and How the Government It Forged Survived." We did this as an after-school project with eight kids who volunteered. We interviewed what we defined as "swamp Yankees" and I think the kids interviewed sixty people. At the time they were going to build a nuclear power plant in Charlestown, Rhode Island, right on the beach. We concentrated on the public issue of a nuclear power plant in our backyard and how the Rhode Island town meeting form of government could deal with such a big national issue at the time of the energy crisis. A couple of years after I started at South Kingston High School, I worked with an English teacher who was teaching a community project class—remember this was in the 1970s when we had a lot of miniclasses— and the class was a mixture of twelve to fourteen tenth-, eleventh- and twelfth-grade students and met once a day for about nine weeks. That was the project about the 1938 hurricane. It was done a year before the fortieth anniversary of the hurricane and dealt with the building of homes on barrier beaches.

Glenn Whitman: Why did you choose to integrate oral history into the curriculum?

Gerry Albarelli: I was supposed to be teaching them English and I was also interested in the people in the neighborhood in Providence. It was really kind of wonderful. We came across a family of Cambodians in a tree who were picking apples and we got them to come down and be interviewed. As soon as we found these Cambodians in a tree, I knew it would be nice to find other kinds of people, there were so many different kinds of people living in Providence that these kids could talk to. Some of the new immigrants, some who had been there for a long time. So when they did that publication, of course, on the cover there was a picture of Cambodians in a tree. Since they were fourth graders I transcribed and than gave them the transcripts and they wrote stories based on the transcripts.

Judy Gulledge: It was a dream that I've had about five or six years prior to the project. I read *Foxfire*, and prior to that I had taken a course at Old Dominion University and was shown a video of a school in western Virginia that shows kids doing an oral history project that they simply bound. But I can remember how excited those kids were when they got their finished product back, having something in their hands that they had done, and I just thought that was something I wanted to experience. I took these kids on these island trips and they had the opportunity to visit with the people that lived a life so different from theirs, and it just seemed like the perfect fit. It took finding an English teacher willing to put forth the same amount of effort that I was willing to put forth. And the principal at that time helped arrange my interdisciplinary team to include Christine. Our curriculum was strongly environmental science and since there is so much change over time in terms of our environment and interviewing these folks who lived on Smith Island, my students were able to see how in the lifetime of these people, how the changes we had studied in the classroom were seen by those who experienced these changes first-hand. Especially with our study of the decreased population of oysters in the bay in the past hundred years and how this has impacted water quality. Oysters are such a keystone organism and how that has changed water clarity, therefore underwater grasses and therefore fish and crabs. To study that, read about it and talk about it is one thing, but then to go and in the process of interviewing these folks who talk about years when there were so many oysters and crabs and how they could run out to the end of the docks and play this game where you could see the bottom and dive down to get things and then my kids are at the end of those very same docks and they can't even see a meter down, is another. It just really brought it home to them, what was happening to the environment.

Dan Whetzel: I have an interest in local history, and that is crucial to having a sense of what is going on with the town and the people. Beyond the interest, I think it is an excellent educational tool for a number of reasons. It's interdisciplinary, the students are doing work on a level that I didn't do until my junior year in college. We spent hours on microfilm at the university to confirm stories. The theater book in particular, when did the theater open, when did the theater close? So the students are using primary research materials, they're interviewing people, and that is a learning experience, how to interview, how to approach people in a professional manner. Then once the interviews are transcribed you have photocopies and newspapers, interview transcripts, articles, artifacts people will bring in, and the authors will have to examine these materials, write an article and reach a conclusion. It's writing, reading, interviewing, interper-

sonal skills, it encompasses what I like to call authentic learning. It reaches students on so many levels. It's a wonderful way to teach and I don't know why more people don't do that because so many kids today are disconnected. The pillars of a society are the family, the religious institution, and the school. Schools can connect kids with the community. It is real easy for a kid to throw a rock through a window or write graffiti on a building if they don't know what lives there or what is connected to it. Get these kids out and talking to people and looking them in the eye, it makes all these connections and creates respect.

Glenn Whitman: What was the first formal oral history project you assigned to your students?

Francisco Guajardo: In 1992, I began training students in a very crude way. So we would do a mock oral history in the class, we would invite some old-timers from the community, go into someone's house, where the kids would be observing, taking notes, and learning. I should say that I don't have any of that in my possession. Beginning in the fall of 1997 we began to do it in a much more sophisticated way, holding on to it and processing it. We're studying the Second Continental Congress, so we are in 1776, Philadelphia, and Carlos Garcia, who was in my U.S. history class, raises his hand and says, "Mr. Guajardo, were Mexicans around when Thomas Jefferson was crafting the Declaration of Independence?" And I said to Carlos, "You know they were around," and he looks down at his book and he points at his book and he says, "Prove it to me." He caught me. I say, "Carlos, I cannot prove it to you." What do you do as a teacher? I responded by bringing Carlos into the fold and putting together a proposal to write the books, having us being active agents in history. Essentially we weren't in the books, actually, we were in the appendix or in an insert, they bring in people like Pancho Villa, but not as an integral part of it. It was not about doing World War II veterans, it was not about doing women from a certain period, it was about "prove it to me" that we are in history. So it was much broader than a specific research project, it was actually about creating ourselves, it was essentially about our own existence. It was also about building skills, building leadership, reversing the hemorrhaging of talent from our community. It was for valuing people's lives and stories, for celebrating people.

Glenn Whitman: How did you decide on the appropriate project?

Gerry Albarelli: In both Brooklyn and Chinatown the project was initially sponsored by Columbia University. It was Mary Marshall Clark, who is the director of the Columbia Oral History Research Office (COHO), who came up with the "Telling Lives" title. It was my idea to conduct the project at the School for International Studies, which I did with Amy Starecheski, who is an interviewer for COHO. Amy and I also did the project in Chinatown. The reason I had that idea was I had interviewed Tom Roderick from Educators for Social Responsibility and in the course of that interview he told me about problems at schools between kids, which I have heard of through other interviews, after September 11. Those problems were basically underreported, Arab kids getting beaten up and abused. Schools tended not to want to talk about what was going on and tended to say to the Arab-American Family Support Center, for instance, "we can handle it." Meanwhile there was a lot of trouble in the schools, especially in Brooklyn, especially in the Cobble Hill section where there are so many Arab students. At this school there were a couple incidents of violence related to September 11. The Arabic-speaking kids were in self-contained Arabic-language classrooms, so they were kind of isolated to start with. After September 11 there was one incident of someone stabbing someone else, lots of fights. The school's response was to assimilate the kids—there are no more Arabic-language classrooms—they try to get them into the general population. They also had educators come in and put on this Cultural Day that was a complete failure because some kids read pro-Palestinian poetry and teachers found it to be anti-Semitic. So I thought this would be a really interesting place to do an oral history project because there are so many different experiences of September 11 and because even in general, in doing the Narrative and Memory Oral History Project [sponsored by Columbia University] of September 11 what we were asking people was, "Who were you before September 11 and how does that story continue to play itself out long after September 11?" "What are some of the stories that you know that aren't being reported in the media?" So we had a meeting with the principal and he was all for this project. He said, "I'd rather talk about the problems that are happening here." The school was basically new, it was formerly called the Nathan Hale School but did poorly, and so it has a new philosophy and oral history makes perfect sense because they want to make educational use of the fact that kids come from such diverse backgrounds. He liked the idea of trying this as an after-school program and than maybe thinking of ways to make it part of the school program next year.

Judy Gulledge: There were three island communities which we usually went to but this one included our stay in homes in the little town of Tylerton. It is such a small town that the kids had free rein in moving around this community; you could walk from one side of the island to the other in ten minutes. We set up the kids' initial interviews but in the day or two afterwards if they had additional questions they were able to walk on down the path and find the person they interviewed and ask further questions.

Delia Perez: I first decided on an oral history project to demonstrate that history can be learned outside of the four-walled classroom and that students can learn by going into and talking to people in the community. The cross-generational project was to help students realize the importance of maintaining their ancestral language and to possibly inspire them to revive their Spanish-speaking skills. One day I came to class and asked the students when was the last time they had a conversation with their grandparents? They commented that they often did not talk with their grandparents because "I cannot speak Spanish." The project would force them to reconnect with people in the community, including their grandparents.

Dan Whetzel: The mill just came about; the theaters came about through a student suggestion. After the theater book we began to reflect on the age of people who could recollect. We decided that the '20s were basically gone. We also decided that this was the last hurrah for the Great Depression so we decided to proceed in a chronological manner beginning with the '30s. We tried to reach back as far as we could to capture stories; we call it "capturing a moment in time." After we complete the Vietnam War we're not sure what we're gong to do. There will probably be a place for an occupation, or downtown Cumberland.

Linda Wood: I don't know where the ideas come from. The '50s project was a real strain for me. I kept trying to do something on the '50s but I couldn't quite get hold of the decade and I don't think we ever did. I don't think that was a good project though, there were some really good parts to it. The 1968 and Grandma projects were great.

Glenn Whitman: What training in oral history did you have prior to conducting your first project?

Gerry Albarelli: I didn't have any formal training. When I taught at Brown as a teaching assistant, I just started using some oral history texts because I found them really good in a fiction writing class. For instance, Danilo Dolci's *Sicilian Lives*, and that was maybe the second writing assignment I gave my class. I read some of those stories and said write a story in the voice of someone where the voice is so strong it determines the shape of the story. I had been interviewing people on my own since I was a little kid. How I got to Columbia is that eventually I made my way back to New York and in 1990 I was making a film about a gay cop. I had just bought a video camera and was very informally interviewing this cop, and I would ask him to tell me about his job. I showed the footage to Mary Marshall Clark of the Columbia Oral History Research Office and she said that while you're making your film and interviewing cops why don't you interview gay cops for our collection. I interviewed thirty-five cops and I learned about oral history formally at that time. I also did a lot of reading. I read Portelli and I just recently sat in on Ron Grele's graduate seminar at Columbia.

Francisco Guajardo: I went through the best training. It was my parents training me. No academic institution could have done a better job than the job my parents and my community did in training me as an interviewer, as somebody who is community-minded, as someone who valued stories, as somebody who could be a part of a revitalization and community effort. In fact, the university did everything to strip me of it. Because of every single textbook that was given to me, because of the very formal methodology and research classes . . . When I was an undergraduate, I remember calling home and talking to my father about the profound dearth of materials. I was looking for primary sources of Mexican people in this country and I just couldn't find them. It was mostly works that had been written by scholars and institutions about Mexican people in this country and that was unsatisfactory at every turn. It was filled with stereotypes; it was another reality from the one I lived. I remember telling my father that the stories he had shared with us as kids were so rich but I wasn't finding them in any books. My father went to the fourth grade in rural Mexico. And I challenged my father to write them down. So he wrote his autobiography. That was great training for me; that was a real model. And the way people looked after me and other people as I was growing up in that community, those were things that were training me. The whole oral history process, if it

isn't about looking after each other then the whole process is missing out on so much. At the university, if I had been taught how to do field research, there was nothing taught about looking after each other in the methodology I was studying. It wasn't about reciprocity and building and continuing with the relationship as a lifelong endeavor. It was mostly about going and collecting the data and being true to the data. But it misses out on the principles that should inform the collection of the data and what you should do with it. The principles of valuing people, not violating them in a very imperialistic way. The principles of caring, the principles of love, the principles of building the relationship for a long time. The university didn't do that for me. It was about my community teaching me through their example of taking care of me and my parents. That was the training for me.

Judy Gulledge: It was learning as we went which was probably tougher on the kids. They did their original transcriptions, that probably took them until February with the trip to Smith Island taking place in November. They had to do it on their own time. What kinds of format we were going to put this in required us to experiment one way and then, all of a sudden, we decided to go another. The kids hung in there, they stuck with us. It was nice because we taught those kids for two years and we chose students who had a strong work ethic.

Dan Whetzel: I had no formal training other than what I would read on my own. However, Barry Lanman [president of the Consortium of Oral History Educators], was very helpful. Before the books began, Frostburg State University called because they were commemorating the fiftieth anniversary of the end of World War II and they were going to invite nationally known people like Dr. Spock and they wanted a local component. We decided to interview veterans, not just about being veterans but about the postwar experience, the years 1945–1947. I got some students who were interested and we looked at race relations, we interviewed a Tuskeegee airman, who after serving could only get job offers to be a janitor. We interviewed a judge, a housewife. I just knew that I was getting into something I didn't know much about. So I wrote to the Humanities Council and someone recommended we get a grant, which I knew nothing about, but part of the process was to secure expertise. Barry came up for two sessions with the kids and me, which got me headed in the right direction. Reading Studs Terkel and, of course, the Foxfire program helped.

Linda Wood: Really none, except for Jim Findlay coming in and being an adviser or, as the humanities grant requires, a "humanist scholar."

Glenn Whitman: What type of support did you receive (administrative, financial)?

Francisco Guajardo: Once we hit the big money there was no turning back, as there was all types of money out there. In terms of support, if you interview certain people for political reasons you can have their support. If one pretends that this is just about an academic exercise we're missing a very large component of it. For me it is very much about community, building young leaders. It is not about collecting stories; it is about building young leaders, it is about community revitalization, it's about all the other things and we just use oral history as a way to do it. And it is about responding to Carlos's question, "Where are we?" And I don't know if I could respond to that question with other strategies or techniques. The administration, and a lot of teachers, were very reluctant and continue to be very reluctant. By no means do we have a buy in from everybody or support from everybody. This flies right in the face of the whole standardization movement (TEKS). You need to have principals and teachers who want to take risks, community members who want to be innovative. There is very little that is interesting about the standards movements and teaching to the test. That crushes people's spirits. We have had seven superintendents and six principals and the Oral History Project continues. A lot of faculty members see this as way too much work. And it is. You must really be willing to invest a lot of creative energy.

Judy Gulledge: We had a share of a fairly large grant from the Virginia General Assembly, about $300,000, and one of the things we proposed that we would do was this book [Perrywinkle]. This is how much we believe in our kids' ability. And the school administration was very open to the project. The staff at the schools also helped the kids in the editing process because Christine and I found it to be far too overwhelming for just the two of us to do it. The kids were paired, and each pair had a teacher-mentor that they could run things past. So the staff, even the principal, was involved in giving feedback to the students about their work.

Dan Whetzel: The first year was on our own; it didn't require any change of schedule but there were unavoidable publishing costs. So I went to Biederlack, which is a German company that opened a factory there and they make blankets and this was my idea.

Biederlack makes blankets; therefore, they should be interested in an old silk mill. I went out with a student and made a presentation, and after going through all my reasons for needing $500 I said we were willing to offer him the space on our back cover for advertising. He said, "No, I don't want that. I don't want to junk up your book. I don't want any credit for this but I will give you the money." With the course, we've had general support from our school administration, which is necessary for scheduling purposes, because the number of students grew that we needed for the two of us instructors to be present in the same room at the same time.

Linda Wood: I tried to sell oral history to social studies teachers, which seems the most logical, but I could never sell it to them because they were so tied into the curriculum and they had so much to cover in such a short period of time that they couldn't really break away from their traditional curriculum. You can't do an oral history project as a three-day assignment, or even a two-week assignment. I was an English teacher for several years before becoming a librarian, so I approached an English teacher—Judi Scott—who seemed very flexible and who was interested in teaching English as a process rather than content. In the English classes we tied the subject together with all kinds of related material, so when the students were doing their research for the oral histories, they were also doing their English assignments. Securing grant aid was helped by the success of our first project, and you have to remember Rhode Island is a very small state and if you build up a reputation, and you write a good grant, you can get the money. The Grandma project received a humanities grant for $14,000.

Glenn Whitman: What advice do you give to teachers searching for grant support for an oral history project?

Linda Wood: I think there is money available; if you can do it with even a couple of hundred bucks, or your department budget, then do it. People love oral history and they will come to the public programs or read your newsletter or whatever you're putting out with it. If you can establish that baseline of support with something successful then it will be easier the next time. But it doesn't cost a lot of money to do an oral history project with the largest cost often transcribing.

Glenn Whitman: What was the initial reaction of students when they were told of this project?

Gerry Albarelli: The kids were a pretty select group, originally ten. There was a kid from Guatemala who had really interesting stories but he had very little English and I think he felt left out. The first week our assignment to them was to go home and have someone tell you a story and come back and tell it to us. When he came back the next week he claimed that he didn't have a story but then, towards the end, somehow, it became clear that he did have a really interesting story about crossing the border into the country illegally with his mother. The kids reacted pretty well. We kept asking the kids, "Where do you want to go?" In the beginning we thought we would ask the kids for their input all the time, that we would have them determine a lot of what we were going to do. It then became clear that they needed our help. In the beginning we would ask where would you like to go and they would just stare back at us. But then we started taking them out and when we took them out, when they were actually doing it, they suddenly had ideas. So one of the Arab kids said, "Let's go to that Jewish store over there and interview the owner." The Arab kids were really interested in the African American stories. At one point, when we first started talking about oral history, I had asked something about the slave narratives and the history or oral history and then asked, "So now what would you like to do?" One kid said he wanted to interview ex-slaves. So then they were really interested, and remained interested, in the civil rights period because they saw a connection between their own experience as Arab Americans at this point in time. So we found people who could talk about that to them. They interviewed an older woman about her experiences growing up in the segregated South, and she knew Martin Luther King, and the next time we met they wanted to interview Rosa Parks. But I said she doesn't live in New York. One kid responded by saying, "That's all right, we can get a van and go and find her."

Judy Gulledge: When they were first told about it, it didn't seem like that big of a deal to them. When they developed a relationship with the people that they met and interviewed, all of a sudden it became very personal to them. Especially with the stark differences, not just in their ages, but you've got urban kids who go to this island community where they don't even lock their doors, where some of our students literally don't go out and play once they get home to their neighborhood because it's not safe. For them to walk down these pathways and see people leave their homes open, and their stuff around and keys in their little golf carts the students' first reaction is "these stupid people, somebody is going to steal it." But look at them, they all know each other so well they don't even need a po-

lice force here. These people really connected with the students as well. These people opened up so much and shared so much of their life, which actually kind of surprised me, they just seemed to really thrive on having somebody listen and to be curious about their life, even though I don't think they believed that we were really going to put this into a book.

Delia Perez: They were skeptical about the idea of learning outside of class and didn't quite know what to expect. In fact, they thought I was making it up, though they were excited to get out of class eight times during the year.

Glenn Whitman: What do you hope to accomplish with your project?

Gerry Albarelli: I really would like to see it become part of their regular school day. The different backgrounds of the students and the resources that they have . . . once they were engaged, the students took us to their own communities and had a lot of good ideas about people who should be interviewed. We just recently put together this publication called *Brooklyn Stories*, which includes five or six of the stories the kids collected and illustrated. It makes me think, as we are about to start another phase of this with a new group of kids, it would be wonderful to have many Brooklyn stories from many schools in the Brooklyn neighborhood recorded by students. It would be a history of Brooklyn recorded by students. We do hope to have the kids realize the importance of their role as oral historians by talking to other kids just starting this work.

Glenn Whitman: How did you find your interviewees?

Francisco Guajardo: We went about identifying people in a very organic way. It wasn't that we developed a scheme to find who came during the Mexican Revolution or who were the people who dug up the earth to build Delta Lake. It was about who is interesting. So names would come up and we would go to those people's homes, we talk with them, we build a relationship with them—by the way, we seldom did an oral history with people who we just met. It was about doing it in a very relational way. So you had to meet somebody, most of the people we already knew, but it wasn't about going into their houses or having them come into the classroom and putting the mike in front of them, it was about building a certain sense of trust. Once we got to talking to people they gave us leads. "Have you talked to this person or that person?" We never took a very thematic approach to the oral history process. It was about allowing it to grow in a very organic way. We were all over the place and, in retrospect—we continue to do it—that's a really good way to do it because you are honoring people as researchers, people as leaders. Someone might say, "Have you interviewed Donesa vel Teerez?" and we would say no, tell us about Donesa vel Teerez and the old man would say he was the founder of Edcouch. Let's go to Donesa vel Teerez, and we ask what can we do for you, we would like to interview you and we wind up fixing the roof in his house, which is part of the reciprocity. You have got to do something. You cannot just be the traditional researcher. The whole concept of research can be very perverse. Historically, research has been about going in and taking stuff and that just really violates the whole relational process. So we are very sensitive to that.

Judy Gulledge: The guides for the Chesapeake Bay Foundation set up the interviews. They had been interviewed quite a bit from other groups, so they were used to being asked a lot of questions but not at such the length my students did. Usually it was ten minutes and my students spent at least two hours in the initial interview, in pairs with little tape recorders and their cameras. Of course my kids were telling them we're going to write a book and these citizens were imaging this little Xeroxed-stapled little book, which, to be perfectly honest when we first began, was maybe how we thought it would happen. It kind of serendipitously fell into place.

Delia Perez: I went to area elderly day care centers and explained to either the manager or owner that I wanted to bring twenty-five to thirty high school sophomores to talk to those who attended the center. There was little pairing up of student with interviewee because persons who came by the center were always changing. I placed students in pairs based on language dominance and they interviewed someone together.

Dan Whetzel: Just by living here in a small town, we have learned through these hundreds of interviews key people. Then it becomes referral, word of mouth. We found a man who was at the Battle of the Bulge and he said, "You should talk to so and so who was there too." And so it goes.

Linda Wood: If you get the word out in a small town, the local paper or even the *Providence Journal*—would help you especially since we were so successful with our first two projects. Libraries were great and the

kids' parents were great and pretty soon you have more interviewees than you can imagine. We then had to sort and pick through them so we had a representative sample.

Glenn Whitman: What did you have to give up, in terms of curriculum, by integrating an oral history project?

Francisco Guajardo: I think everyone has got to come up with their own weaving. To me, the kind of skills that were being built were so much more important than covering every single period of American history. So I didn't mind skipping over Progressivism because there was going to be some interviews and some writing skills that were really important to develop. There has got to be a give-and-take, I am not going to suggest that you can cover it all and still do an oral history; that is way too ambitious. To me it is about who is in front of me and what can we do together. When I graduated from high school I knew very little about FDR and the Gilded Age but the kind of skills that I built in high school were skills that I would not trade, the interpersonal, the relational, the communication skills—I didn't go through an oral history process—now my students go through an oral history process and they develop the interviewing and they develop the writing and they develop the technology and they develop the community sense and that kind of stuff is there for life. You can interview some of my former students in college and they will tell you, "I am going back home." They would not say that kind of stuff had they not gone through that learning process.

Judy Gulledge: In the English class, those kids knew they had to get through other parts of their lessons just a little quicker than students not involved in the project in order to leave time to do some work during the school day. But they also had to be willing to put in after school and weekend time. We put incredible hours in—all of us did. And there were things I gave less time to in the science class and I was a bit concerned about their test scores. But, I have learned from doing these kinds of things that are really authentic, that usually your tests are fine because kids are so intensely involved.

Delia Perez: In order to conduct the oral history project I had to give up depth of coverage as well as some selected topics. In the end I felt students would be better able to identify with the material and the relevance of history through an interview rather than covering, as an example, the unification of Germany.

Glenn Whitman: How did you prepare students to be oral historians?

Gerry Albarelli: We did interviews in class. We introduced them to the equipment during the first week and also had them use it by interviewing one another briefly. We then talked about what oral histories are, and I talked about the history of oral history. We then played them some interviews and had them read along the transcripts and tried to point out where there were some missed opportunities for questions, where somebody wanted to tell a story. They also went home and collected stories and told them to us. And then we had a teacher come in from the school and she was interviewed by the kids. That was good because she was part of the history of the school. She had been there for thirty-five years.

Francisco Guajardo: We did some role-playing; we did some mock interviews. The kids would interview me or we would interview each other or we would bring somebody in. It was really an experiential thing. In terms of reading, we haven't done a whole lot of reading. There's been the Studs Terkel stuff, very useful, but it's been really a lot of practical application.

Judy Gulledge: We had talked about the project in the spring of their seventh grade year and we wanted them to be thinking about that. In their English classes in their eighth grade year, they did some practice interviewing early in the school year. Christine had different people come into her classroom and discussed how the students would interview them and she set it up so that they just answer yes to questions that don't encourage people to give more than one or two word responses. They discussed how they should change their questions and how to come back to a topic you felt wasn't fully explored the first time. Practice also included little things, like how to use the tape recorder, in order to avoid problems when doing the real thing.

Delia Perez: Students prepared themselves by interviewing one another, thus everyone experienced what it was like to be interviewed, as well as what it was like to conduct an interview. These interviews were very enlightening, as students who might have been going to school together for years learned new things about each other. Students were also required to read relevant textbook chapters and primary source materials in order to understand the history and terminology of events such as World War II and the Great Depression that were to be a focus of their interviews. There was

no formal research paper but a lot of reading and talking, which included the brainstorming of potential questions to ask interviewees.

Dan Whetzel: We always have a small group of tenth graders working their way through the program. In that way, they can be the mentors. I sit down with the kids and explain to them how to ask open-ended questions. I am there for virtually every interview or my colleague is. We stress open-ended questions, don't you be the star, don't stop people when they get off track, rather gently get them back on the subject matter, being very courteous. What we find is that we have kids who really become proficient, after eight or twelve interviews these kids go in without any notes or questions. We work with them on practice interviews. What they lack is a sense of the time period. What we've done in the past is have, in the case of last year, a military historian come into class and lecture on World War II for two periods to give an overview of the war; this expert help at the beginning of the year helps set the tone.

Linda Wood: Because I am a librarian I tried to thoroughly prepare them for the interviews through research. I taught them the process of oral history while the teacher gave them the content they needed for the background. While they were reading a book like *A Catcher in the Rye* for the '50s project, and watching some film from the '50s, I would be teaching them how to ask questions, how to conduct an interview and helping them do research on the '50s. And again, as part of the Humanities grant, we had outside scholars come in and talk to the students about the '50s . . . the thing that takes the most time is the research. I emphasize they won't know everything but they don't want to ask really stupid questions in the interview. If the interviewee brings up something about Saigon, the student has got to know what Saigon is and where it is. The kids are so smart these days they can master the technology in a wink. Two more things that come to mind are (1) The questions that they ask, not just the content of their questions and what kinds of questions that they ask. We do a lot of preparation on how to ask and what kinds of questions to ask. We won't just let them ask questions about dates and places. (2) If you are going to transcribe the interview, or even just part of it, the amount of information you can get in an hour interview can be overwhelming. It is very difficult for students to get the important, significant content from the interview, throwing out the chaff and cutting right to the meat and importance of it all. You don't want to get misled by somebody's very interesting story but which has no real relationship to your project. I really used our scholars on that to work with our students in finding the most important parts of the interview.

Glenn Whitman: What equipment did the students use to conduct their interviews?

Gerry Albarelli: DVD and also video, though the video is pretty rough.

Francisco Guajardo: We used to do just the paper and pencil thing and than we graduated to the Sony tape recorder. Today we do most of our stuff digitally; we actually do all of our stuff on video now which creates a whole new dimension which could potentially alter the story. That is why we don't do an oral history with someone we don't know. From there we convert the video to audio and then from the audio we go through the transcription process.

Judy Gulledge: They used tape recorders with the little embedded microphone. They were the ones, and we felt this was a mistake, that when no sound is recorded they kind of turn themselves off. So we had to make sure the kids disabled that. We pretty much discovered that in our practicing.

Dan Whetzel: We have a Sony digital video camera as most interviews are recorded and then transcribed and burned to a CD, which is of better quality than an audio cassette.

Glenn Whitman: What have been the responses from the interviewees?

Francisco Guajardo: Equally profound and maybe more, than the students. The elders in the community really have never felt a sense of their importance in their story. We have seen time and again people's self worth raised . . . people respond to us differently because we valued their stories.

Judy Gulledge: After receiving copies of the book, they were absolutely floored, they were so proud, they sell it on the island, they sell it in the little museum across the way. I have had so many people comment, as I take other groups there, of how much it has meant to them.

Dan Whetzel: You can sense it, you can see it, you can feel it. A lot of people who are older just love to talk about the past; it makes them feel necessary, vital, and important and it validates what they did. It makes them feel good and important. On many occasions I

have seen people cry during an interview. I remember one gentleman talk about the Great Depression and he cried while talking about his family not having any food. They are so proud. It certainly has an impact on both the interviewer and interviewee.

Glenn Whitman: What were the biggest challenges for the students?

Gerry Albarelli: They struggle with what is the difference between oral history, journalism, and where chronology fit into this. Chronology is a hard thing for seventh and eighth graders to get a handle on. At one point, one new student once said, "I have a question for you, why are stories so important?" I think because stories have been trivialized in general by the culture that there is a little trouble with that. Then a student from Chinatown said to me recently when we were leaving the police station—the kids interviewed five or six cops in teams of two or three—"I have figured something out about oral history, you can't have a good interview unless you have a good interviewee." In a sense that has been a problem, and you sometimes have to screen people as you search for dynamic and interesting people and sometimes they're not. A lot of times I preinterview people just to give them a sense of what we are looking for though some people think they have to tell kids that forty years ago it was much better and these are the things you should do, they become very didactic.

Judy Gulledge: For middle school students we had to be very careful about going back—I discovered this by mistake—and taking their transcription and their tape home and listening to it in order to ensure that what they transcribed was true to what was on the tape. There were some kids who had really long interviews and just decided they were done when there was still thirty minutes left on the tape. The heavy dialect of the interviewees made it tough for the kids to hear it right so we had to listen to the tape a few times. We wanted to make sure what was said was really what the kids were getting down. During the actual interviewing process, a couple of the teams had a hard time getting the person they were interviewing to talk enough. Christine and I went with two of the groups that we knew were probably the shyest kids, but there was one particular group that when they returned knew that everything they asked their interviewee only came with three or four words and so we had to talk that through and see if they could go back and get more from the interview. We had the students go back in a different kind of setting as she was more outgoing when more people were around. There were times when kids were shy and I was with them and I found myself jumping in and asking a question I thought they should ask.

Delia Perez: Language and a lack of experience with respect to interviewing. Most students approached their earlier interviews in a very formal and structured manner instead of seeing it as a conversation with an open direction. Students also had a tendency to stick only to the questions they developed before the interview which led to some missed opportunities for further information.

Dan Whetzel: Getting students placed in the position that they are the most effective. Some students are effective in interviewing but not at writing. We have people who write beautifully but they seldom speak or feel comfortable holding conversations with people. Oral history methodology is also important, the training period for how to ask questions. Logistically, since we live in a rural area, especially with the theater book, we had to go all the way down to Georgia's Creek because each little town had a theater, so we needed help. Fortunately, there was a service learning person at the Board of Education who physically took the students to those sites. The kids sometimes can't get to the interview, so we take them. During school there was also an issue with one research team that had to get to Frostburg State, but to do that during school you need cooperation from parents, the administration, and colleagues.

Linda Wood: The research was hard for the kids. But I think they found the whole thing really rewarding and fun. It is great to hear the anecdotes; they came back really thrilled declaring, "Let me tell you what I heard last night" or "My narrator told us . . ."

Glenn Whitman: What were some of the biggest challenges you faced as an oral history educator?

Gerry Albarelli: I found it very necessary as the teacher to go and do preinterviews. That means it was really time consuming putting this project together. As an after-school program, working with a teacher who was really committed too, and that teacher is in position to reinforce what we are doing only one time per week. Another challenge with a diverse group of kids is that some of them are interested in certain stories and some of them are not. And there are mistakes, especially when the firefighter came and despite the fact the students were told not to interrupt, everybody was interrupting. Since he was talking about September 11—because that is the idea behind this Telling Lives Project—the kids will talk to people who lived through various historical crises and adversity and get a sense of how those people have overcome or lived through history and then maybe be in a better position to talk about September 11 by putting it into historical perspective. We had the firefighter come in at the very end of the program in Brooklyn, after they had already heard about the Second World War and the Great Depression, and we had a really interesting discussion. The students interviewed the firefighter and Debbie Almontaser, who was teaching that day at the same time and they had two very different experiences on September 11, she being Muslim. She was teaching that day early in the morning. People came and told her what had happened and not to tell the kids. Little by little the students found out about it and one said to her, "We found out who did it, it was those dumb Arabs." In which she responded, "I'm an Arab." In the end she had to be escorted out of the school where a parent was also attacked.

Delia Perez: First, I should not have provided a list of interview questions for the students because they did not encourage enough natural conversation and questioning in the interview. Second, due to time pressures associated with both conducting the oral history project and covering course content I did not allow enough time for the students to reflect and discuss their experience.

Linda Wood: There are lots of mistakes we make but it is all part of the learning. The mistake with the '50s was not having enough of a focus for the project. I think making students transcribe can be a problem. I think now if I was going to do a project I would have them work more as teams with each other, I don't think you need to transcribe the whole interview and as teams they could work together picking out what's important. I also think the sharing of information is something I didn't do enough. If I was doing it again I would have a lot more sharing. Each kid got to do their interview but they didn't get to hear the other kids' interviews or stories. I think that needs to be an important part of a project but you run out of time; but I also wasn't smart enough to build in the time.

Glenn Whitman: What form did the final product take?

Judy Gulledge: Our final product was the book, *Pennywinkle*. Finding somebody, when it came time to have [our book] printed, was a challenge. We found this place around 4:30 in the afternoon where we met the president of the company who was so friendly and took the time to sit down with us and he saw what we had and what our dream was. He said, "I want you to bring me one chapter, with the photos you want, I want to show you what I can do with this." Two weeks later we came by to get it and we were like "Oh my God, we have got to do this." He gave us a real wonderful price for it. I ended up having to ask the art teacher to help us with the book cover.

Delia Perez: Each interview transcription was the basis for a narrative created by the students as well as a second grade lesson plan. The project was shared with the community and those who were interviewed at a cultural arts festival where the students performed dramatizations of the narratives developed from their interviews.

Glenn Whitman: How did you assess the work of your students?

Delia Perez: Students were assessed on a portfolio of work that included (1) an essay that reflected on each interview, (2) the narrative students created based on their interview transcription, (3) lesson plans that each student developed for second grade students based upon material generated from their interviews.

Linda Wood: We had devised a point system for scoring everybody [see the appendix in Linda Wood, *Oral History in the Classroom*]. On the content, she gave writing assignments and listening assignments. The students were also graded on the interview, the questions and how they chose their topic for the story that was based on the interview. There were quizzes once a week on the classroom content. She would test both the content as well as their reading.

Glenn Whitman: What impact does an oral history project have on students?

Judy Gulledge: I went to Russia with four of the students who are all seniors. The Russians were amazed by this student-centered learning and then for my students to come with me and to share, looking back on their school career, what has been the most memorable thing that you've ever done in school? I had four *Pennywinkle* authors who all said "this book" and one happened to have it with them. They said there will never be anything they can think of that will ever come close.

Delia Perez: It allows students to develop interpersonal skills—where even the shyest student begins to feel comfortable talking with strangers—as well as their critical thinking and writing skills. Students also experienced how to write grants and raise money for the cultural arts festival.

Linda Wood: They have all used the oral history class when they write their applications for college. I think the impact is due to the "reality learning" that for them is very meaningful. They are actually becoming part of history by asking questions, and the way they interpret the answers. They grasp that very quickly. They become historians and they have actually contributed to the history of that period.

Dan Whetzel: On the first day of class I talk about tradition, high expectations, and how this book has changed student's lives. The fact that the quality of their work will be judged not just by me or my colleague Mr. White but by the community. We make it clear that these expectations and the burden of the work will be on them. We have something else going for us and that is a core of really nice kids in Allegany. Although we are a very poor area, we are rich in history and we have a stable community. For most of the students I teach I either know their father, their mother, or taught their brother or sister. We have a sense of community there and consequently we get support from people who now know us and what we are doing but also the business community. Mead Westeco, who publishes high quality paper, supported us five years ago after I went to meet with the public relations director about the notion for a book. I asked, "If she could please donate a thousand dollars worth of paper?" Now, they can't get it to us fast enough, and other people are the same way; they go out of their way to help us. It has changed students' lives. We had one student work on two books and he applied to a number of schools, one of them being Pepperdine. The interview was supposed to be fifteen minutes, but it ended up being an hour because they wanted to know about the book. It's a great recommendation for a student.

Glenn Whitman: What happens to the projects when they are completed? How is the material shared with the larger community?

Delia Perez: Currently the archives of the audio tapes can be found at my house with the video archives and transcripts available at the center.

Dan Whetzel: We have excellent cooperation with the local newspaper, the *Cumberland Times*. When we were working on the World War II book, we wanted to make sure veterans knew we were searching for stories. They provided a feature article in the paper. We have a book signing in which interviewees are invited along with other people in the community. Anyone who is interviewed receives a free book and it generates a lot of excitement. It is held in the library and we have light refreshments. The students are arranged in the order of how the photographs appear in the book so individuals can go down the line and have the students sign the book. People hang around and talk, share stories, especially last year with the veterans. It gives you a real good feeling.

Linda Wood: In the case of the Hurricane Project, we transcribed all the interviews and put them in a spiral bound book. There is no story, no photographs, just the transcripts. And we gave a book to every public library in Rhode Island and maybe a dozen schools. We also put a copy in the Rhode Island Historical Society because they were our cosponsors for the project.

Glenn Whitman: What advice do you have for teachers considering implementing an oral history project?

Gerry Albarelli: That experience of interviewing Mrs. Hadden who knew Martin Luther King, the kids are still talking about it as if suddenly someone came to life from the pages of the textbook. Just do it!

Francisco Guajardo: Create this sort of work in a collaborative way. It is essential to have support from administration and from community before you engage in this kind of work. It has to be a collaborative, participatory process when creating it. The process, how it is created and implemented, must be democratic.

Judy Gulledge: Teachers are pretty amazed when we share this project, claiming there is no way they could duplicate this because they see the amount of work that is involved. What we try to help them understand is the value of what the students are going through, even if it is on a small scale, of a process like this. There

are two things we have done with the book: How and why you would do oral history with the students and how can you use a book like *Pennywinkle* in your classroom. It's pretty powerful when you use it with kids and just the idea that this was written by somebody their age. What's neat is that I will have that as one resource in a science classroom. I don't know if I could have done the project without Christine and the support of the staff and our administration for what we were doing. The amount of personal time is just incredible, but it was such a big dream, but that is probably why there has not been a second one. There are several reasons for doing this type of project. One, writing is so vital to any child, if you want to talk about standards that's the power standard. If students don't graduate from high school with the ability to write, you've done them a disservice. The other thing is the connection you make with other people, looking at things from another person's perspective, having empathy for another person and even the self-knowledge you gain from this is incredible. It was one of the things in taking this trip to Russia that these four seniors who had been involved in this oral history project brought with them. I watched them interact with the hosts of ours and how simple their [the hosts] lives were and how less these people had. But the students were able to see the things that were really important and those four kids picked up on it to a far deeper extent than the other four kids who went with me.

Delia Perez: I would recommend an oral history project as it is a great experience for both teachers and students. Students who were in my class might forget the facts and dates they read in their textbook but they never forget who they interviewed. An oral history project is useful to inspire students and to build links with the larger community.

Dan Whetzel: Oral history makes history more meaningful, it brings it alive, it brings the past to the present. That to me is the most effective way to teach history.

Linda Wood: Do it!

CHAPTER 7

Voices from the Field:
The Student Oral Historian

IN THE FALL OF 2002, I WAS WALKING THROUGH THE Dupont Circle section of Washington, D.C., when I ran into a former student. Since this book was on my mind, I thought I would continue an informal survey I have conducted for the past five years. After the traditional exchange of pleasantries, I asked this student, "Do you remember who you interviewed for your oral history project?" This question was followed by another, "Which western senator was considered the Great Compromiser?" Not surprisingly, the first question was answered with as much confidence as if I asked what day she was born. Unfortunately the Great Compromiser, Henry Clay, was not so enduring. Such an exchange highlights a fundamental question faced by every educator: How best do students learn?

When developing an oral history project, consider what students think about their experience as oral historians. Such reflection often yields important insight as students reveal an enhanced understanding of their self-worth and a firsthand experience of what history is. In addition, students also reveal their frustrations as first-time interview transcribers, such as not asking the right questions, working harder and longer than on any other classroom project, or of letting their enthusiasm to learn more lead to interrupting their interviewees.

Over the course of writing this book I had the opportunity to survey ten years' worth of my students, as well as an impressive number of students who have conducted oral history projects in other parts of the country. Student interviews also included those who used oral history in their National History Day projects. Student reflections on their experience as oral historians provides an important opportunity to hear from those individuals responsible for going into the field and, as Studs Terkel once said, "uncovering the living repositories of our past."[1] Nearly all of the students were responding to my survey at least two years after they had conducted the project, and from their current position as college students. While a majority of these comments reflect the benefits of an oral history project, some students have sought ways around

---

MUSEUM OF LIFE
By A. J. Beck

Museums are collections
So care about who I am
I am a student of life
I am a student of life
Listen to my story and you will see
Just how valuable a collection I can be
I am a museum of life.

Can't assume that I don't have anything to say
Or that I am not worth the time of day
I am mathematics
The sum of all my life lies within
The parenthesis of my body and soul
I am a museum of life.

I am social studies
Examine the diversity reflected in me
Within the multiculturalism of my family tree
I am a museum of life.

I am science
See the blood flowing through my veins
My eyes reflect light and a few aches and pains
I am a museum of life.

I am art
Wonderfully made by the puzzle of who I will be
Original piece of work-a one of a kind, that's me
I am a museum of life.

I am language art
Be curious enough to listen to my story
Watch my wings unfold-writing with my body
I am a museum of life.

Museums are collections
So care about who I am
I am a student of life
I am a student of life
Listen to my story and you will see
Just how valuable a collection can be
I am a museum of life.

Source: Ann Jo Beck wrote "Museum of Life" while completing graduate work at California State University, San Marcos. It was first published in csusm.edu/artscohort/currentproject/museum.html and *Communication del Corazon: Core Communications from the College of Education*, January 2001, 1. She is currently a multilevel teacher for Addison District 4 in Addison, Illinois.

the project by taking a course over the summer that does not have enough time for such work.

THE VALUE OF ORAL HISTORY

James Conklin
Interviewee: A. Wesley Wright, World War II Prisoner of War

I think back on that project very frequently. Perhaps it is because the subject matter (World War II) is still relevant today with all of the current events. I remember really enjoying the project because it forced me to do something I might not have done otherwise. The oral history project gave me a perspective on the history that I could never have gotten from a book or a class. I think that the only downside of a project like this is the potential for an inaccurate view. Having spent the last few years taking statistics courses, I think of the problem as the law of small numbers. That is, if you only have/know one perspective or one belief, than you are much more inclined to believe it unconditionally than if you had several conflicting perspectives. Without a doubt, I think about my conversations with Mr. Wright frequently. While we did not discuss many of the more horrific experiences during the interview, I was able to pick up bits and pieces from what he said. Just knowing the suffering that he must have gone through is enough to make one think twice about wanting to go to war. Having lived in a time when the only war I've seen my country wage was an ocean away, I could never know firsthand the absolute horror of war. So the conversations I had in this interview helped me have a more well-rounded perspective on some issues.

Jen Cantwell
Interviewee: John Edward Nolan, Korean War Veteran

Looking back on my experience as an oral historian one word comes to mind: rewarding. Not only was it beneficial for me, seeing as how it forced me to come out of my shell and interview a complete stranger, but it was also, I feel, rewarding for my interviewee—who I came upon through an article in my local newspaper honoring a decorated Korean War veteran—who was finally given a chance to tell his story. Overcoming my shyness, I gave the man a call, and he graciously agreed to meet with me and share his story. I can honestly say that the answers he provided to my questions would have been impossible to obtain in a history textbook. My initial ignorance as to why the oral history project was so important in my teacher's eyes faded, and I

learned that the people around me had stories to share if I was willing to listen.

Colin Pinkham
Interviewee: Vincent Van Allen, African American Korean War Veteran

The oral history of Mr. Van Allen's experience is valuable to the study of history because not only is it told from the point of view of a soldier as opposed to a historian, but also as an African American during times of racial tension. These two outlooks, that of a soldier and a minority, are two points of view that students are not accustomed to encountering, and which do not appear very frequently in most historical sources.

ON BECOMING ORAL HISTORIANS

Ben Cantwell
Interviewee: William Phillips Talbot, Vietnam Veteran

The oral history project provided me with one of the most rewarding experiences in my high school career. At first, when the project is described and presented to us students, we shudder and think that we can't possibly produce a successful outcome. We are immediately struck by the daunting task set before us. To produce a quality project we know that it will take time and patience, organization and perseverance. We know at times the road may be rocky and we will be stuck researching instead of being out playing soccer or engaging in other more favorable activities. But we also know that at the end, when the project has been presented, we will be stronger and better people for it. For me, the reward that came by the end of the project is priceless: confidence. History aside, this project taught me about life and relationships. It showed me that I can tackle any task, no matter how daunting. I will take the confidence given to me from this project and I will apply it in life—in my travels to China next fall, a completely strange and alien world [just like the oral history project].

Elizabeth Ballou
Interviewee: Urszula Krzych, 1950s Polish Immigrant

The Oral History Project is a valuable teaching tool because it forces the student to go beyond the subject to learn about life. It challenges the student to be a thorough researcher, to be objective, and to think critically about the story being told. However, all this can be achieved by studying other primary or secondary sources. The strength of the oral history project is that it brings the student into contact with the immediacy of history. This is particularly difficult to achieve with teenagers, who are still making that transition from a self-centered universe to one where there is a world outside of their own experience. By immersing themselves in the lives of their interviewees, students can begin to bridge the gap between their own lives and the past.

Meredith Coyle
Interviewee: Jim Gibson on Atlanta's Race Riots

The coolest part about being an oral historian was knowing that what I was making was real. It was not just another research paper based on other primary and secondary sources, but rather, what I made was a primary source.

Tyler Basen
Interviewee: Claudia Ansah,
Head Start Program Participant

Remembering back on the oral history project, I think the main thought I had in my mind was that I am doing this for my interviewee, not for myself. I was recording somebody's own life on to paper. I interviewed a woman who worked for the Head Start Program, and as Studs Terkel said, sometimes inter-

viewing the noncelebrated or nonrecognized citizens of society can be the most rewarding. So it was my job to inform others about her importance and her role in this society. Although she is not well-known, she contributed and helped make things better.

WHAT WE LEARNED

Stiliana Dimkova
Interviewee: Warren Allen Smith,
1969 Stonewall Riots Greenwich Village, New York

The interview itself was the most enlightening part of all and I think that if I had a chance I would love to have a discussion with Mr. Smith about many other issues aside from the gay rights movement because he is one of the most fascinating men I have ever met. I found the transcription process extremely tedious but now understand that without writing out and closely listening to his responses I would not have the understanding of the topic that I now have. I think, overall, the experience of actually going to a new city, and meeting a complete stranger and asking him such personal questions has taught me that I am very good at communicating with people and demonstrating my seriousness in a given field. In further examining our conversation, I now realize that it has given me a

Figure 7.1. St. Andrew's Episcopal School student Stiliana Dimkova posing with interviewee Warren Allen Smith at the Stonewall Memorial, Greenwich Village, New York, following an interview on the Stonewall Riots in 1969. (Photo by Iana Dimkova)

whole new outlook on humans rights and gay rights in particular.

Paige Kobert
Interviewee: New Jersey Governor
Christine Todd Whitman

I really think that project was memorable and rewarding. I remember how nervous I was interviewing Christie, since at the time I didn't know her as well as I do now. Thinking of how close I've grown with her over the past seven or more years I find it hard to imagine being so nervous in front of someone who is honestly now like family to me, and I can't think that the project itself didn't help initiate our relationship. In addition, I wasn't a very outgoing individual in high school when it came to dealing with adults. I think this project forced me to step out of my comfort level. Having to actually conduct an interview, with not only someone older than myself, but a highly regarded politician, was a great challenge for me. And, of course, at the time I don't think I valued what I might take from that experience, but I can look back and smile, since such a project made me so extremely nervous, and now in my job I find myself speaking in front of much larger groups and far from uneasy. I also feel that hearing someone's perspective, and in this case on the changing role of women in politics, is a great change from merely researching a topic. In high school and college I wrote numerous papers in which I was blindly learning from research found in books or articles but to hear of a person's experience firsthand, and to be able to ask them any question that came to me, was far from the norm. When can you ever ask your history book how it felt to actually be there, or what was running through their mind at the time? And furthermore, I think it's great to have the experiences and thoughts of such individuals that have been interviewed over the years through this project written down. Far too many times, someone's story does not get told or not written down to share with others in the future.

Elizabeth Kiernan
Interviewee: Kiyo Finucane,
a Japanese American World War II Internee

Oral history is unlike any other method of studying history. No other way can impact a person quite so much, connect the historian so closely to an event, or give an event such humanity. The most important points in my interview are the lessons that Mrs. Finucane learned from her own experiences, those that she

felt it was important to teach me. Because of this interview I feel I am looking at the stories I find in texts differently. After seeing how a huge event affected one single person, I find myself thinking of all the single people who were effected by other events I learn about.

Erin Schwall
Interviewee: Kenneth Keenan,
Vietnam War Conscientious Objector

Textbooks tend to tell the story through the eyes of the winners or those in power. Although our textbook, *A Short History of the American Nation*, by John Garraty, does talk for one page about the antiwar movement, there is not one mention of conscientious objectors and what they had to go through. This is why the oral history interview with Kenneth Keenan is so important; it shows what life was like for someone who went against the government, fought for what he believed in, took an unpopular stance, and how this affected his life and how he won even though the country lost the war. For students to study this period without interviews of COs would be incomplete.

Amy Helms
Interviewee: Rosalie Iadorala
on Women in the 1950s

In the case of my project, examining the role of women in the 1950s, my interview totally contradicted my research. I could not understand why this woman did not hate staying at home raising five children with no career or educational opportunities. I thought that I had done something wrong. What I learned, however, is that her story was one that had never been told. I told her story.

CHALLENGES FACED AND OVERCOME

Austin Saylor
Interviewee: Lieutenant Colonel Woodrow W. Crocket,
Tuskeegee Airman

I think that many students (and I would definitely include myself in this group) make the critical mistake of limiting, consciously or not, the list of potential interview subjects. I don't know about recent years, but from what I can remember only a handful of interviews dealt with lesser known historical events and/or marginalized perspectives. World War II, Vietnam, and the civil rights movement are all extremely important parts of our history, but maybe not the best focus for this project (unless the interview narrows to a specific, less prominent aspect of these events). I do remember you warning us of this, but I don't think it sunk in. Also, while many people might have steered clear of famous people, I don't think many of us were as wary of famous *events*. I guess part of the dilemma is in whether to select for interviewee or event, but even so I feel that too few of us focused on marginalized histories. Looking back, it seems to me that the oral history project was unique not only because it allowed for an alternative perspective on history, but also because it demanded a significant amount of individual initiative and independent thought. Much more so than other high school assignments. Taking a tape recorder out into the "field," prepared yet ultimately vulnerable, cemented the transformation from high school student to oral historian.

Lauren Connelly
Interviewee: Helen Thomas, White House Reporter

The oral historian can only completely learn through experience how to best receive the knowledge his or her interviewee holds. However, to check the tape recorder and tape previously must surely be common sense. In this part I failed miserably. An hour before the interview, I had a tape recorder that I didn't know how to work and mini-video cassettes instead of the audio tape I needed. I still cringe when I hear my actual interview. The transcription, while time-consuming, was nothing in comparison to my chagrin in hearing the magnitude of my mistakes. If I had only allowed her to finish her thoughts! If I had only followed up with that question! Then there's the obvious blunder where I asked her what it was like growing up in the 1950s when she would have been in her thirties at the time. Through this interview I made an emotional connection to history and engaged in a dialogue with the past that has yet to end.

APPLYING THE EXPERIENCE

Rachel L. Danjczek
Interviewee: Congressman Paul McHale

As for the experience, I have never forgotten it. Being given the task of speaking with someone about their experience with a historical event was both challenging and fascinating. It was a challenge because I had to track down someone who had not only experienced "history," but also was able and willing to converse about it with me. It was fascinating because it was more edifying than I thought it would be. I chose Congressman McHale because, honestly, I thought his

title would be impressive. I chose the subject of his experience in Desert Storm because it was a recent historical event that I didn't know much about. In my conversations with McHale, I heard about his firsthand account of the burning oil and the conditions U.S. soldiers were in while serving in the Middle East. My eyes were opened to a subject I had little thought about or cared for. I still have my write-up of our interview, and find it interesting to read over today. My project has actually returned into my thoughts as of late due to the rising tensions that are occurring once again in the Mid East. McHale had mentioned in our conversation that he felt the U.S. did not finish the job, and it turns out he was right.

Sarah Kmieciak
Interviewee: Preston Williams
on the Home Front during World War I

Has the oral history project impacted me in anyway beyond St. Andrew's? Yes. It is the reason that I am a history major now. History had always been my favorite class, but the oral history project really made me look at it differently. Talking to a person about what they lived through, and how it affected them had a much stronger effect on me then anything that I ever could have read. It made me appreciate the secondary sources that we read for class in a different way, and it made me analyze information differently. I wish that I could have done another project, it was that interesting to me.

Olga Chistyakov
Interviewee: Thu-Ha-Nguyen,
Vietnam War Refugee

The project was such an eye opener and played a huge role in my academic development. I refer back to it rather often when discussing history and writing and when I am talking to historical persons. As a matter of fact, I am going back home (to Moscow) in a few days and will be bringing a tape recorder to capture my grandmother's experience during WWII in Russia. I have always been interested in learning more about it from her, and now, having read a lot of different literature from both the American and Russian perspectives, I would like to finally see what my grandmother has to share, if she is willing to. I definitely have only positive thoughts and recollections of my experience with the project. I remember that November (I think it was November) day, when you handed out the assignment, and I thought to myself that it would be the hardest task to get an A on this project. I thought that because English was my second language, this project would be even more difficult for me. But taking it step by step as you instructed us, proved to be the key to timely success. I interviewed a Vietnam War refugee, who has made a successful life as a World Bank employee. It was an amazing experience both in terms of getting to know someone who suffered due to serious political error of the time, and learning to interpret history from my own perspective. Learning about the formal process of creating the right questions, about the importance of body language during an interview, about following up, transcribing, creating a summary, and analyzing was indeed an incredibly valuable experience without which I would be a completely different person. The project developed in me the ability to question history, facts, happenings, and to not trust the media fully. It aroused my curiosity and made me look beyond the textbook in searching for answers. Overall, I believe that the oral history project changed my writing and research style, and made me much more inquisitive about the world—an active participant in thinking, rather than a passive one who simply accepts what others say. It isn't just about history. It was learning about the world, social interactions, emotions hidden behind people's words, reading between the lines, learning who I am through interaction with other people. I think it is an amazing way to learn and if I had the opportunity, I would do it all over again a million times, interview a million different people from a million different walks of life! Alas, we only have so much time!

AN AUTHENTIC ASSESSMENT

Elizabeth Barringer
Interviewee: Elizabeth Campbell,
Founder of Public Television Station WETA

At the time of the project, I can remember complaining profusely to anyone who would listen about how laborious oral history—in particular, transcription—is. Here I will grudgingly admit that in this case, that which did not kill me made me stronger. Reflecting back, my memories of the oral history project are mostly positive. I think that it was probably the first (mostly) independent research project that I had done. At the time, the idea of tackling something like the oral history project was incredibly daunting but also hugely liberating. I say daunting, because the project required an uncomfortable amount of personal involvement. It is one thing to be given a topic, to formulate a thesis, and write a five-, ten-, or even twenty-page research paper. It is quite another to be made accountable for

someone's life. The project was also daunting from an academic perspective. I can clearly remember staying up until three in the morning with my siblings as we all tried to get our final projects done. It was a thorough lesson in academic pacing. It was also a lesson in how to approach the content of an extended research project. There is no textbook answer when dealing with oral history, because it is by nature personal. In analyzing it then, we are forced to independently define and justify our own standards of historical significance. Learning how to do this is learning how to think. It is not academic regurgitation. The oral history project was a challenging and a rewarding experience. It was a valuable teacher of several academic lessons, but more importantly, it had the broader effects of expanding my awareness of history as a process, and myself as both a participant and a critic of that evolution. Most significantly, it provides a relatively safe arena for learning the art of thinking.

ORAL HISTORY AND NATIONAL HISTORY DAY

Oral history has become an integral part of students' research and presentations for National History Day. As a seventh and eighth grader at Fruitvale Junior High School in Bakersfield, California, Allison Tate conducted numerous oral history interviews with individuals for her projects on Jackie Robinson and the free speech movement at Berkeley.

Oral history interviews actually helped my project and was one of the reasons I got as far as I did in the National History Day Competition. It also helped me in my life as I begin to feel more comfortable talking to adults. With the free speech movement, being able to listen to these people and hear what they went through, I can picture myself being there and protesting with them. Being able to talk to the person makes history more real though it is also really important to research the documents. I was really afraid in my first interview with Tommy Lasorda. I got the interview by calling 411 and asked for the LA Dodgers and then I called the stadium and they gave me his hotel number in Florida where he was helping with spring training. It is amazing what you can do with 411! Most of the people I interviewed were happy to talk to me about their experience to someone as young as me who is trying to learn about their history. This experience with National History Day and oral history is very different from class where I sit and listen. Without the interviews I don't think I would be involved with the history as I am, I also think my projects would be boring and the history I presented would be less effective. Having to interview somebody gives more perspectives than just reading from a book or the Internet, and I learned a lot more from my interviews than I did from my books. I have also gained a lot of confidence in my ability to talk with adults. For those students thinking about using interviews for their National History Day projects, I would tell them to get all their courage together and pick up the phone and call somebody and see what that person thinks, it will be worth it.

A PARENT PERSPECTIVE

Over the years parents have played an important role supporting their student oral historians. Parental support has come in many forms, from driving their children to an interview, listening and exchanging ideas with their children about their work at the dinner table, or supporting them through each phase of the project. The following is an excerpt from a letter written by St. Andrew's Episcopal School parent Leslie Downey to the *Washington Post*, inviting the paper to cover the Oral History Coffee House while also celebrating the work of her daughter.

I would love to see ALL high schools, public and private, adopt such a project as part of their history curriculum. My daughter has not been St. Andrew's most avid history scholar, but the oral history project has increased her interest in history tenfold! The project has made history seem so much more real. And she has developed a great respect for and friendship with her interviewee, a Sudeten German woman who was forced to flee her country at the end of World War II. Besides helping the student to see history through the eyes of the person who "lived through it," another benefit of an oral history project is the sense of empowerment felt by the student in *finding and choosing* his or her interviewee. Since students in families of all income levels are surrounded by people who have "lived through history," this project does not require a high income. Furthermore, the reading level of the student is not the key criterion for success—rather, *initiative*, I believe, is that criterion.

NOTE

1. Studs Terkel, *My American Century* (New York: New Press, 1997), 481.

CHAPTER 8

The American Century Project

In their rememberings are their truths.

—Studs Terkel

WHAT FOLLOWS IS A CHRONOLOGICAL PRESENTATION OF EXCERPTED PORTIONS of nine of the three hundred interviews made by my students over the last decade.[1] Each interview was selected for its insight into effective interviewing techniques described through marginal notes, as well as its historical significance. Many of the difficulties students encounter during interviews—asking more than one question at a time, asking closed questions, failing to follow up on a response, sticking to the list of prepared questions—are reflected in each of the excerpts, as are their strengths.

Student interviews have included veterans from each of America's twentieth-century wars, participants in the rights revolution of the 1960s, immigrants from all corners of the world, Holocaust survivors, and politicians. In essence, they are generating microhistories of individuals that help create a more complete national history. Interestingly, nearly an equal number of girls and boys chose topics on war, which is not the case for topics dealing with feminist issues. Over the years a significant number of interviews have been conducted with "Rosie the Riveters," women of the 1950s who challenged the "feminine mystique" or were beneficiaries of Title IX. The selection of such topics, primarily by female students, emphasizes two important aspects of an oral history project. First, it gives voice to more than half America's population that does not receive comparable coverage in textbooks. Second, it allows female students to create an intergenerational bridge with those who came before them to help advance the fight for women's equality.

Over the years, my students have independently secured interviews with prominent individuals, including Marion Barry, former mayor of Washington, D.C.; Supreme Court Justice Sandra Day O'Connor; Jack Valenti, special assistant to Lyndon Johnson and third president of the Motion Picture Association of America; Helen Thomas, White House news reporter; and John Lewis, civil rights leader and congressman. Despite having been interviewed before, or, in some cases, having books written about their lives, interviewees often express a fresh point of view to a student interviewer. This was particularly evident with an interviewee, a Holocaust survivor who was interviewed as part of Steven Spielberg's Shoah Project. Away from the lights and cameras, the student was able to draw out new information because of the unique teacher–student relationship that emerged between interviewee and interviewer.

At the age of 104, Preston Williams was the oldest individual ever interviewed for this project and the only interviewee who could share his experience on World War I. Sarah Kmieciak's 1997 interview with Mr. Williams highlights both the importance of collecting this workingman's perspective and the challenges faced by student oral historians.

Sarah Kmieciak: What was Washington like when you moved there in 1916?

Preston Williams: Washington had a population of 55,000. My job was $0.21 an hour and I worked 12–16 hours a day, 365 days a year. We'd have done anything in those days to have a job. I rented a three-room apartment at 14th and Florida Avenue for $10 a month, utilities furnished. I bought a house in 1922 over near the Old Soldiers Home on Park Road then I bought a bigger house on Aspen street. I bought that in the Depression for $7,200, sold it in 1967. I passed by it a few months ago and they had if for sale, asking $267,000.

SK: In 1916, Woodrow Wilson was president; what did you think of him, was he a good president?

PW: Yes, he was a good president.

SK: For a while the president didn't want to go to war [World War I]. Was this a popular opinion then?

PW: Yes, it was a hard time. I remember the Depression, I would see people with a bucket standing in a line two blocks long at the coal yard.

SK: What did you think about World War I?

PW: I don't think it ever should have been. It was just the rich men that caused it all.

AN INTERVIEW WITH JOSEPHINE (JOEY) THOMPSON

St. Andrew's Episcopal School student Amy Petersen interviewed Josephine Thompson in 1998 on her experience receiving polio treatment, along with President Franklin Delano Roosevelt, at the Warm Springs Resort in Georgia. This interview goes a long way in supporting Louis Starr's definition of oral history, "As primary source material obtained by recording the spoken words . . . of persons deemed to harbor hitherto unavailable information worth preserving."[2]

Amy Petersen: What year was it when you got polio?

Josephine Thompson: 1931. I was born in 1926; I was five at the time. I got it on my birthday, they diagnosed it on my birthday, and my parents got divorced at that point, and I went to Warm Springs, so it was fairly eventful.

AP: How did your family find out about Warm Springs?

JT: I don't know how my father found out about it except that it was Roosevelt who started it and it was very famous because it helped a lot of people. I think if you could pay for it you could go.

COMMENT: This is a very good way to start an interview, with a broad, "open-ended" question that is easy to respond to. This technique allows interviewees to get comfortable with the oral history process and with talking about their experiences. Other open-ended questions include

- Can you tell me about . . . ?
- How did you feel about . . . ?
- Why did you choose . . . ?
- What was a typical day like?
- What can you recall about . . . ?
- What was it like . . . ?
- And then what happened . . . ?

COMMENT: This is an example of a "closed question" that often yields short responses. Other types of closed questions include:

- How many . . . ?
- What year . . . ?
- Did you like . . . ?
- How much . . . ?
- When . . . ?

COMMENT: Responses that yield little information should be followed up with other questions, in this case, by asking, "Why was he a good president?" or "Can you explain your thoughts on President Wilson further?"

COMMENT: In this example, the interviewee confuses the time period in which the question is based. The interviewer does a good job refocusing the interviewee on the World War I period in the next question.

AP: What were your initial reactions to Warm Springs when you finally got there?

JT: There was an old-fashioned, rickety, wooden hotel called the Merriweather Inn or something like that. In it I was going to have to have blood taken out of my ear, that's how they did it then, and I was just paralyzed with fear and I made this terrible scene so I spent the night there and they did it the next day but because I was so awful they couldn't do it. But that was my initial reaction, that this was not a good place. I quickly changed.

AP: When you first arrived in Warm Springs, did you know who FDR was?

JT: Well, I doubt that I knew who he was before I got there, he was governor of New York, but once there I immediately became very conscious of who he was in the big picture. He was running for president the same year and he gave us these little teddy bears with FDR shirts and sweaters. We were so happy with them and we called him "Gov" for governor of New York.

AP: When you got to Warm Springs did you know if he was there?

JT: He was coming all the time. The cottage that I lived in was the first place he lived, but he built what he called the Little White House down there, and that's where he stayed with his wife and secretary. I remember once, when he was president, going down to meet his plane or train, and him sitting in his open car with his jaunty way and his cigarette thing going up like this (gesturing with fingers). He was such an ideal role model for kids, we had no idea that he kept this "splendid deception" from the rest of the world. They thought if you had something wrong with you physically, something was wrong with your brain, you weren't running on all four cylinders, you wouldn't have a chance. But we didn't know that; we thought anybody could be president of the United States, we could be elected from a wheelchair. FDR was in a wheelchair down there, you see, and no effort was made to hide it. How could he? I mean we all had polio together.

AP: What was your initial reaction to him?

JT: Like everyone else, I just adored him. I thought he was the most wonderful man there ever was, and he was so cute with the kids, wonderful with children. He played with them in the pool.

AP: Did he seem to enjoy his political life or did it seem to be a burden?

JT: No, he seemed to love it. You have to keep remembering that I was only five, six, or seven but I have a very good memory for back then, but I have no memory of what happened yesterday.

AN INTERVIEW WITH ROBERT VIGDERHOUSE

As an army medic in World War II, Robert Vigderhouse participated in two major battles in the European theater. Mr. Vigderhouse arrived at Normandy two days after the invasion and continued on to help his unit at the Battle of the Bulge. In 2001, Mr. Vigderhouse, who was awarded the Medal of Jubilee on the fiftieth anniversary of Operation Overlord, shared his story with St. Andrew's Episcopal School student Doug Bower.

COMMENT: A follow up question along the lines of, "What led to the change of your initial reaction?" would have drawn more depth out of the interviewee's response.

COMMENT: Early in an interview it is important to establish where the interviewee was or what her role was in this event. This is essential in order to determine if she was an eyewitness to an event or is basing her response on information gained from others.

COMMENT: Nonverbal communication or movements are noted in parentheses.

COMMENT: This is a phrase that is often used by historians to describe FDR's "cover-up" of his polio and should have emerged in the student's research. This could have led to a great follow-up question regarding how FDR presented himself to the public.

COMMENT: The validity, as well as fallibility, of an interviewee's memory is often challenged by critics of oral history. Like all historical sources, the accuracy of an oral history interview must be verified by more traditional historical sources. In this case, verifying the interviewee's memory with respect to FDR at Warm Springs requires an evaluation of more traditional—written—sources.

COMMENT: This is a question that nearly all students who interview World War II vets should ask, as it allows for the comparing of responses. It also establishes an individual's place in time.

COMMENT: Good use of research of local "newspapers of the day." This question leads to a response that only a few other men could provide and demonstrates the uniqueness of oral history.

COMMENT: It is important to clarify any reference for the reader. This can be done in two ways, by adding [bracketed] information in the text or providing an informational footnote.

Doug Bower: What was your reaction to Pearl Harbor?

Robert Vigderhouse: Very frankly, I didn't know what Pearl Harbor was. We were having dinner that evening at home, and I was devastated to hear that Pearl Harbor was bombed and all those people were killed.

DB: How did you become an army medic?

RV: I wanted to go. I wanted to help and do anything I could to protect this country and I went over there, I was overseas for four years . . . I was taking premed in college; therefore, they put me in the medical corps when I got in the army.

DB: Can you describe D-Day?

RV: Well, I was very young at the time, I think twenty-one. I was, I'll tell you honestly, frightened. I thought maybe I would get killed because all I could hear was shooting and going around picking up dead and wounded, everybody was moaning and crying, and they still shot at us though I had red crosses all over my helmet. I said I went through hell during the invasion of Normandy, and that's what I did, I went through hell.

DB: In the newspaper interview you said that you have a story involving German nurses.

RV: During the Battle of the Bulge there were about twenty of us on either side of the road, going forward, somewhere in Belgium. We see six people come toward us. From far away, we couldn't tell what they were or who they were. At first, they came up to us and it was six German nurses, who somehow got away from their unit, lost. The Geneva Treaty[3] says that you can't put male and female prisoners together. We had no way of taking these German nurses prisoners. So we had a radio that you turned the dial and finally we got the German lines. Some German officer got on and spoke better English than either you or I. We told him what happened. The major made a deal with them to stop shooting on both sides at three o'clock until the nurses came back. So, sure enough, at three o'clock there was no shooting, no nothing. The major comes up to me and says, "Sergeant, get an ambulance, get a driver and take these nurses back to the German lines." Oh man, I was really upset. First of all, they were killing medics, shooting them in the back of the head even though they had red crosses. So I said, "Major, you don't need me, I'll get a driver and he can take them back." He says, "I'm not asking you to go, I'm telling you to go. This is a direct order." So I get in the ambulance with this fellow from Oklahoma, his name is Elmer Craig . . . and the nurses are in the back and we get about three miles up the road. We come to a cul-de-sac, you can't go any further, just pull around. So I get out of the ambulance and I was filthy, dirty and musty . . . and there was this German officer who saluted me and said, "On behalf of the Third Reich, thank you for bringing our nurses back to us." He said, "Sergeant, how would you like some hot soup?" And man, I hadn't had anything hot to eat and I started to say yes and Elmer said, "We can't eat that soup, it may be poisoned." So much as it hurt me I saluted and said, "Thank you sir but we have to get back to our unit." We got back in the ambulance and go down the road about a half mile and the Germans started shooting the

88s (a big mortar) over us. They never tried to kill us. We got out of the ambulance and got in a bomb crater and stayed there until they stopped shooting. We finally got back in the ambulance and back to our unit. We looked around and everybody was dead. They killed everybody in my outfit. The Germans evidently got our position either from the radio or from the German nurses. I think this was all set up. I really believe that they [the nurses] were as vicious as the men.

AN INTERVIEW WITH ROSALIE IADAROLA

In 2001 St. Andrew's student Amy Helms took her self-declared feminist views with her to interview Rosalie Iadarola. As Amy conveyed at the end of the project, "One of my greatest challenges, one that all historians face, was to be objective. As a young feminist of the twenty-first century I battled my biases." As you read this interview, see if Amy's view of the 1950s as an oppressive period for women makes an impact on the interview.

Amy Helms: Are you familiar with historian David Halberstam, who calls the 1950s "a ten-year PTA meeting?"

Rosalie Iadarola: Yeah, that's all we did. I had five different PTA meetings I had to go to at one time with my children the way they were spaced. I was a den mother for Paul [son], Girl Scout leader for my daughter. That's what you oriented yourself around. Your children and your husband.

> COMMENT: This is an effective use of research as it allows the interviewee—one who experienced the time period firsthand—to respond to one of the leading historians of the period through a "statement question."

AH: I have an excerpt from a high school home economics textbook. I want to know what you think about it?

RI: I think if you have to do all these things on a conscious level, say good-bye to your marriage. If you can't relax and use your common sense for making a good environment at home, forget it. After all, that was your main job then. So you automatically took into consideration certain things. You would always have dinner; after all, your children were also hungry. You would try to have a congenial atmosphere at the dinner table. That was mainly it but, dear God, use common sense. (Reading from the text) "Don't complain if he's late for dinner, arrange his clothes, offer to take off his shoes." He can do that himself! (Reading from text) "Speak in a low, soft, soothing and pleasant voice." Now that is real stupid. I did listen to him, yes, that was important . . .

AH: Are you familiar with Betty Friedan's *The Feminine Mystique*; this is an excerpt?

> COMMENT: Here the interviewer allows the interviewee time to read the excerpt and respond. An effective questioning technique.

RI: I told you that I was really busy. I never felt cheated; I was happy caring for my children's needs, my husband's needs. And, of course, in the '60s I got very involved, starting in '66, with my son Robert who was retarded and my husband and I had to pay for private school for him . . . the thought came to me that if my son Robert was normal he would be occupying a seat in the public school. So I went to the Department of Education in the district and asked them to pay me the amount that it cost them to keep a child in school . . . Stanley Jackson [head of the Department of Special Education] called me and said that a parent wanting approximately what I had asked him for was going to make a presentation in front

> COMMENT: This bracketed information was added to the interviewee's response for clarification. Information that was not part of the interviewee's original response needs to be bracketed.

of the board of education. Stanley called because he had a child, a girl, in Forest Haven, which was the district's institution for the mentally retarded. It was an infamous place . . . During the '50s, when my children were being raised, there was rumor, but I think a lot of people who felt like this about the Vietnam War. We really didn't know what it was all about. It wasn't clear-cut what was going on over there. We used to listen and read; when you have four little children in your charge and there are so many things you have to do every day that are more important than anything else.

AH: Well, the Vietnam War was a bit later, but I want to go back to what you were saying about the infamous institute in Washington, D.C. What was that like?

AN INTERVIEW WITH VINCENT VAN ALLEN

When St. Andrew's Episcopal School student Colin Pinkham set out to interview Vincent Van Allen in 2001, his intention was to focus on Mr. Van Allen's experience as a black man fighting to defend democracy during the Korean War. Little did Colin realize that Mr. Van Allen had something to say about his experience fighting racism in America following the war during the 1960s protests. Fortunately, Colin's preinterview research was broad enough to cover issues of race both in Korea and at home. This interview also highlighted another important benefit of an oral history project, especially in schools that in this case are predominately composed of white middle- and upper-class students. Students now have the opportunity to interact with individuals who are of a different race or class, which humanizes an experience that they often read about in books and discuss in class but never deal directly with themselves. This can be a very powerful and enduring teaching tool.

Colin Pinkham: What was it like growing up in Brooklyn, New York?

Vincent Van Allen: Oh, my (pause) difficult. (laughs) Difficult, well, I'm an old man now, and at ten years old I worked on the ice truck because we didn't have refrigerators then, and then in the wintertime we delivered coal in bags, because everything was coal then. Oil wasn't that predominant with heating. But anyway, that's how it was, and the movies were a dime, and if you got there early you got popcorn, and you had to get out of there by six o'clock because the adults came then. And they gave you big plates and cups, oh boy. It was growing up but it was wonderful because, well, you have to know New York. And in the summer there was always Coney Island and Nathan's hot dogs for a dime, and this is quite a while ago. Luna Park. And then that burnt down, and then they built Steeple Chase. I was the first African American lifeguard at Bay Nine at Coney Island.

CP: Did you ever experience racism growing up?

VVA: Oh, of course. That was a way of life when we're talking about America in that time, in the '30s and the '40s. Growing up in Brooklyn, New York, we grew up with everybody, Jews, Germans, Japanese, Chinese, you name it . . . your father had as much authority over me as my father had over you, no hanging on the back of the trolley unless you

COMMENT: One of the biggest challenges for a student oral historian is keeping the interviewee focused on the question. While going off on tangents should be expected, and often yields new, sometimes unexpected insight into the person or event, the interviewer effectively refocuses her interviewee.

COMMENT: On the original recording it was "Okay. So, Mr. Allen, what was it like growing up in Brooklyn."

COMMENT: In the end, the question was never answered by the interviewee. A follow-up question should have been, "What type of racism did you experience growing up?"

want to get your legs cut off. It was just a way of life, but authority and respect of the elders was a way of life, a habit . . .

CP: How did you first become involved in the military?

VVA: After school the war was getting close to being over and I just decided to go.

CP: Why did you choose the air force over the other branches?

VVA: I went into the army because they didn't have an air force then; they had an Army Air Corps. This was the early '40s. So I went into the army at Fort Jackson, South Carolina. The army, now you talk about racism and prejudice. It was horrendous. I was just turning seventeen and coming from Brooklyn, New York, I didn't know anything about water fountains that say "colored only" or "white only" or "don't do this" because I was never exposed to it. I'll never forget, I went into the J.C. Penney clothing store as a buck private, khakis crisp and starched; I was dying of thirst because the temperature must've been 110 outside—this is Columbia, South Carolina, in the middle of the summer. And I saw this water fountain . . . So I'm at this water fountain, just slurping up this wonderful water, and something grabbed me in the back of my collar and the back of my belt and just practically picked me up off the ground and started me toward the door. So I says, "What are you doing?" And he said, "Nigger, don't you know you can't drink any water here, can't you see the fountain says, "White only?" And I never went back to Columbia anymore till we were going overseas [laughs]. Cause I was scared to death. At that time the South was very cruel and very brutal, believe it or not. In the late '40s they were lynching. That's the truth. If you look in the books, that's a fact. But I never forgot that, and I'm an old man now. But I know how it was.

CP: How do you feel about Executive Order 9981, the order that desegregated the armed forces?

VVA: Explain that again.

COMMENT: While the interviewee knew about the desegregation of the armed forces, he did not know it by its official title (Executive Order 9981). Thus the interviewee had to clarify the question.

CP: Sorry. What do you remember about Truman's decision to desegregate the armed forces?

VVA: Well, that was overdue. He realized that with the world as it was developing, he said, "Hey, what is this one here and over there? We're in the same army, we're in the same mess hall, we're in the same everything." And he did it. And the integration, as I said earlier, they thought it would be like a battle. There was no battle. There was a period of adjustment . . . And they became the best of friends. Saved each other's lives.

AN INTERVIEW WITH JACK VALENTI

Each year when the project is first introduced students immediately think of someone famous they can interview, which is enhanced by living in the Washington, D.C., area. While they are reminded that the best interviews are often with those who have never shared their story before, a certain percentage of students want the challenge of interviewing an elite individual. In 2001 Cat O'Dell interviewed Jack Valenti—special assistant to President Lyndon Johnson and third president of the Motion

Picture Association of America—on his relationship with the former president. Valenti was with Kennedy in Dallas on November 23, 1963, and was beside Lyndon Johnson as he was sworn in as president aboard Air Force One. While Valenti has been interviewed numerous times before, we see the unique teacher–student relationship that emerges in this interview as well as the unique questions developed by a student. Moreover, this interview gives us a different perspective on President Johnson.

COMMENT: Interviewers should ask one question at a time.

Cat O'Dell: What was going through your mind when Kennedy was shot, when you found out you had to work for Johnson, and the plane ride?

Jack Valenti: Well, disbelief mostly. I mean, you couldn't believe this happened. The thing that I remember most is I thought I was in a nightmare, and I thought I was going to wake up, and of course, you wake up and it wasn't a nightmare. Disbelief, consternation, and most of all a kind of numbness. I didn't know what being on a staff meant, all I know is that I'm going to fly to Washington. Matter of fact, I asked two dumb questions, when the president told me he wanted me on his staff. I said, "Well Mr. President, I don't have any clothes; I just have one night's clothes." And he said, "Well, call your wife and have her send some up, and you can buy some when you get there." And then I said, "I don't have a place to live," and he said, "Well you can live with me until your wife comes up." As a matter of fact, I lived for eleven days at his private home and then when he moved into the White House, I also moved in to the White House. I lived on the third floor of the mansion . . . I found out later that there have only been two special assistants to a president to ever actually live at the White House; the other was Harry Hopkins, who was assistant to President Franklin Roosevelt. So if ever you're on Jeopardy and they ask you the question, you got the answer. And if it's *Double Jeopardy*, I want 10 percent of your winnings (laughs).

COMMENT: Such banter reflects the relaxed environment created by interviewer and interviewee. It is also important to note laughter in the transcription because it explains the tone of the response. Laughter, smiles, cries are all noted with parentheses but are best heard by listening to the recording of the interview.

CO: When you were on Air Force One—there's the picture of Johnson being sworn in, and you're in the picture—what was that like?

JV: At the time I had no idea that the picture was even being taken, for goodness sakes. This picture . . . I got over on the right-hand side of Johnson just to see what was going on and I was standing there no more than six feet away from him. It's a strange thing. I didn't have any sense of the monumental and immense historical significance of that. I just know that I was there, and I was watching this man I had known and now I was going to work for, being sworn in, raising his right hand. Then, later on in that plane ride, I began to think about how Johnson spoke the same words and swore to the same oath that George Washington did 174 years earlier, and it struck me as being miraculous that a piece of parchment that all these old guys [created] worked . . . Mrs. Kennedy came forward to be in the picture and I don't know how she withstood that . . . it was a moment that was so fraught with poignancy and grief and despair that it's all etched in her face in that photograph.

COMMENT: The use of an image to stir one's memory is a very effective interviewing technique. While the image is one of the most famous in American history, connecting it to someone who was present at the time gives it more meaning.

CO: If you had to write about your experiences with Johnson and his administration in a textbook for high school students, what would you want them to remember?

COMMENT: This question certainly reflects the interviewee's place in time and is one the interviewee probably had not experienced during numerous professional interviews. It reflects the unique opportunities that emerge when prominent individuals are interviewed by students. Each student in the class was required to ask this question.

Figure 8.1.   Lyndon B. Johnson being sworn in on Air Force One, November 22, 1963. Jack Valenti is pictured to the left of President Johnson. (LBJ Library Photo by Cecil Stoughton)

JV: I think I would want them to know that he came into office with convictions, from which he did not diverge, and that he wanted to lift the quality of life in this country for the uneducated young, the poor and old, the sick and the black. He never diverged from it, he never failed, he never hesitated. What really counts is whether or not twenty-five to forty years after his death it matters to the country that he lived and served. I got a letter from Mayor Williams, of Washington, D.C., about two weeks ago. I had a little dinner at my house in his honor, and he wrote me a letter thanking me for the wonderful time and I had told some LBJ stories at the dinner and he wrote, in his own hand, "Jack, I'm a living example of what LBJ did, because if it hadn't been for LBJ thousands of officeholders like myself would never have held office." That's what I would try to tell young people.

AN INTERVIEW WITH BOB RAST

In 1997, twenty-seven years after being drafted into the Vietnam War, veteran Bob Rast spoke, for the first time, about his experiences to St. Andrew's Episcopal School student Alex O'Flinn.

Alex O'Flinn: What was your knowledge of the war prior to being drafted?

Bob Rast: The war wasn't all-consuming. We didn't sit around freaking out about the war all day. We were playing music, going to school, chasing girls. I figured that I was in college so I was one of the privileged guys. One of the reasons I went straight to college was to try to avoid the draft. But I screwed around too much and didn't keep my grades up.

AO: Did you feel properly trained?

BR: The whole process of turning civilians into soldiers is pretty well oiled. It is one in which basically the idea is to depersonalize the recruit, so that you don't question authority. Coming from a period in which we questioned authority, I found the whole basic training thing to be really difficult. I had to spend a lot of time doing push-ups for talking back along with everybody else. For what we did, yeah, I felt adequately trained. But you don't know whether you're going to Korea or where until you get your orders. And I would say I was kind of freaked out when I got my orders for Vietnam. But I had some time off and then when I got on that plane, I think it was TWA at that time, I landed in Saigon. You get out of this air-conditioned plane and the heat hits you, the humidity hits you, and you're in this big city with all this military equipment around you, and it's just confusing and weird. The 93rd Medivac Unit consisted of four pointy-shaped huts. I got assigned to a crew and off we went. My job was usually to be one of three field medics on a helicopter, and we basically spent our days flying into situations and bringing people back.

AO: What was that like?

COMMENT: A simple yet important follow-up question.

BR: Constant fear. You're so wildly afraid that at some point you just get beyond it, and you do what you have to.

AO: So you overcame that fear?

BR: You do your job. I mean we saved more people than died, but when you are out there with somebody who is nineteen or twenty, and they have been hurt and they are shot, and they are terrified, you do the best you can to try and make them feel comfortable. But after you see a lot of people die something inside of you gets rolled off. And one of the things that has stuck with you is the ability to turn off my emotions. It was very hard to make friends because you didn't want to get really close to anybody. And I lost a lot of really good friends.

AO: Did your opinion of the war change once you went to Vietnam?

BR: Well, I didn't agree with it to begin with. And I felt that after a couple of months of going out and picking people up from the same damn piece of ground, I felt like the people back home, the politicians had no idea what they were doing, and we were out there just spinning our wheels . . . We would cope with constant fear and a feeling of frustration. And some people get hurt. I mean what a waste. I keep coming back to this, but you really turn off, and you compartmentalize things. You shut off parts of yourself, you become less sensitive to things. You just take certain things for granted after a while when you see another guy die. Well, that's it, zip up the bag. You can't understand the war. You can't understand what it's like to be covered in somebody's blood, to put your hand in somebody's body stuffing their guts back in. You can't understand it unless you've been in the middle of it. When you are actually being shot at, there is an incredible rush when you get back out of it and realize that you made it. You are about as alive as you're ever going to be. When I got back I basically shut all the doors, tried to put it behind me and tried not to think about it. I had nightmares, horrible nightmares for years. I think I became a very hard-hearted person. I think that I probably drank too much to numb the pain. And I think that's very characteristic of a lot of guys who were in Vietnam.

AO: Do you ever think you'll be able to open those doors, to talk about your experience more?

BR: I really don't know. I'd probably be a healthier person mentally if I could but it's frightening to me, sometimes the flood of emotion that comes out. One thing that I will say after fifteen or twenty years of nightmares, things seemed to kind of go away. I think it's one of those things that will always be locked up. And as far as being part of history, well, we're all part of history. There are other parts of my life that I feel are better parts of history, some of my journalism stuff that I've done. Vietnam was a part of history I wish I wasn't part of. I wish it never happened. I wish it never happened to this country. We came from a period where we thought we could change the world, and peace and love, and the Age of Aquarius was upon us. And then, all of a sudden, Kennedy gets killed and Martin Luther King Jr. gets killed and the drug scene went to hell. And this war split the country and the race riots and everything else. As a country I guess we had to go through those things, but that was a painful time in America. It went from really good to really bad in a big damn hurry. It's very strange when we pulled out of Vietnam, that last helicopter. Watching that thing on the news, I was sitting around with a couple of guys, I was in school then, and I was just closing the door and you're going it's great that we're out of there, but what about all those guys? And all those families? I keep coming back to the same phrase, what a waste. What a waste. That sums it up.

AN INTERVIEW WITH VIET XI DO

Over the years many students have conducted interviews focusing on the theme of immigration. Nat Ward's 1999 interview of Viet Xi Do highlights an important challenge when transcribing an interview with someone whose first language is not English.

Nathaniel Ward: I think we should start with some background information.

Viet Do: Okay. Do you want me to give my name and my _____ [??].

COMMENT: When a word or phrase is unintelligible or inaudible, ask someone else to listen. If it remains unintelligible, note it with ___??. When multiple words are unintelligible note it by ___??+.

I'm thirty-three years old, and I'm originally from South Vietnam. I was born in 1967 in a city called Vunhtau, which is V-u-n-h-t-a-u [now spelled VungTau], which is the southernmost tip, city, in South Vietnam—There was the Vietnam War—South Vietnam was a democracy, North Vietnam was communist. Actually, you probably know more about the war than I do, because I don't have any desire to know more about the history than what I gleaned from the ordinary course of life. We left when I was eight years old. We were on one of the last boats to leave the shore, as they were shooting at us on the dock. At dawn we left as the Vietcongs were shooting at us from the shore. I actually saw the boat next to us was blown up, with about fifty people on there, obviously they were dying or dead. A Philippines tanker picked us up and took us to Guam where we stayed for about three months before we got refugee papers from America. We were flown to a place called Fort Chaffee, Arkansas, and from there, a Catholic church in Tulsa, Oklahoma, sponsored us and brought us to Tulsa.[4]

AN INTERVIEW WITH EUGENIA KIESLING

On March 3, 1976, the women's crew team at Yale staged a protest for their rights to have equal athletic facilities as men, as defined by Title IX. In 2000, St. Andrew's Episcopal School student Emily Clark traveled to the Army War College in Carlisle, Pennsylvania, to interview historian Eugenia Kiesling, one of the Yale crew team members who stripped in the office of the Yale female athletic director, Joni Barnett, to reveal "Title IX" written on their bare backs and chests claiming, "These are the bodies Yale is exploiting."[5] This story was the basis for the video documentary *A Hero for Daisy.*

Emily Clark: In 1969 I know that Yale just started to admit women. What year did you begin to attend Yale?

Eugenia Kiesling: I matriculated in 1974.

EC: Before you went to Yale, you went to high school in California. Did you play a lot of sports at your high school?

EK: Actually, I was forbidden to play sports in my high school, by the high school administration, because they said I was "physically and mentally unfit for girls' physical education." In my freshman and sophomore years I had played on the basketball, softball, and the volleyball teams. I played with great enthusiasm and I took PE classes very seriously. I was very interested in things being organized and disciplined, to play hard. And that was not appreciated, so, when I played seriously girls accused me of cheating, I would respond violently and be thrown out of the game. So the school told me, basically, I didn't have to do PE, which was illegal. They said I could do independent PE. So I wrote up a contract and every day lifted weights or ran or did something athletic. I had a regular training schedule and the result of that was I graduated high school a very fit person but very bitter about women's sports.

EC: Did you know about Title IX when it came about in 1972?

EK: I had never heard of it. The school that I went to, Los Altos High School, actually had very good facilities for girls. We had lots of teams, we had uniforms, we weren't discriminated against. The problem was attitude, and particularly among the girls who didn't want to be there.

EC: What got you interested in crew [at Yale]?

EK: Well, I'd always been interested in being very fit but I'd never heard of crew and I'd never seen it. I happened to be walking to the freshman commons for dinner about my third night on campus. The crew coach was standing in front of the dining hall next to a sixty-four-foot shell, a racing eight, which he used as fly paper to attract candidates.

EC: Did you know about Title IX as a rower?

EK: I knew that it existed. I was aware that rowing was a new program, that it's a very expensive program and that it takes time to develop facilities. So, I didn't expect Yale to [produce], out of thin air, all sorts of new boats and a boathouse and things. I was always rather impressed with what we did get. My first year I thought the university was trying to do the right thing, especially when they did provide us with a modified house trailer that had showers and toilets so that we could change at the boathouse. I was more bitter in the second year when it seemed time to build us a locker room and the complaints we had were met with such disdain. And when we said to the men, "Look, it's not fair," their attitude was "well we've been here 150 years and you haven't." It was an ugly tone. I began to think why should we have to wait 150 years.

EC: Before the protest, what was the feeling among the teammates?

EK: It happened extremely suddenly. When we started rowing in late February, or perhaps the beginning of March, we were surprised there was no shower facility there [at the boathouse] for us, and for several days we just put up with it. And then one day on the bus, out of nowhere came the idea. I remember the conversation because Chris Ernst and Anne Warner and I were the three people most involved in the conversation, that the first thought was to throw Joni Barnett in the river because then she'll see how cold we are. Then we said that's not very practical. Let's make a statement by going into her office after practice with buckets of water and use her office as a shower. We thought, well, that's not very practical because she won't be in her office after practice. So, we thought, we'll go and take our clothes off in her office anyway before practice. But it evolved very quickly . . . this was not a long planned mutiny.

EC: Describe for me the event as it happened.

EK: We were frightened and we were very intense. We were going to do this and we were going to do it right. We didn't know what was going to happen but we knew this was a big thing to do. . . . We took off our uniforms and all of our clothes. We painted or inked Title IX on our chests and our backs and there were some comments then about how good we looked. And this is one of the most important parts about the whole event; we were very proud of our athleticism and our bodies. One of the reasons we wanted to take our clothes off is because we wanted to make a feminist statement that we're proud of ourselves as athletes but we are not interested in being pretty; we're interested in being big and strong. And then we put on our sweat suits, which were new and nice at that time of the year, and we went into the office in two files, very quiet, very somber, very serious. We stripped off our clothes and we had a man from the *New York Times* there. Chris [Ernst] read the statement and Joni Barnett didn't react.[6] And we immediately marched out.

EC: That's basically all my questions, is there anything I should have asked you that I haven't?

COMMENT: This is an effective way to conclude an interview by using what is referred to as a "summary question." This gives the interviewee a chance to have the last word and add anything that did not come out in the questions. If necessary, be willing to return to another interview session if requested by the interviewee or if after listening to the initial tape more information is needed. Another good summary question: Is there anything you wanted to talk about that we didn't get to?

COMMENT: This response highlights the importance of having a "plan of attack" not only for the interviewee and how such preparation, especially in this case, not only earns the confidence of the interviewee but also leads to a historically valuable transcript.

EK: I am very impressed by your questions; you obviously had done a lot of research before. Interviews are worthless unless the interviewer has a plan. So tell your teacher that I thought you planned this interview very well, very professionally. I think you gave me a chance to say everything that I had on my mind.

NOTES

1. A complete list of interviewees, including full transcripts, can be found at the project's website, www.americancenturyproject.org.
2. Louis Starr, "Oral History," quoted in David K. Dunaway and Willa K. Baum, eds., *Oral History: An Interdisciplinary Anthology*, 2d ed. (Walnut Creek, Calif.: AltaMira, 1996), 40.
3. An informational footnote helps clarify references made by the interviewee. In the case of the Geneva Treaty, it was signed in 1864 and subsequently amended to protect more persons in time of war under the banner "international humanitarian law."
4. The St. Bernard Catholic Church in Tulsa was a major sponsor of Vietnamese immigrants from Fort Chaffee.
5. "Yale Women Strip to Protest a Lack of Crew's Showers," *New York Times*, March 3, 1976, E5. See also Eugenia Kiesling, interview by Emily Clark, Carlisle, Pa., December 21, 2000.
6. Chris Ernst was the women's crew team captain.

CHAPTER 9

Meeting Standards

Oral historians have a responsibility to maintain the highest professional standards in the conduct of their work and to uphold the standards of the various disciplines and professions with which they are affiliated.

—*Principles and Standards of the Oral History Association*

IN 1987, THE ORAL HISTORY ASSOCIATION COMMITTEE on Teaching conducted a survey of the use of oral history in the K–12 classroom. Sixty-nine percent of the respondents identified time and scheduling as the "most substantial obstacle to classroom use."[1] While time and scheduling continue to challenge an educator's ability to integrate new educational methodologies, since that survey, a new obstacle has emerged: national and state academic standards. These are standards, established at the national level, by professional organizations such as the National Center for History in the Schools, National Council for the Social Studies, and the National Council for History Education (formerly the Bradley Commission) that often serve as guidelines for state standards. In most states, students are held accountable to such standards through standardized tests. Depending on the organization or state, reference to academic standards might appear as "standards of learning," "curriculum standards," "basic understandings," "content standards," "core knowledge and/or skills," and "core learning goals."[2]

In order to meet these standards educators often resort to traditional means of covering material, as well as deploying the "drill and kill" exam preparation technique that reinforces the negative attitude many students have toward their classes. Ironically, despite many educators' fear that an alternative assessment such as an oral history project takes too much time away from preparing for national and state academic standards, many of those same educators realize that such a project reinvigorates the teaching and studying of history and is a more authentic way to learn. Thus, how do we reconcile the need to meet established academic standards, as well as professional standards established by the Oral History Association, while at the same time providing students with meaningful, enduring learning opportunities?

ORAL HISTORY AS AN ALTERNATIVE ASSESSMENT

As I developed the American Century Project, high and clear standards, established when the project is first introduced, emerged at three different levels: in my own classroom as I assess each student's progress in accordance with the Oral History Association's principles and standards and as defined by national as well as state academic standards. Such standards play an integral role not only in ensuring the quality of the final product but also in preparing students for standardized tests. In my own classroom, I have conducted an oral history project with Advanced Placement U.S. History students each year I have taught the course. When I present this project at AP workshops and conferences, teachers wonder how I can cover all that is required for the AP exam and still conduct an oral history project for nearly three months of the school year. Inevitably they ask, "Don't your scores suffer?" My response is twofold. First, I do not attempt to cover every aspect of U.S. history nor do students read every chapter of our textbook. Like all historians, I must also be selective in determining what is essential for my students to know. Second, the oral history project takes place in the context of our survey of U.S. history, reinforcing and exposing material traditionally covered through textbook readings and lectures.[3] At various points in our study of the American century there emerges a student who is in the process of conducting an interview on the same subject we are covering in class. The student invariably becomes a coteacher for the course and is often better able to connect his peers to the material through what he uncovered in his interview.

As for my students' scores, I argue that an oral history project actually enables them to do better because of the higher level of historical thinking and writing that is expected of them. While the research on the cognitive benefits of an oral history project in comparison to more traditional methods of teaching is limited, a study at an urban high school in Baltimore County concluded that "oral history did prove to be a legitimate method of teaching the course content of immigration and black history. This finding refutes critics who have made substantial and off-the-record comments that oral history is inferior, when compared to traditional instruction, for developing the cognitive domain of United States history."[4] An analysis of the entire survey indicated that oral history was also an effective motivator when compared with traditional educational methodologies. As the survey pointed out, "The most significant area of support for oral history, by the total group, appeared to be in the way in which students believed the method increased their participation and involvement in history . . . the potential therefore exists that increased affective attitudes, acquired through oral history, might also assist an improved cognitive performance."[5]

The challenge remains in how to properly assess the multiple skills and intelligence that an oral history project demands. Over the years two educational theories reinforced the value and time I commit to an oral history project while helping me to more clearly define the essential knowledge, skills, and understanding students can gain from such work. Howard Gardner's identification of multiple intelligences and Benjamin Bloom's taxonomy—which remains "one of the most systematic approaches of studying the cognitive processes for the purpose of assessing learning outcomes"—highlight the value of an oral history project regardless of the varied abilities or learning styles that exist every classroom.[6] The following table measures how Gardner's and Bloom's ideas fit into each phase of a student's work as an oral historian (see table 9.1).

Daniel Goleman's work on emotional intelligence indicates how an oral history project can develop much more than a student's cognitive ability. Emotional intelligence is essential for the oral historian because it is a social skill that features quite prominently throughout each phase of the oral history project process. According to Goleman, emotional intelligences include self-awareness, self-regulation, motivation, empathy, and social skills. Since emotional intelligence is not fixed at birth, an oral history project provides an important opportunity for students to further develop this essential capability, which has been identified as being as important in determining future success as IQ intelligence.[7]

Such educational theory helped shape an assessment rubric (see appendix 15) that provides students with effective feedback that they can apply to other assignments that demand similar skills. It is important to note that the rubric is distributed when the project is first introduced in order to give students a clear vision of what they are working toward and how they will be evaluated.

At various points, students are also provided with three "visions of excellence" in order to have a clear understanding of excellence as it pertains to this type of assessment: (1) students read and interpret professional oral histories such as Studs Terkel's to learn to identify excellence in the field of oral history; (2) students review oral histories from previous years that are archived in the library in order to identify exemplary aspects of each; (3) students receive informal and formal feedback from both teacher and peers throughout each phase of the project to ensure they are meeting the expectations and standards for the project. Providing continuous, quality feedback and assessment allows students to refine the variety of skills that this project demands, to ensure the highest quality for the project and to meet the "professional" expectations placed on each of them. Such feedback—early and often—is essential to help students earn a successful outcome. More often than not, students not only achieve but surpass established standards. The extended hard work challenges their confidence as students and their abilities as historians. Best of all, it often has a waterfall effect into their other academic responsibilities.

The Oral History Project rubric I designed is helpful to the teacher as well as the students. One of the most important benefits of a rubric is my ability to assess a student's progress more objectively through clearly defined standards. I have also found A History Rubric for Alternative Assessment as another excellent model for assessing the three dimensions of students' historical literacy: their knowledge, ability to reason, and ability to communicate their historical knowledge and reasoning to others.[8] Possibly the greatest benefit of a carefully designed rubric is to identify a student's strengths and weaknesses. In the case of an oral history project, students with strong research and interpersonal skills might excel in their historical contextualization paper and interview but struggle with the analysis of their project due to poor reasoning skills. An alternative means to assess a student's progress as an oral historian is by developing an interview portfolio

Table 9.1. Applying Gardner's Multiple Intelligences and Bloom's Taxonomy to An Oral History Project

	Interviewee Selection	Preinterview	Research/Content Background	Interview Questions	Interview Release Form Legal/Ethical Issues	Interview	Transcription	Analysis/Interpretation	Products/Public Presentation	Archiving/Preservation	Oral History Method Training
Gardner's Multiple Intelligences[1]											
Linguistic (Syntax, phonology, semantics, pragmatics)	x	x				x	x		x		x
Musical (Pitch, rhythm, timbre)	x	x	x			x	x		x		
Logical-Mathematical (Number, categorization, relations)			x	x					x	x	x
Spatial (Accurate mental visualization, mental transformation of images)				x	x		x		x		
Bodily-Kinesthetic (Control of one's own body, control in handling objects)							x		x		x
Interpersonal (Awareness of others' feelings, emotions, goals, motivations)		x		x	x	x	x	x	x	x	x
Intrapersonal (Awareness of one's own feelings, emotions, goals, motivations)	x	x	x	x			x	x	x	x		x
Naturalist (Recognition and classification of objects in the environment)	x		x								
Bloom's Taxonomy[2]											
Knowledge (Of terminology; specific facts; ways and means of dealing with specifics; defined as the rememberings [recalling] of appropriate, previously learned information)	x	x	x	x	x	x	x	x	x		x
Comprehension (Grasping [understanding] the meaning of informational materials)		x	x	x	x	x	x	x	x		x
Application (The use of previously learned information in new and concrete situations to solve problems that have single or best answers)					x		x		x	x	x
Analysis (The breaking down of informational materials into their component parts, examining [and trying to understand the organizational structure of] such information to develop divergent conclusions by identifying motives or causes, making inferences, and/or finding evidence to support generalizations)		x	x	x		x	x	x	x		x
Synthesis (Creatively or divergently applying prior knowledge and skills to produce a new or original whole)	x		x	x		x	x		x	x	x
Evaluation (Judging the value of material based on personal values/opinions, resulting in an end product, with a given purpose, without real right or wrong answers)			x						x	x	x

Notes:
1. Howard Gardner, *Multiple Intelligences: The Theory in Practice* (New York: Basic, 1993). See also Thomas Armstrong, *Multiple Intelligences in the Classroom* (Arlington, Va.: Association for Supervision and Curriculum Development, 1994); and Project Summit: Schools Using Multiple Intelligence Theory, www.pz.harvard.edu/sumit/MISUMIT.HTM.
2. Benjamin S. Bloom, *Taxonomy of Educational Objectives: The Classification of Educational Goals* (New York, 1956). See also the "six facets of understanding" (explanation, interpretation, application, perspective, empathy, and self-knowledge) established by Grant Wiggins and Jay McTighe in *Understanding by Design* (Alexandria, Va.: Association for Supervision and Curriculum Development, 1998), 44–62.

(see appendix 17). In the end, whatever way you choose to evaluate the work of the student oral historian, being able to objectively identify a project's strengths and weaknesses allows for the establishment of appropriate strategies for developing all areas of students' historical literacy.

PRINCIPLES AND STANDARDS OF THE ORAL HISTORY ASSOCIATION

In addition to distributing an assessment rubric early in the project, I carefully review with the students the principles and standards of the Oral History Association.[9] The distribution of the OHA standards highlights the professional nature of the project and begins to establish quality control on their work with respect to the conduct of the interviewee, interviewer, and the preservation of project materials. The OHA also outlined guidelines for educators, which serve as an important reminder of our responsibilities as oral history educators (see table 9.2).

As we work through these standards I remind students that these are the same expectations of "professional" oral historians. When students realize that they are doing the work of professionals, this enhances the importance and quality of their work as well as its usability.

There is an additional, underlying benefit to the use of professional standards that is often overlooked. The OHA standards not only ensure the highest quality interview but also remind oral historians of their legal and ethical responsibility to the interviewees as well as to the public and the profession. In addition to the OHA standards, the American Association for State and Local History established a statement of professional ethics for its members, which more

broadly addresses all areas of historical study, including oral history. Similarly, the American Historical Association (AHA) has a very useful statement on interviewing for historical documentation. These ethical standards allow educators to use an oral history project as an opportunity to meet the dual responsibility of shaping both a student's historical mind as well as their character.

MEETING NATIONAL STANDARDS

The proliferation of national and state academic standards is probably the most contentious educational debate since the push for the integration of schools that began in the 1950s. The impetus for the standards movement began with the eye-opening report, *A Nation at Risk: The Imperative for Educational Reform* (1983), and received increased attention following President Bush's 1989 declaration "to establish clear and national performance goals, goals that will make us internationally competitive [and] second to none in the twenty-first century."[10] This goal was furthered by both the 1996 National Education Summit of the nation's governors and business leaders during the Clinton administration and by the second Bush administration's No Child Left

Table 9.2. Educator and Student Guidelines from the Oral History Association

Has the educator:

a. Become familiar with the oral history evaluation guidelines and conveyed their substance to the student?
b. Ensured that each student is properly prepared before going into the community to conduct oral history interviews, including familiarization with the ethical issues surrounding oral history and the obligation to seek the informed consent of the interviewee?
c. Become familiar with the literature, recording equipment, techniques, and processes of oral history so that the best possible instruction can be presented to the student?
d. Worked with other professionals and organizations to provide the best oral history experience for the student?
e. Considered that the project may merit preservation and worked with other professionals and repositories to preserve and disseminate these collected materials?
f. Shown willingness to share expertise with other educators, associations, and organizations?

Source: Oral History Association, *Oral History Evaluation Guidelines: Program/Project Guideline,* omega.dickinson.edu/organizations/oha/pub_eg.html.

Behind Act. However, teachers often feel trapped by academic standards that they believe limit their ability to engage students in meaningful ways and forces them to "teach to the test." Such constraints were recognized and overcome by Eliot Wigginton. Wigginton's model oral history program for language arts that began in 1966, Foxfire, enabled students to capture the stories that shaped their community, which were first published in a magazine and then in a series of Foxfire books. At the same time that students were preserving their community's stories they were also learning fundamental research and writing skills while meeting Georgia's basic skills requirements. In the end, Wigginton was able to overcome presumed challenges to a teacher's ability to create alternative and empowering classroom assessments, despite his concern that standards "deintellectualize" schools.[11]

While an oral history project is a natural fit into national and state guidelines established for history and social studies, the flexibility associated with project topics, interviewee selection, research, writing, editing, active listening, questioning, and analyzing skills are applicable to standards across the curriculum. The best standards assess students' factual understanding, skill development, and ability to apply the knowledge they have acquired. At the national level, the National Council for History Education (NCHE; formerly the Bradley Commission [1988]), the National Center for History in the Schools (NCHS-1994, revised 1996), and the National Council for the Social Studies (NCSS-1994) have all established historical knowledge, skill, and thinking standards that can easily be matched to an oral history project.

In the case of the Bradley Commission, an oral history project can be created to meet one or more of the six vital themes and narratives that help organize U.S. history as well as all thirteen habits of mind that aid in a student's historical thinking (see table 9.3). A table that helps educators match their oral history project to national and state academic standards is also available in appendix 3 in this volume.

The Bradley Commission on History in Schools established an important framework, *Building a History Curriculum: Guidelines for Teaching History in Schools* (1988), from which grew the NCHE, NCHS, and NCSS standards. Again, these standards not only allow for but emphasize the value of a classroom oral history project because of the multiple skills and broad knowledge and understanding that can be gained through such work. In the case of the NCHS,[12] an oral history project fits easily into the guidelines established for historical thinking and understanding: (1) chronological thinking, (2) historical comprehension, (3) historical analysis and interpretation, (4) historical research capabilities, (5) historical issues analysis and decision making.[13] As pointed out by the authors of the national history standards, "The thinking skills standards take an explicit stand against any official history and invite continued reassessment and reinterpretation of U.S. and World History."[14] Each new oral history project provides opportunities to reassess and reinterpret the past, especially when a voice is finally extended to marginalized groups in history—one of the true values of oral history as a historical and educational methodology. Such discovery fosters continual reassessment of the story of the United States and the world. The importance states place on seeing the past from multiple perspectives is highlighted by the Michigan Curriculum Framework for Social Studies, which recommends that history students use "credible reconstruction of the past that draws upon a variety of records and compares interpretations that reveal more than one perspective on events."[15]

With respect to the historical understanding standards, the flexibility associated with creating the appropriate topic for your course or program enables you to meet various standards at different points in the year. As an example, NCHS Standard 1B for U.S. history (Era 10: Contemporary United States 1968–present) for grades 9–12 expects students to "explain why labor unionism has declined in recent decades [interrogate historical data]."[16] An oral history project in which students interview, rather than "interrogate," individuals who chose to be in, or resisted being part of, a labor union would allow them to make a human connection with the challenges faced by workers.

SIX VITAL THEMES AND NARRATIVES OF THE BRADLEY COMMISSION

1. Civilization, cultural diffusion, and innovation
2. Human interaction with the environment
3. Values, beliefs, political ideas, and institutions
4. Conflict and cooperation
5. Comparative history of major developments
6. Patterns of social and political interaction

Table 9.3. Matching an Oral History Project to the Bradley Commission's Habits of Mind

Bradley Commission Habits of Mind	Interviewee Selection	Preinterview	Research/Content Background	Interview Questions	Interview Release Form Legal/Ethical Issues	Interview	Transcription	Analysis/Interpretation	Products/ Public Presentation	Archiving/Preservation	Oral History Method Training
Understand the significance of the past to their own lives, both private and public, and to their society.	x				x	x	x	x	x	x	
Distinguish between the important and the inconsequential, to develop the "discriminating memory" needed for a discerning judgment in public and personal life.			x	X		x		x	x		x
Perceive past events and issues as they were experienced by people at the time, to develop historical empathy as opposed to present-mindedness.	x	x	x	X		x		x	x	x	x
Acquire at one and the same time a comprehension of diverse cultures and of shared humanity.	x	x	x			x					
Understand how things happen and how things change, how human intentions matter, but also how their consequences are shaped by the means of carrying them out, in a tangle of purpose and process.			x			x					x
Comprehend the interplay of change and continuity, and avoid assuming that either is somehow more natural, or more to be expected than the other.			x			x					
Prepare to live with uncertainties and exasperating, even perilous, unfinished business, realizing that not all problems have solutions.			x			x		x			x
Grasp the complexity of historical causation, respect particularity, and avoid excessively abstract generalization.		x	x	X		x		x	x		x
Appreciate the often tentative nature of judgments about the past and thereby avoid the temptation to seize upon particular "lessons" of history as cures for present ills.			x			x		x	x		x
Recognize the importance of individuals who have made a difference in history, and the significance of personal character for both good and ill.	x	x	x	X	x	x		x	x	x	
Appreciate the force of the non-rational, the irrational, the accidental, in history and human affairs.			x			x		x	x		x
Understand the relationship between geography and history as a matrix of time and place, and as context for events.			x								
Read widely and critically in order to recognize the difference between fact and conjecture, between evidence and assertion, and thereby to frame useful questions.			x	x							x

Source: Paul Gagnon, ed., and the Bradley Commission on History in Schools, *Historical Literacy: The Case for History in American Education* (New York: Macmillan, 1989), 25.

The world history standards provide equal opportunity for students to engage with individuals who were part of, or who witnessed history. Interviewing individuals to meet world history standards allows students to engage with individuals whose lives were shaped outside of the United States. For example, NCHS Standard 1B (Era 9: The Twentieth Century since 1945: Promises and Paradoxes) expects that "the student understands why global power shifts took place and the Cold War broke out in the aftermath of World War II." A student in grades 7–12 is able to meet this standard through an oral history project by "analyzing major differences in the political ideologies and values of the Western democracies and the Soviet bloc. [Compare and contrast different ideas, values, and institutions]" through interviews with individuals from both sides of the global divide.

In the *Curriculum Standards for Social Studies* established by the NCSS, an oral history project provides an excellent means to cover one or more of the ten thematic strands for middle and high school.

The wide range of disciplines that fall under the social studies banner provides for some authentic interdisciplinary opportunities. The essential skills for social studies can also easily be applied to all aspects of an oral history project. Those skills include acquiring information, organizing and using information, and interpersonal and social participation.[17] At the same time an oral history project meets all aspects of these essential skills, it is also particularly well suited to putting established standards into practice. Table 9.4 demonstrates how oral history projects can fit the NCSS standards and performance expectations for middle grades and high school.

The application of national standards to an oral history project should not be limited to social studies or history. The ability to integrate an oral history project across the curriculum is validated by examining national and state standards in English and language arts established by the National Council for teachers of English, foreign languages (American Council on the Teaching of Foreign Languages), science (National Research Council), and disciplines that fall under the purview of social studies—civics (Center for Civic Education), geography (National Council for Geographic Education), and economics (National Council on Economic Education). In the end, every discipline is shaped by individuals who all have stories waiting to be uncovered by students.

MEETING STATE STANDARDS

National standards are, by definition, voluntary, because education in the United States is principally the responsibility of the state and their localities. The authors of the national history standards point out that the national standards are not intended to be prescriptive. As former Colorado governor Roy Romer, a member of the planning committee for the 1996 educational summit, declared, the Bradley Commission, NCHS and NCSS provide "a national framework to give guidance to state efforts. They are national, not federal."[18] For example, the American Century Project, while it fits areas of each of the national standards for history and social studies, meets a number of the criteria established by the Maryland Department of Education for high school students in language arts and science (see tables 9.5–8).

In New York, teachers Elizabeth Hoffman and Michael Barker of the Johanna Perrin Middle School in Fairport created an oral history learning module— "Experiencing Oral History"—for eighth grade social studies classes. This project was recognized in 2003 through the Oral History Association's Martha Ross Teaching Award. Students studied the techniques and value of oral history through a series of activities and projects. As pointed out in the module, "each of the skills involved in collecting and analyzing oral history is scaffolded over a series of four or five activities throughout the school year." Table 9.9 demonstrates the desired learning outcomes for Experiencing Oral History, including meeting New York state social studies and English language arts standards. (See appendix 18 for module description and grading rubric.)

NCSS TEN THEMATIC STRANDS IN SOCIAL STUDIES

I.   Culture
II.   Time, continuity, and change
III. People, places, and environments
IV.   Individual development and identity
V.   Individuals, groups, and institutions
VI.   Power, authority, and governance
VII. Production, distribution, and consumption
VIII. Science, technology, and society
IX.   Global connections
X.   Civic ideals and practices

Table 9.4. Using An Oral History Project to Meet NCSS Curriculum Standards for Social Studies

	Project Type: Putting Standards into Practice	Thematic Strand	Standards and Performance Expectations Met
Middle Grades	"America's Newest Immigrants" project includes interviews with recent immigrants to the United States from different regions of the world: Europe, Asia, and Africa	Culture Related Strands • People, Places, and Environments • Individual Development and Identity • Individuals, Groups, and Institutions • Global Connections	a. compare similarities and differences in the way groups, societies, and cultures meet human needs and concerns; b. explain how information and experiences may be interpreted by people from diverse cultural perspectives and frames of reference; c. explain and give examples of how language, literature, the arts, architecture, other artifacts, traditions, beliefs, values, and behaviors contribute to the development and transmission of culture; d. explain why individuals and groups respond differently to their physical and social environments and/or changes to them on the basis of shared assumptions, values, and beliefs; e. articulate the implications of cultural diversity, as well as cohesion, within and across groups.
Middle Grades	As part of your school's 50th anniversary students preserve "Our School's History" by conducting interviews with former teachers, administrators, staff, and personnel.	Individuals, Groups, and Institutions Related Strands • Time, Continuity, and Change • People, Places, and Environments • Power, Authority, and Governance	a. demonstrate an understanding of concepts such as role, status, and social class in describing the interactions of individuals and social groups; b. analyze group and institutional influences on people, events, and elements of culture; c. describe the various forms institutions take and the interactions of people with institutions; d. identify and analyze examples of tensions between expressions of individuality and group or institutional efforts to promote social conformity; e. describe the role of institutions in furthering both continuity and change; f. apply knowledge of how groups and institutions work to meet individual needs and promote the common good.

| High School | As part of their study of the Dust Bowl and Great Depression in their social studies class and land use in their science class, students conduct "A Life on the Farm" project that includes interviews with farming families. This project can also be incorporated into an English class reading of *The Grapes of Wrath*. | People, Places, and Environment Related Strands

 • Culture
 • Time, Continuity, and Change
 • Individual Development and Identity
 • Individuals, Groups, and Institutions
 • Production, Distribution, and Consumption
 • Science, Technology, and Society | a. refine mental maps of locales, regions, and the world that demonstrate understanding of relative location, direction, size, and shape;
 b. calculate distance, scale, area, and density, and distinguish spatial distribution patterns; describe, differentiate, and explain the relationships among various regional and global patterns of geographic phenomena such as landforms, soils, climate, vegetation, natural resources, and population;
 c. use knowledge of physical system changes as seasons, climate and weather, and the water cycle to explain geographic phenomena;
 d. describe and compare how people create places that reflect culture, human needs, government policy, and current values and ideals as they design and build specialized buildings, neighborhoods, shopping centers, urban centers, industrial parks, and the like;
 e. examine, interpret, and analyze physical and cultural patterns and their interactions, such as land use, settlement patterns, cultural transmission of customs and ideas, and ecosystem changes;
 f. describe and assess ways that historical events have been influenced by, and have influenced, physical and human geographic factors in local, regional, national, and global settings;
 g. analyze and evaluate social and economic effects of environmental changes and crises resulting from phenomena such as floods, storms, and drought;
 h. propose, compare, and evaluate alternative policies for the use of land and other resources in communities, regions, nations, and the world. |

Source: National Council for Social Studies, *Expectations of Excellence: Curriculum Standards for Social Studies* (Maryland: National Council for Social Studies, 1994).

Table 9.5. The American Century Project and Maryland's High Assessment Core Learning Goals (2004): Social Studies Skills

Social Studies Skills	Interviewee Selection	Preinterview	Research/Content Background	Interview Questions	Interview Release Form Legal/Ethical Issues	Interview	Transcription	Analysis/Interpretation	Products/Public Presentation	Archiving/Preservation	Oral History Method Training
Content Standards–Social Studies, Grade 12 Standard 1:											
assess the credibility of primary and secondary sources, assessing the accuracy and adequacy of the author's details to support claims and noting instances of bias, propaganda, and stereotyping, and draw sound conclusions		x	x			x		x			x
analyze the connections, causal and otherwise, between particular historical events and larger social, economic, and political trends and developments			x	x		x	x	x	x		
analyze decisions made in the area of public policy, evaluate alternatives and consequences			x			x		x			
evaluate issues by stating and summarizing the issue, and drawing conclusions based on conflicting data								x			
explain different viewpoints in historical accounts of controversial events and determine the context in which the statements were made, including but not limited to, the questions asked, the sources used, and the author's perspective	x		x	x		x		x	x		x
use clear research questions and coherent research methodology to elicit and present evidence from primary and secondary sources using available library, electronic, and human resources	x	x	x	x	x	x					x
identify community resources that preserve historical information and know how to access this knowledge (e.g., libraries, museums, historical societies, courthouse, World Wide Web, family records, elders)	x	x	x	x		x			x	x	
synthesize information from multiple sources, evaluating each source in terms of the author's viewpoint or bias and use of evidence, identifying complexities and discrepancies in the information, and making distinctions between sound generalizations and misleading oversimplifications			x					x	x		
explain different points of view in historical accounts of controversial events and determine the context in which the statements were made (e.g., the questions asked, the sources used, the author's perspective)			x	x		x		x	x		

Source: Content Standards Grade 12, Social Studies. mdk12.org/scripts/worksheets/gradebook_worksheet.plx?ContentArea=Social+Studies&GradeCode=12&redirect=1&Template=gradebook_form_template3.html.

Table 9.6. The American Century Project and Maryland's High Assessment Core Learning Goals (2004): English/Language Arts Standards

English/Language Arts Standards — A high school (grades 9–12) student will be able to:	Interviewee Selection	Preinterview	Research/Content Background	Interview Questions	Interview Release Form Legal/Ethical Issues	Interview	Transcription	Analysis/Interpretation	Products/Public Presentation	Archiving/Preservation	Oral History Method Training
Standard 1: Reading											
synthesize the content and ideas from several sources dealing with a single issue or written by a single author, producing evidence of comprehension by clarifying the ideas and connecting them to other sources, related topics, or prior experience			x					x			
extend ideas presented in primary or secondary sources through original analysis, evaluation, and elaboration			x	x		x		x	x		
make warranted and responsible assertions about significant patterns, motifs, and perspectives, using elements of text to defend and clarify interpretations			x	x		x		x	x		
Standard 3: Writing											
establish a controlling impression or coherent thesis that conveys a clear and distinctive perspective on the subject and maintains a consistent tone and focus throughout the piece of writing			x					x			
support thesis or judgments with techniques such as analogies, paraphrases, quotations, and opinions from authorities			x					x			
develop key ideas by integrating complex connections among ample supporting evidence such as descriptions, personal experiences, observations, and/or research-based information			x	x		x		x			
use clear research questions and coherent research methodology to elicit and present evidence from primary and secondary sources using available library, electronic, and human resources			x	x					x		x
synthesize information from multiple sources and identify complexities and discrepancies in the information and how each medium offers a different perspective							x	x	x		
use appropriate conventions for in-text documentation, notes, and bibliographies, adhering to style manuals			x				x	x	x		
improve the style, sentence variety, controlling perspective, precision of word choice, and tone in light of the purpose, audience, and formality of the context											x
self-edit and refine writing using knowledge of standard English conventions of language and appropriate print and non-print resources (e.g., dictionary, thesaurus, spell-check software)			x					x	x		
prepare writing for publication by integrating illuminating graphics and format and appropriate traditional and electronic resources to enhance the final product and create an easily read final product									x		
Standard 4: Language											
use all conventions of standard English grammar, usage, and mechanics to communicate clearly			x					x	x		x

(continued)

Table 9.6. The American Century Project and Maryland's High Assessment Core Learning Goals (2004): English/Language Arts Standards (*continued*)

English/Language Arts Standards A high school (grades 9–12) student will be able to:	Interviewee Selection	Preinterview	Research/Content Background	Interview Questions	Interview Release Form Legal/Ethical Issues	Interview	Transcription	Analysis/Interpretation	Products/Public Presentation	Archiving/Preservation	Oral History Method Training
Standard 5: Listening apply listening skills appropriately in a variety of settings and for a variety of purposes including the use of print, non-print, and emerging technology and media						x					x
evaluate the credibility of a speaker and the coherence and logic of an oral presentation						x	x	x			x
analyze how the effects of language sounds (e.g., rhyming patterns, meter, regional and social language variations) contribute to meaning						x	x	x			

Source: mdk12.org/practices/support_success/hsa/language_arts/instructional.html.

Table 9.7. The American Century Project and Maryland's High Assessment Core Learning Goals (2004): Science Standards

Science Standards A high school (grades 9–12) student will be able to:	Interviewee Selection	Preinterview	Research/Content Background	Interview Questions	Interview Release Form Legal/Ethical Issues	Interview	Transcription	Analysis/Interpretation	Products/Public Presentation	Archiving/Preservation	Oral History Method Training
Standard 1: Skills and Processes access and process information from readings, investigations, and/or oral communications	x					x		x	x	x	x
formulate questions that lead to a testable hypothesis, which demonstrates the logical connections between the scientific concepts and the design of an investigation			x	x		x					
use observations, research, and select appropriate scientific information to form predictions and hypotheses		x						x			
critique scientific information in order to detect bias and analyze the source of the bias				x		x		x			
analyze the adequacy of the supporting evidence used to form conclusions, devise a plan, or solve a practical problem				x		x		x			
the student will apply skills, processes, and concepts of biology, chemistry, physics, and earth/space science to societal issues	x		x	x		x		x	x		

Source: mdk12.org/practices/support_success/hsa/biology/skills_processes.html.

Table 9.8.   Matching Maryland State Content Standards to the American Century Project Topics

Social Studies Content: Students will examine significant ideas, beliefs, and themes; organize patterns and events; and analyze how individuals and societies have changed over time in Maryland and the United States. A grade 12 student will be able to[1]:	Relevant interview topics/themes from the American Century Project[2] that fit Maryland state content standards for social studies and science
analyze the enduring effects of the Civil War and Reconstruction on the relationships between individuals and groups	Leaders and "foot soldiers" in the civil rights movement
analyze the relationship between governmental authority and individual liberty	Vietnam war conscientious objectors Civil rights protesters Labor unions
analyze current examples of contributions of individuals and groups to initiate change in governmental policies and institutions	Antiwar protestors in Vietnam Demonstrators at the 1968 Democratic National Convention National, state, and local politicians Women in the factories during World War II
analyze issues regarding the meaning and importance of social rights, economic rights, and political rights in the United States	Women who pursued the rights defined by Title IX Freedom Summer 1964 Migrant farmers
analyze the conflicts between cultural traditions and cultural change	The Beat Generation Women who challenged the feminine mystique Woodstock and hippies
evaluate conflicts among and within cultures	Vietnamese boat refugees Those who seek to immigrate to the United States Perspectives on the Cold War
analyze situations that illustrate decisions of conscience taking precedence over respect for authority	Vietnam War draft dodgers Communists during the 1950s Sit-in movement
analyze issues related to polarization and unity in pluralistic societies	The 1950s
evaluate the manifestations of prejudice and discrimination on individuals and groups	Civil rights movement (Tuskegee Airmen) Native Americans Title IX
Standard 5: Concepts of Physics	
describe developments in modern physics (i.e., nuclear fission, photoelectric effect, wave-particles duality, energy of light) and their applications (e.g., nuclear power, MRI) (i.e., semi-conductors).	The Manhattan Project Los Alamos
Standard 6: Concepts of Environmental Science	
investigate and analyze environmental issues from local to global perspectives (e.g., world population, food production and distribution, pollution and epidemics, biodiversity) to develop an action project that protects, sustains, or enhances the natural environment.	Nuclear power Three Mile Island Farmers

Notes:
1. mdk12.org/practices/support_success/hsa/index.html.
2. A complete list of project topics can be found at www.americancentury.org.

Table 9.9. Matching New York State Learning Standards to Experiencing Oral History

Social Studies Standards Relevant to Experiencing Oral History	English Language Arts Standards Relevant to Experiencing Oral History
Standard 1: History of the United States and New York: Students will use a variety of intellectual skills to demonstrate their understanding of major ideas, eras, themes, developments, and turning points in the history of the United States and New York.	Standard 1: Language for Information and Understanding: Students will listen, speak, read, and write for information and understanding. As listeners and readers, students will collect data, facts, and ideas; discover relationships, concepts, and generalizations; and use knowledge generated from oral, written, and electronically produced texts. As speakers and writers, they will use oral and written language that follows the accepted conventions of the English language to acquire, interpret, apply, and transmit information.
Standard 2: World History: Students will use a variety of intellectual skills to demonstrate their understanding of major ideas, eras, themes, developments, and turning points in world history and examine the broad sweep of history from a variety of perspectives.	Standard 2: Language for Literary Response and Expression: Students will read and listen to oral, written, and electronically produced texts and performances from American and world literature; relate texts and performances to their own lives; and develop an understanding of the diverse social, historical, and cultural dimensions the texts and performances represent. As speakers and writers, students will use oral and written language that follows the accepted conventions of the English language for self-expression and artistic creation.
Standard 3: Geography: Students will use a variety of intellectual skills to demonstrate their understanding of the geography of the interdependent world in which we live—local, national, and global—including the distribution of people, places, and environments over the Earth's surface.	Standard 3: Language for Critical Analysis and Evaluation: Students will listen, speak, read, and write for critical analysis and evaluation. As listeners and readers, students will analyze experiences, ideas, information, and issues presented by others using a variety of established criteria. As speakers and writers, they will use oral and written language that follows the accepted conventions of the English language to present, from a variety of perspectives, their opinions and judgments on experiences, ideas, information, and issues.
Standard 5: Civics, Citizenship, and Government: Students will use a variety of intellectual skills to demonstrate their understanding of the necessity for establishing governments; the governmental system of the United States and other nations; the United States Constitution; the basic civic values of American constitutional democracy; and the roles, rights, and responsibilities of citizenship, including avenues of participation.	Standard 4: Language for Social Interaction: Students will listen, speak, read, and write for social interaction. Students will use oral and written language that follows the accepted conventions of the English language for effective social communication with a wide variety of people. As readers and listeners, they will use the social communications of others to enrich their understanding of people and their views.

Source: NYS Learning Standards, New York State Academy for Teaching and Learning, www.nysatl.nysed.gov/standards.html. Contact Elizabeth Hoffman and Michael Barker at Johanna Perrin Middle School.

An examination of state academic standards (other than Maryland's and New York's) demonstrates that states share many of the same content and skill objectives. A survey of standards across the country yields similarities that fit into each phase of an oral history project. One of the best comparative studies of the correlation between national academic standards and states for high school students was conducted by the General Educational Development (GED) Testing Service in 1996 (see table 9.10). The cross-section of states included Colorado, Maryland, Massachusetts, Michigan, Oregon, Texas, Vermont, and Wisconsin. While many aspects of the historical knowledge standards can help shape an oral history topic, all of the historical thinking skills are met through a oral history project. With respect to the need to present the past through multiple perspectives, an oral history project becomes an effective way to achieve such standards.

Table 9.10. **Matching National Standards for History with State Summaries of History/Social Studies Standards for CO, MD, MA, MI, OR, TX, VT, WI**

Historical Knowledge	Historical Thinking Skills
Both national and state standards expect high school graduates to know and be able to do the following: • Understand and use chronology as an organizing principle • Acquire knowledge about local, regional, national, and world history, including the origins of ideas from the documents that influenced the development of U.S. constitutional democracy • Understand history from global, Western civilization, and regional perspectives • Understand and apply perspectives in the study of history, including social, political, scientific/technological, economic, philosophical/religious, and aesthetic/cultural	Both national and state standards expect high school graduates to show ability in the following areas: • Critical thinking • Chronological thinking • Comprehension Multiple perspectives Nontraditional voices Spheres of human activity Variety of sources • Historical analysis and interpretation: multiple causation

Source: Katherine S. Woodward, *Alignment of National and State Standards: A Report by the GED Testing Service* (Washington, D.C.: GED Testing Service, 1999), 233, 238.

CONCLUSION

What is the function of standards in an oral history project? The ability to match national and state standards to an oral history project should provide educators with the reassurance that, in fact, an alternative assessment can not only achieve but supersede the historical knowledge and thinking skills that define a student's historical literacy. Moreover, the standards and skills of an oral history project are better preparing our students for the twenty-first century and providing them with an authentic opportunity to preserve the stories and give meaning to the lives that have shaped the past. As Foxfire creator Eliot Wigginton points out, as an educator, "you have to look at the state [and national] guidelines themselves, and you have to remind yourself not to fall into the old trap that tells you that these guidelines and these skills can only be acquired by the use of the state-mandated workbooks and tests."[19]

NOTES

1. Barry A. Lanman, "The Use of Oral History in the Classroom: A Comparative Analysis of the 1974 and 1987 Oral History Association Surveys," *Oral History Review*, Spring 1989, 218–19.
2. Katherine S. Woodward, ed., *Alignment of National and State Standards: A Report by the GED Testing Service* (Washington, D.C.: GED Testing Service, 1999), 192.
3. I am often asked whether or not there is a textbook that works best when conducting an oral history project with students. My response is that I continually search for the shortest textbook that surveys U.S. history in order to free up students' time from reading textbook chapters to conduct work such as an oral history project. In the past I have found John Garraty, *The Short American Nation*, and David Kennedy, *The Brief American Pageant*, best suited for this objective.
4. Lanman, "Oral History as an Educational Tool for Teaching Immigration and Black History in American High Schools: Findings and Queries," *International Oral History Review*, June 1987, 128.
5. Lanman, "Oral History," 129–30.
6. Lanman, "Oral History," 134.
7. Daniel Goleman, *Emotional Intelligence: Why It Can Matter More Than IQ* (New York: Bantam, 1997).
8. Frederick D. Drake, "Using Alternative Assessment to Improve the Teaching and Learning of History," *ERIC Digest*, June 1997, www.ericfacility.net/ericdigests/ed412170.html. The history rubric for alternative assessment can be found at Frederick D. Drake and Lawrence W. McBride, "Reinvigorating the Teaching of History through Alternative Assessment," *History Teacher*, February 1997, 145–73.
9. The principles and standards of the OHA are available at omega.dickinson.edu/organizations/oha.
10. Quoted in Gary Nash, Charlotte Crabtree, and Ross E. Dunn, *History on Trial: Culture Wars and the Teaching of the Past* (New York: Knopf, 1997), 149.
11. Eliot Wigginton and Christopher Crawford, "Foxfire and the Educational Mainstream," in Rebecca Sharpless and David Stricklin, eds., *The Past Meets the Present: Essays on Oral History* (Lanham, Md.: University Press of America, 1988): 101–18. Available at Baylor University's Institute for Oral History Workshop on the Web: www3.baylor.edu/Oral_History/Workshop.htm. See also Barbara

Combs and Christy Stevens with Linda Koch, eds., *Considering Assessment and Evaluation: A Foxfire Teacher Reader* (Mountain City, Ga.: Foxfire Fund, 1999). *From Thinking to Doing: Constructing a Framework to Teach Mandates through Experience-Based Learning, Considering Reflection, and Considering Imagination and Creativity* are available through Foxfire at www.foxfire.org.

12. *National Standards for History: Basic Edition* (National Center for History in the Schools, 1996), www.sscnet .ucla.edu/nchs/standards.

13. *National Standards for History.*

14. Woodward, *Alignment of National and State Standards,* 192.

15. Woodward, *Alignment of National and State Standards,* 239.

16. National Center for History in the Schools, United States History Standards for Grades 5–12, www.sscnet .ucla.edu/nchs/standards/era10-5-12.html.

17. *Expectations of Excellence: Curriculum Standards for Social Studies,* National Council for the Social Studies (Maryland: National Council for the Social Studies, 1994), 147–49.

18. Woodward, *Alignment of National and State Standards,* 15.

19. Wigginton and Crawford, "Foxfire and the Educational Mainstream," 106.

CHAPTER 10

Going Public: Linking Curriculum and Community

The oral history experience taught me a lot about myself and the people I live around and my community. A lot of students just want to get out of here but I realized through the interviews the importance of carrying on traditions and this community's history. I learned that we were not merely living in a barren, desolate desert town at the tip of Texas. I also experienced the powerful emotions associated with events that took place here and the uniqueness of our culture. Oral history brings history alive; it makes you excited about the past and how it affects you and teaches you. An author of a textbook has no connection to our town, the material is not geared to our personal history, but I could understand me and my community more by doing the interviews.

—Gilberto Perales, Student,
Edcouch-Elsa High School, Edcouch, Texas

THROUGHOUT THIS BOOK I HAVE ARGUED THAT THE WORK of the student oral historian can make for a more complete and democratized historical record while increasing a student's understanding of the past. This understanding, however, should not be limited to the student but shared with the larger community. An important consideration when developing a project is what you are going to do with the finished materials, as it is inherently the responsibility of the oral historian to go public with his or her work. After you formally present your work to the community, archive the projects in the library of your school or institution or publish them on the Web.[1] Also consider what other institutions would benefit from a copy of the project. In the case of two St. Andrews Episcopal students, their interviews are archived in the school library as well as the National Baseball Hall of Fame and Museum in Cooperstown, New York, and a county historical society. Too often projects are entombed in boxes and never see the light of day and thus are of no use to future historians. In short, creating an archive is not just an added part of an oral history project but a responsibility of the oral historian to ensure that original interviews are preserved and accessible to historians.

I have also argued that an oral history project alters the traditional way in which students learn. Unlike most school projects that are often developed for an audience of one—the teacher—and are complete after receiving a grade, an oral history project has the unique ability to expand the boundaries of a school by fostering collaboration with organizations in the local community. The rich collection of oral histories that have been generated by the American Century Project are shared through three very different public presentations. First, at the annual Oral History Coffee House, members of the community, as well as each interviewee, are invited to listen to student readings of excerpted portions of interviews and view museum-like exhibitions of student projects that outline the exhibition hall. This annual event celebrates both the work of the students and the stories each interviewee shared to further develop our understanding of the American century. Second, each project is permanently archived in the school library and accessible to researchers.

Third, our student-designed website, www.americancenturyproject.org, allows these important contributions to America's collective memory to be viewed by a worldwide audience (figure 10.1). This website is a resource for students, educators, and researchers. An interesting by-product of publishing on the Web is that students take even more ownership of their work, usually resulting in better final products, because they are preserving history for a larger audience. Any archive should include both a typed transcript and the original recording of the interview, as each serves a different purpose for historians. More importantly, a typed transcript provides an important backup to analog or magnetic tape that has a lifespan of twenty to thirty years. A project archive can be developed in conjunction with a school librarian or archivist or can be outsourced to a local museum, community library, or historical society that can bring its own expertise, time, and financial assistance to this aspect of the project. Such

Figure 10.1. Homepage for student-designed and -built American Century Project website www.americancenturyproject.org.

potential collaboration is an important reminder to educators of the strong support network in place to help them through a project.

In addition to creating an archive, across the country educators have developed innovative ways to share their work with the community. An essential component of making your project public is also the need to publicize the existence of the materials. Local newspaper and radio stations provide excellent vehicles for getting the word out. At Central Alternative High School in Dubuque, Iowa, students raised money with the support of Loras College, community businesses, and organizations to present a public seminar as part

of their research project on the Little Rock Nine (they conducted a similar seminar in 2002 for their project on the Tuskegee Airmen). The seminar featured three members of the Little Rock Nine, a National Guard Soldier who protected one of the black students, and a white Little Rock student who supported the integration; all were interviewed for the project. Allegany High School students have produced five magazines based on their oral history interviews, which are eagerly awaited by area residents and are presented to the public at an annual book signing by the student oral historians and book authors. The books have been used as educational materials in area high schools and community colleges. Holy Child teacher Ken Woodard linked up with Montgomery County, Maryland, public access television, which provided the training and equipment that allowed him and his students to produce a thirty-four-minute video documentary, *Mercy in Vietnam: U.S. Military Nurses Tell Their Story.* The latter project was conducted as part of an Advanced Placement U.S. History class where coverage of material often supersedes uncovering events and individuals such as nurses in Vietnam with such depth. When the school day was over, Roy Barber, along with his students, conducted interviews with South Africans suffering from AIDS and Washington, D.C., gay and lesbian teenagers. They converted the interviews with gay and lesbian teens into New Musical Theater performances such as "I Want to Tell You." This production focuses on the special vulnerability of sexual minority youth in high school and, as Barber believes, "bears witness and gives voice to the

---

THINGS TO CONSIDER WHEN ARCHIVING AN ORAL HISTORY PROJECT

- Use quality equipment (especially a microphone) in recording the interview to create the most useable materials.
- What are the costs of creating an archive and what are potential sources of funding?
- Use a backup tape for transcription and the original for archiving.
- While all projects should include a tape log, this is especially important if a recorded interview has not been transcribed.
- What space is available for transcripts and tapes?
- What are the storing conditions for the materials (room temperature, storage materials)?
- Who will maintain the archives?
- How will you publicize the collection?
- Make sure all materials are properly labeled, including the format an interview was conducted in.
- A website is not a permanent archive.

---

voiceless." The goal of the performance is to make schools safe for all students.

An oral history project also has a unique ability to create community partnerships between schools, state and local historical societies, museums, area colleges, libraries, and universities. Such partnerships allow educators to share the challenges associated with planning, conducting, and completing a project. State and local historical societies, as well as state humanities councils, are an excellent source of financial support and provide various types of grants to oral history projects.[2] They also provide an institutional base that is necessary for writing grants. Students can make one of three contributions to existing state and local history by supplementing, complementing, or even creating original sources that become part of the existing collection.[3] For example, students in Maryland contribute to an oral history collection at the Montgomery County Historical Society on civil rights in the region. The American Folk Life Center at the Library of Congress is the central archive of the Veterans History Project that relies on student interviews to preserve the voices of those who served in America's wars. It also produces a project kit (www.loc.gov/folklife/vets/) and conducts free workshops for schools and organizations. Students at Harwich High School were part of a cooperative project with the Brooks Museum and local Channel 19, which began in 1995 and has students preserve Harwich's history through videotaped interviews with community residents (see www.harwich.edu/depts/history/BAM).

One of the best examples of how an oral history project extends the boundaries of the traditional classroom is Community History, a joint project of Marion High School (Marion, Indiana) and the Marion Public Library (www.marion.lib.in.us/history/index.html). Like most states, Indiana requires students to understand local history, which fits well into the library's mission to provide educational resources for the community. The student interviews became those resources. Over the years, students have conducted oral history projects such as *Rough Times*, which became a book based on interviews with Grant County area men and women who lived and worked in the first half of the twentieth century. They also produced videos, including *Weaver: Community at the Crossroads*, which was the story of an early African American community in Grant County that can be checked out of the library. The W. K. Kellogg foundation awarded a grant of $45,000 to Marion Public Library and Marion Community Schools to support the student research; the

Community Foundation of Grant County served as fiscal agent. Cooperation with the local public library proved to be flexible and productive. Moreover, the library is the central archive for all the interviews students have conducted over the years.

Some excellent collaboration has taken place between schools and local universities. The Williams Center for Oral History at Louisiana State University linked up with a summer program conducted at McKinley High School that resulted in two local oral histories: "Visions: The Soul & Spirit of South Baton Rouge Churches" and "Pictures in My Mind: An Oral History of South Baton Rouge Community Business and the Business Community" (www.lib.lsu.edu/special/williams). As part of the Miami Valley Cultural Heritage Project at Miami University of Ohio, English and economics students from Middletown Senior High School conducted an oral history entitled "Women at Work," available at www.cola.wright.edu/publichistory/welcome/index.html. English students in Kingstown, Rhode Island, conducted two oral history projects entitled The Whole World Was Watching: An Oral History of 1968 and What Did You Do in the War, Grandma? An Oral History of Rhode Island Women During World War II. With the assistance of Brown University's Scholarly Technology Group, student transcripts and audio are accessible to a worldwide audience at www.stg.brown.edu/projects/1968.

The Rhode Island project identifies an important benefit of Web publication as well as a major methodological debate among oral historians. If you examine oral history sites on the Web, you will notice that many only provide a copy of the interview transcription. However, as the 1968 project demonstrates, with the proper software, as well as support, oral history websites can also include the actual recorded interview. The ability to combine the oral with the written form of the interview restores the orality to oral history. Text and sound capture the emotion and feelings that emanate through the spoken word and are unique to oral history sources but not yielded through a transcript. The posting of oral history on the Web highlights the increased application of new technologies to oral history projects by a new generation of oral historians who are much more media savvy. Despite these benefits, the placement of oral history interviews on the Web raises enormous legal, ethical, and professional concerns, in particular because the use of such material is less easily controlled than if accessible solely through an institutional archive. It therefore needs to be made very clear to the interviewee—before an interview takes place—whether or not any materials derived from the interview will be posted to the Web or successor technologies (projects conducted prior to the emergence or consideration of the Web require a new release form). It is imperative that a release form include such a possibility while allowing an interviewee to restrict such use. Ethical concerns with electronic publication of oral histories led to a revision of the Oral History Association's *Standards, Principles, and Guidelines,* highlighting the responsibility to the interviewee "to be informed of the wide range of potential uses of their interviews given the rapid development of new technologies."[4] The Web adds a new and exciting dimension to oral history. However, "no matter how the technology evolves, the human element will remain crucial to the future of the oral history field."[5]

SERVICE LEARNING: THINK HISTORICALLY, RESEARCH LOCALLY

The benefits of an oral history project extend far beyond providing students with an opportunity to be historians. An oral history project allows students to give back to the communities in which they live and study by making people feel that their history is worth something. This is highlighted by one interviewee who commented after she returned home from being interviewed about her role in the 1960s student movement that "no one had ever been so interested in my life story before." As Paul Thompson wrote in his book, *The Voice of the Past: Oral History,*

> Interviewing can bring together people from different social classes and age groups who would otherwise rarely meet, let alone get to know each other closely. Much of the widespread hostility to students is based on little knowledge of what they actually like or do, and these meetings can bring an

appreciation of the serious-mindedness and idealism which is widespread among them . . . Conversely, teachers and students can become more directly aware of the image which they present to the wider public. And through entering into the lives of their informants, they gain more understanding of values which they do not share, and often respect for courage shown in lives less privileged than their own.[6]

An oral history project becomes an opportunity not just to participate in the preservation of the past but also to provide a service to a community while learning in a more authentic and enduring manner. It also fosters a better understanding of who we are, since we are all significantly influenced by the place in which we live.

An exciting project that links students with their communities and builds intergenerational bridges is Tell Me Your Stories: An Oral History Curriculum for High School and Middle Schools Involving Students with Their Family and Community developed by the Living Legacies Historical Foundation (tellmeyourstories.org).

A local oral history project becomes even more important in societies whose history is predominately preserved through the oral tradition. This is particularly true for Native American societies and is highlighted in the Suquamish Oral History Project, *A Guide for Oral History in the Native American Community,* which provides important points about oral history in Native American communities. The history of these marginalized societies, which tend to be poor and rural and reliant on the oral tradition to pass along their stories, will be forever lost unless interviews are conducted to learn about the people, places, and events that shaped the community. Theda Perdue points out in her book, which organized the less known Federal Writers' Project oral history interviews with Native Americans, "Oral history represents the democratization of a discipline which too often has been elitist by peopling the past with individuals who never led armies, never served in Congress, never invented the cotton gin or steamboat, and never wrote a great book as well as with people who did."[7] As an old African saying goes, "An old man dies . . . a book is lost."[8]

Preserving the voices of a community through oral history also provides a therapeutic and psychological use for interviewees, since someone is willing to listen to their story. In this case, curriculum builds community and community builds curriculum. Students can now "use their historical knowledge to become more effective, self-aware, and ethical participants in the life of their communities."[9] For example, teacher Alison Parker at Christa McAuliffe Elementary School in Bakersfield, California, has her sixth grade students conduct oral history interviews with residents of an assisted living center. This service-learning project helped students meet the history/social science framework for California public schools, in particular "becoming active participants in their community and in history."[10]

The importance of giving back something to the community, as well as learning from living resources in the community, is evident in the use of a student-driven oral history project as part of place-based education that "enlarges student learning and improves community life by better connecting rural schools and communities and by engaging students in community-based public work."[11] Oral history becomes a method to meet this objective and is effectively demonstrated by the Bland County History Archives (www.bland.k12.va.us/bland/rocky/gap .html), which include over four hundred interviews conducted by Rocky Gap High School students from Rocky Gap, Virginia. This interdisciplinary project allows the student interviews—conducted by junior U.S. history students—to be published on the Web with the support of students from the technology class. The community-building nature of oral history is also an essential part of service learning programs that "involves serving the community in a way that achieves academic goals and objectives, while providing students with a unique experience to learn, serve, and teach as they examine society at a primary level. It is based on the reciprocal relationship in which the service reinforces the learning as the learning reinforces and strengthens the service. It also fosters the development of the intangibles such as empathy, personal values, awareness of others, self-confidence and social responsibility, and helps create a sense of caring for others."[12]

An excellent example of the promise of oral history to both the student and the community is reflected in a collaboration between New Mexico State University, Las Cruces, and Panther Achievement Center (PAC), Gadsden High School, Anthony, New Mexico, titled Preserving Community/Cuentos del Varrio (web .nmsu.edu/~publhist/ohindex.htm#Introduction). The purpose of the project was to record the heritage of southern New Mexico. PAC is an alternative learning center for students who experienced difficulties in traditional high school classes, ranging from disciplinary problems with school and law officials to employment conflicts, problems with school attendance, and being high school parents. As the project's website attests, "The project teaches high school students how to interview the elders of their communities to capture the local history and language of the region and to empower the participants as they explore their ancestry and cultural background." It grew out of a proposal to teach oral history to teens considered at risk. This project highlights the value of an oral history project to students—regardless of their perceived ability or labels—and to the community in a geographically isolated part of the country. In the end, this collaboration seized on one of our most life-shaping influences: the communities in which we live.

Students are also preserving the history of community families. More than once, students have conducted an interview with an individual who had yet to convey the full account of their life to his or her family. Thus the student serves as an important conduit between the interviewee and the family and becomes the preserver of the family's history. This is reinforced by one student, reflecting on his work:

One other thing you may find interesting about my experience as an oral historian was a comment I heard almost a year after doing it. I was talking to a relative of my interviewee who I knew quite well and she told me that he had never opened up or talked to anybody about the experiences he had while a POW. As far as I know, I was the first and last person to hear some of those stories. This is not to say that he did not talk at all about his time in Europe, but some of the things he told me he had never discussed before—even with family.

Such reflection highlights not only the important contributions students can make to their communities but also how a carefully designed oral history project can empower students with their own learning and at the same time reinvigorate the teaching and studying of history while meeting national and state standards of learning. Without the student oral historian, far too many stories would be lost, or, as Donald A. Ritchie once expressed to one of my classes, "It would be like a library burning down."

NOTES

1. Archiving an oral history project in a school library or special archive must also include having the project catalogued on the Web in order to create access for a worldwide community of scholars. Project websites, such as www.americancenturyproject.org, should also be linked to a library's electronic catalogue in order to create multiple entry points into the oral history project's collection. Not only is the school or program enriched by this collection, but so is the larger historical community, which is always seeking out original sources.
2. See Laurie Mercier and Madeline Buckendorf, *Using Oral History in Community History Projects* (Carlisle, Pa.: Oral History Association, 1992).
3. Barbara Allen, *From Memory to History: Using Oral History in Local Historical Research* (American Association for State and Local History, 1981), 15.
4. Oral History Association, *Principles and Standards* and *Evaluation Guidelines* are available at omega.dickinson.edu/organizations/oha.
5. Donald Ritchie, quoted in Sherna Berger Gluck, "Reflections on Oral History in the New Millennium," *Oral History Review*, Summer–Fall, 1999, 25.
6. Paul Thompson, *The Voice of the Past: Oral History* (London: Oxford University Press, 1988), 11.
7. Theda Perdue, *Nations Remembered: An Oral History of the Five Civilized Tribes, 1865–1907* (Westport, Conn.: Greenwood, 1980), xix.
8. Hugo Slim and Paul Thompson, *Listening for a Change: Oral Testimony and Community Development* (Philadelphia, Pa.: New Society Publishers, 1995), 40.
9. Larry E. Hudson Jr. and Ellen Durrigan Santora, "Oral History: An Inclusive Highway to the Past," *History Teacher* 36, no. 2 (2003): 208, quoting Gerland E. Schenk and David Takacs, "History and Civic Participation: An Example of the Scholarship of Teaching and Learning," *Perspectives* 40, no. 4 (2002): 30.
10. Alison Parker, "Visiting and Interviewing Older Adults: Service Learning in the Sixth Grade," *Middle Level Learning*, September 2002, M3–M7. Supplement to National Council for the Social Studies Publications, no. 15
11. Rural School and Community Trust, www.ruraledu.org/index.html.
12. Elsa A. Nystrom, "Remembrance of Things Past: Service Leaning Opportunities in U.S. History," *Oral History Review*, Summer–Fall 2002, 61–62.

APPENDIXES

THESE APPENDIXES ARE PROVIDED TO MAKE IT EASIER FOR EDUCATORS TO BEGIN USING ORAL HISTORY IN THEIR CLASSROOMS or programs. Some of the materials are also available for downloading and adaptation at www.american centuryproject.org.

The American Century Project
(www.americancenturyproject.org)

PROJECT OBJECTIVES

FIRST, TO PROVIDE STUDENTS THE OPPORTUNITY TO CREATE AND PRESERVE A PRIMARY SOURCE THROUGH AN ORAL HISTORY interview.

Second, to develop an understanding of the oral history process and the strengths and weakness of this historical methodology in comparison to more traditional historical sources.

PROJECT DESCRIPTION

According to historian Henry Luce, the twentieth century was the "American century." This was a dynamic time in history shaped by the lives and experiences of Americans from different backgrounds who do not receive equal recognition in the history of this period. This project provides students the opportunity to further uncover the American century through interviews with individuals who helped shape or witnessed events or periods that form the American experience. Students are required to interview a nonfamily member about a particular period or event of the American century. The project allows students to probe deeper into a content area of their choosing while at the same time utilizing many of the skills that are evaluated on the AP exam and in college history courses. This project is an extension of our history studies and not a separate entity of the course. Interviewees have ranged from war veterans, civil rights activists, politicians, and restaurant waitresses to survivors of the Great Depression and the Holocaust. The breadth of interview subjects supports the traditional coverage of each period or event, leading to a fuller understanding of American history. In order for students to become excited about history, they must see the relevancy of the past to their own lives. Oral history provides such an opportunity as students go into the "field" and, as oral historian Studs Terkel once said, they uncover the "living repositories of our past."

Historian James Hoopes once said that "every good history course includes work meant to give [students] the experience of doing history. This is often a research paper, and it should be the most interesting, stimulating aspect of the course. Too often, though, it is tedious, not because it is hard work, but because the challenge to human sympathy and imagination is neglected."[1] In the case of this oral history project, a traditional research paper is no longer the final product but rather a necessary stepping-stone from which students go into the field and interact with people who were part of, or possibly even made, history. Unlike most of the work done in conventional history classes in which projects are often developed for an audience of one—the teacher—and are complete after receiving a grade, the rich archives that your project will become a part of are shared with the larger community through the annual Oral History Coffee House and published on the World Wide Web at www.americancenturyproject.org.

Like all historical sources, oral history cannot stand by itself and has its pitfalls. Therefore, this project draws from a wide range of primary and secondary historical sources to ensure not only historical accuracy but also the most complete presentation possible. After selecting and receiving written permission for an interview, students will thoroughly research the history surrounding the period or event in a seven to ten-page research paper using a minimum of eight sources. Students use their research as a basis in formulating open-ended interview questions that not only focus on gaps in the existing literature but also challenge the interviewee to address the complexities surrounding historical events. Each project concludes with analysis of the historical value of the interview, and where it fits into the history of a period or event in American history.

THE AMERICAN CENTURY PROJECT PROCESS AND PRODUCTS

1. You must select an individual—who is not related to you—to interview. Take risks in selecting someone to interview. The interviewee must be cleared by the instructor and must be willing to sign both the release form

and additional materials form, though restrictions can be attached. Inform your interviewee of this requirement immediately.

- Establish date, time, and place of the interview well in advance. You may wish to call and remind the interviewee a few days before you appointment.
- Establish informal banter with your interviewee. You do not want to show up, turn the tape recorder to play, and start taping. The more your interviewee becomes comfortable with you, the better the interview will be.
- Clearly state the purpose of the interview at the beginning and show the interviewee the end result on the project website, www.americancenturyproject.org. Explain why this class is doing the project and all the components of it. You might have to convince him or her of the importance of the story to creating a complete picture of America's past.

2. Your interview must focus on a particular period or event that your interviewee either witnessed or was part of. You are required to broadly research the period or event, using at least seven sources (minimum of four print sources). This research will allow you to develop sophisticated, open-ended questions. Begin developing questions throughout your research. Photographs, speeches, and video can also be helpful in engaging the interviewee.

3. Each interview needs to be recorded either on tape or minidisk or, in certain instances, with a video recorder, and must be conducted in person. The beginning of the tape must include your name, the interviewee's name, the date and location of the interview. The tape must be labeled accordingly. Do this prior to the interview.

4. You are expected to take notes during the interview to serve as reference points when doing your analysis as well as for helping to develop follow-up questions.

5. You are responsible for transcribing the questions you asked and the response of the individual while trying to maintain the tone of the responses. Expect six hours of transcription for each hour of interview.

6. You will analyze the historical value of the interview. What was its value as a historical source? Where does it fit into the existing history, the sources you researched? Can it be useful in better understanding our past?

The final project will be bound and ordered as follows:

Part I: Title page, followed by interview releases.
Part II: Table of contents.
Part III: Statement of purpose of the project and your interview (provide setting, dates, and location).
Part IV: Biography with photo. Introduce the reader to your interviewee by supplying a short (one page) biography. Include a physical description of the interviewee.
Part V: Historical contextualization. You must assume the reader is intelligent but knows nothing about your subject. Therefore, you are responsible for a minimum seven- to ten-page research paper, drawn from a minimum of eight sources (*including newspapers of the day*), that highlights the history surrounding the event or period that the interview covers. It should provide context for better understanding the interview and therefore will need to be revised following the interview.
Part VI: Interview. Transcribed as outlined in class and includes time indexing log.
Part VII: Historical analysis. Possibly the most important aspect of this project because as a historian you must determine the historical value of the interview. Was it biased, glorified? Does the interview shed new light on a particular period or event in America's past? How does it compare with the "traditional" history that you conducted in your historical context?
Part VIII: Photographs, charts, and maps that might clarify responses for the reader can only be used with written permission from the interviewee on the borrowed materials receipt.
Part IX: Works consulted of all sources you used to conduct this project.
Part X: A handwritten thank-you note, which includes the formal invitation to the Oral History Coffee House.
Part XI: Museum exhibition (poster, PowerPoint, web design, theatrical performance, etc.) presented at the annual Oral History Coffee House.
Part XII: Submission of properly labeled disk and tapes.
Part XIII: Baked goods. Each student is required to bake or prepare some food for the annual Oral History Coffee House.

NOTE

1. James Hocpes, "Oral History for Students," in David K. Dunaway and Willia K. Baum, eds., *Oral History: An Interdisciplinary Anthology* (Tennessee: American Association for State and Local History in Cooperation with the Oral History Association, 1984), 349.

Viewing Guide to Nobody's Business

THE PURPOSE IN VIEWING THIS ORAL HISTORY INTERVIEW OF OSCAR BERLINER BY HIS SON, ALAN BERLINER, WHO ALSO produced the film, is to see both the value and challenges associated with oral history as a historical methodology. As you view *Nobody's Business*, keep in mind the following questions.

1. Why do you think Oscar resisted his son's questions?
2. What was the producer's (Alan Berliner) motivation for making this film?
3. What was the most significant event in Oscar's life (were you surprised by his response)?
4. What types of questions were posed by the interviewer (Alan Berliner)?
5. What were some of the challenges faced by the interviewer (Alan Berliner)?
6. What were some of the techniques used by the interviewer (Alan Berliner) to get the interviewee (Oscar Berliner) to talk?
7. What did you learn from watching *Nobody's Business* that you plan to apply to your work as an oral historian?
8. Would you consider this a successful oral history interview? Why or why not?

Standards and Assessments Worksheet (for Educators)

Oral History Process	National Standard	State/Local Standard	Method of Assessment	Resources
Oral history method training				
Interviewee selection				
Preinterview				
Research/content background				
Interview questions		Note: Use chart to justify project with administrators		
Legal/ethical issues		Teachers may want to develop chart on poster board due to size, etc.		
Interview				
Transcription				
Analysis/interpretation				
Products				
Preservation/archiving				

Source: This table was created and used with the permission of Barry A. Lanman, director, Martha Ross Center for Oral History at UMBC, userpages.umbc.edu/~tatarewi/mrc.

Organizational Log (for Educators)

Student Interviewer	Interviewee	Preinterview Release Form	Historical Contextualization	Transcript	Interview Release and Borrowed Materials Receipt	Biography	Analysis	Thank You Note	Museum Exhibition/Public Presentation	Archiving/Preservation
					Due Date					

Materials Tracking Log
(for Students)

Place a check next to each requirement of the project upon its completion.

Student Interviewer: Address:

Interviewee: Telephone:

Name: E-mail:

——— Interviewee contacted   ——— Interview transcribed

——— Preinterview worksheet completed   ——— Interview reviewed by interviewee

——— Interviewee selection approved by teacher ——— Thank-you note written to interviewee

——— Historical contextualization paper   ——— Interview log completed
       submitted
                                              ——— Interview transcription submitted
——— Fifteen Preliminary Questions
                                              ——— Biography and historical analysis paper
——— Preinterview student/teacher conference   completed

——— Interview conducted   ——— Final, bound copy of oral history project
                                                      submitted
——— Picture of interviewee taken or collected
                                              ——— Recording and electronic copy of project
——— Interviewee release form signed   submitted and properly labeled for
                                                      preservation and archiving
——— Borrowed materials release form signed
                                              ——— Museum exhibition completed
——— Recording labeled and saved
                                              ——— Baked goods
——— Backup copy of recording created

Source: Adapted from Judith Moyer, "Interview Tracking Form," in *Step-by-Step Guide to Oral History* (1999), www.dohistory.org.

Preinterview Worksheet

1. Your name: _____

2. The person you intend to interview (full name): _____

3. Interview topic: _____

4. Was the interviewee directly involved in the event or a witness?

   Involved _____   Witness _____

5. Date, time, and location of interview: _____

6. Has the interviewee agreed to sign the release form and be recorded?

   Yes _____   No _____

7. Did you explain the purpose and use of this project?   Yes _____   No _____

8. Has your interviewee been interviewed before?   If yes, on what topic? _____

9. Biographical data of interviewee:

Year and place of birth: _____

Places lived: _____

Married: Yes _____   If yes, what year? _____   No _____

Children: _____

Education: _____

Work experience: _____

Nationality: _____

Interests: _____

---

10. To be completed if interviewing a military veteran:

Branch of service or wartime activity: _____

Battalion, regiment, division, etc.: _____

Highest rank: _____

Drafted or enlisted: Drafted _____   Enlisted _____

Dates of service: _____

Wars in which individual served: _____

Location of military or civilian service: _____

Did the veteran or civilian sustain combat or service-related injuries?   Yes _____   No _____

Medals or special awards: _____

Additional information: Honors/awards, social organizations, political membership, family history, etc.

_____

_____

_____

_____

11. Historical period or event the interview will focus on and what was going on during that period. Be detailed with dates.

_____

_____

_____

_____

12. Why did you choose this interviewee and period of focus?

_____

_____

_____

_____

13. Preliminary works consulted. List a minimum of five print sources you have accessed that will help in your historical contextualization. Use MLA format.

_____

_____

_____

_____

14. Preliminary questions:

_____

_____

_____

_____
Student's signature   date

_____
Instructor's signature   date

Oral History Project
Release Form (Interviewee)

ST. ANDREW'S EPISCOPAL SCHOOL

I, ———————————————————— hereby give and grant to St. Andrew's Episcopal School the
    (interviewee/narrator)
absolute and unqualified right to the use of my oral history memoir conducted by _____
                                                                (student interviewer)
on _____. I understand that the purpose of this project is to collect audio- and videotaped oral
      (date)
histories of firsthand memories of a particular period or event in history as part of the American Century Project.

I understand that these interviews (tapes and transcripts) will be deposited in the St. Andrew's Episcopal
School library and archives for the use by future students, educators, and researchers. Responsibility for
reproduction, distribution, display, and the creation of derivative works will be at the discretion of the librarian,
archivist, and/or project coordinator. I also understand that the tapes and transcripts may be used in public
presentations including, but not limited to, books, audio or video documentaries, slide-tape presentations,
exhibits, articles, public performance, or presentation on the World Wide Web at the project's website,
www.americancenturyproject.org, or successor technologies.

In making this contract, I understand that I am conveying to St. Andrew's Episcopal School library and
archives all legal title and literary property rights that I have or may be deemed to have in my interview as well as
my right, title, and interest in any copyright related to this oral history interview that may be secured under the
laws now or later in force and effect in the United States of America. This gift, however, does not preclude any
use that I myself want to make of the information in these transcripts and recordings.

I herein warrant that I have not assigned or in any manner encumbered or impaired any of the
aforementioned rights in my oral memoir. The only conditions that I place on this unrestricted gift are:

1. _____

2. _____

3. _____

_____

Signature of Interviewee/Donor

_____

Type or Print Name

_____

Address

_____

_____

Date

Oral History Project Release Form (Interviewer)

ST. ANDREW'S EPISCOPAL SCHOOL

I, _____, am a participant in the America Century Project. I understand that the purpose of the American Century Project is to collect audio- and videorecorded oral histories as part of a class project. The documentary materials that include a bound copy of the transcript and supporting materials, interview tapes and recordings, and visual image of my museum exhibition may be deposited in the permanent collections of the St. Andrew's Episcopal School library. The deposited documentary materials will serve as a record of individual experiences and may be used for scholarly and educational purposes. I understand that responsibility for reproduction, distribution, display, and the creation of derivative works will be at the discretion of the librarian, archivist and/or project coordinator. I also understand that the tapes and transcripts may be used in public presentations including, but not limited to, books, audio and video documentaries, PowerPoint presentations, exhibitions, articles, public performance, or presentation on the World Wide Web at the project's website www.americancenturyproject.org or successor technologies.

I herby grant to St. Andrew's Episcopal School and library ownership of the physical property delivered to the library and the right to use the property that is the product of my participation (for example my interview and additional written materials, photographs) as stated above. By giving permission, I understand that I do not give up any copyright or performance rights that I may hold.

I also grant the St. Andrew's Episcopal School library and project coordinator my absolute and irrevocable consent for any photograph(s) provided by me or taken of me in the course of the my participation in the American Century Project to be used, published, and copied by the St. Andrew's Episcopal School library and its assignees in any medium.

I release St. Andrew's Episcopal School and library and project coordinator, its assignees and designees, from any and all claims and demands arising out of or in connection with the use of such recordings, documents, and artifacts, including but not limited to, any claims for defamation, invasion of privacy, or right of publicity.

Accepted and Agreed

_____   _____
Signature of Interviewer/Student   Date

_____
Type or Print Name

_____
_____
_____
Address

_____   _____
Signature of Parent or Guardian (if interviewer is a minor)   Date

_____
Type or Print Name of Parent or Guardian

Borrowed Materials Receipt

ST. ANDREW'S EPISCOPAL SCHOOL

Instructions to the Interviewer:

Additional materials, whether originals or copies, enhance the value of an oral history memoir. Ask the interviewee/lender if you may borrow or keep such materials as personal photographs, newspaper clippings, programs from relevant events, and other mementos. Borrowed materials can be photographed or Xeroxed and then returned. *Make a copy for the interviewee/lender and one copy for yourself.*

Borrowed materials (be specific including condition of materials):

1. _____

2. _____

3. _____

4. _____

5. _____

Conditions for use:

_____

_____

_____

_____

_____

Date for materials return:

Signature of Interviewee/Lender	Signature of Interviewer
Type or Print Name	Type or Print Name
Address	Address
E-mail:	E-mail:
Date	Date

Source: Adapted from McKinley Oral History Project in Pamela Dean, Toby Daspit, and Petra Munro, *Talking Gumbo: A Teacher's Guide to Using Oral History in the Classroom* (Baton Rouge, La.: T. Harry Williams Center for Oral History, 1998), 53.

Interview Reminders

AN ORAL HISTORY INTERVIEW, LIKE A STORY, HAS A BEGINNING, A MIDDLE, AND AN END. AS YOU PREPARE FOR YOUR interview, keep the following steps in mind. Ask yourself what historians living one hundred years from now would want to ask your interviewee if he or she were still alive. As oral historian Donald Ritchie says, "An interview succeeds when the fully engaged interviewer constantly evaluates his interviewee's responses and changes gears." In short, be prepared, be flexible, and be respectful.

1. Have a plan of attack beginning with a careful, logical organization of your fifteen questions, saving the toughest and most sensitive questions for last. Actual recorded interview time should not exceed two hours. Take breaks if necessary and be willing to come back a second or third day. Especially with older interviewees, breaks might be important.

2. Ask open-ended questions. Establish where the interviewee was with respect to the historical period or event being examined: is she a primary source or is she reporting secondhand information? When conducting a project on a particular period, event, or theme, it is important that each interviewee be asked a consistent set of questions for purposes of comparison. Use images in your questioning and quotes from your research. Ask tough, personal questions and be willing to lean into discomfort.

Types of Questions		
Beginning the Interview	*Open-Ended Questions*	*Closed Questions*
• This is _____ and I am interviewing _____ as part of the American Century Oral History Project. The interview took place on _____ at _____.	• Can you tell me about . . . ? • How did you feel about . . . ? • Why did you choose . . . ? • What was a typical day like? • What can you recall about . . . ? • What was it like . . . ? • And then what happened . . . ?	• How many . . . ? • What year . . . ? • Did you like . . . ? • How much . . . ? • When . . . ?
Statement Questions	*Follow-Up Questions*	*Summary Questions (Ending the Interview)*
• What do you think about historian David Halberstam calling the 1950s "a ten-year PTA meeting?" • What can you tell me about this image? • What do you think about Studs Terkel calling World War II "the good war"?	• Silent question • That is interesting, or I didn't know that; can you tell me more? • Can you elaborate on that a bit more?	• Is there anything you wanted to talk about that we didn't get to? • Is there anything that I missed that would help me better understand the subject? • Is there anything I failed to ask you that you think is important for me to know to understand this topic? • Always ask for permission to call if you have further questions.

3. Ask one question at a time. Do not move too quickly to another question; allow for the tactical "silent question" that can lead to further responses. Be prepared to think on your feet by developing follow-up questions to ensure clarity ("can you explain further?"). When you get yes or no responses, ask why or why not?

4. Let the interviewee answer for herself or himself without leading to an answer you expect (i.e., "Didn't you feel sad when Kennedy died?" versus "How did you feel when President Kennedy died?"). Remember your research and perceptions might not parallel those of the interviewee; these differences will be noted in your historical analysis at the project's end. Remember that the purpose of the interview is to find out what that person thinks, not what you think.

5. Listen closely and ask good follow-up questions. In forming new questions, remember that individuals reading your interview may not know what you mean by some terms or references to places and people you and your interviewee might know well. Get interviewee to explain. If another question emerges during an interviewee's response, write it down in order to remember it.

6. Let the interviewee do most of the talking. Interrupt only when the interviewee appears to be going off on a tangent in order to redirect the interview by stating, "Getting back to . . ." Keep in mind that tangents can also lead to new and unsuspecting opportunities.

7. Save controversial questions for the end of the interview, when the interviewee is more comfortable talking with you.

8. Have the release form signed before leaving.

9. Try to transcribe and write up results and notes of the interview as soon as possible after the interview has been completed. Even in rough form, these notes will help you capture the "sense" of what was said, as well as the actual information that was presented.

10. Remember there are only two sides to a tape.

11. Punch out and label tapes following the interview or engage the appropriate switch on a minidisk. (Name of interviewee and interviewer, date and location, project title, institution, and number sequence for each tape.)

12. Remember to maintain good eye contact and concentrated listening. Always remember that the interviewee is sharing his or her life with you.

13. Be flexible with the direction of your interview!

14. Close your interview by leaving room for additional thoughts by your interviewee. An excellent closing question: "Do you have anything you wish to add that we might have missed?"

15. Always end the interview with a spoken thank-you followed by a thank-you note.

Transcribing and Editing Guidelines

- Expect six hours of transcription for every hour of interview depending on the quality of tape and your typing ability.
- Work with a copy of the recording if at all possible. Do not play the master tape.
- In order to protect the recording punch out tabs of each tape or minidisk.
- Listen to the recording for approximately ten to twenty minutes prior to beginning the transcription in order to become familiar with the voices on the tape, patterns of speech, and the questions being asked.
- Create a proper heading for the transcript that includes Interviewee/Narrator, Interviewer, Location of interview, date, and who transcribed the interview if different from the interviewee. If the transcription was edited by the interviewee, that should be noted as well.

Interviewee/Narrator: Grace Whitman

Interviewer: Glenn Whitman

Location: Ms. Whitman's home, Washington, D.C.

Date: April 30, 2004 [date of the interview]

This interview was reviewed and edited by Ms. Whitman

- When formatting the text on the page, use one-inch margins on each side of the paper; number the pages; and double-space the text.
- Identify all speakers at the start of their comments, by typing their full name in bolded letters, followed by a colon with the first questions and than by initials for subsequent questions. If initials are the same, include the middle initial of the interviewee.

Glenn Whitman:

Grace Berdie Whitman:

GW:

GBW:

- Create a verbatim transcript but omit crutch words such as "um" or "ah." Include expressions such as "uh-huh" or "uh-uh" when used to mean "yes" or "no" in response to specific questions.
- Retain the questions posed by the interviewer but pare down rambling questions. Eliminate false starts, fumbling, and superfluous crutch words.
- Do not revise the narrator's words to force them into standard written prose. Leave untouched any sentence fragments, run-on sentences, and incorrect grammar. Commas and dashes may be used to reflect pauses in the spoken words. Correct grammatical errors if they are obviously an error of speech or if the narrator is very sensitive about his or her speech patterns, but aim for the most accurate portrayal of the narrator's speech.
- Preserve chit-chat to indicate the formality or informality of the interview session.
- Leave in repetitions of word, phrases, or stories that show emphasis and/or convey the narrator's feelings and attitudes.
- In order to reflect the tone of the interview, vulgar responses and racial epithets should be retained in the transcript. However, depending on the audience and age of the students involved, educators might consider censoring some of the transcript. Any censorship should be noted in the transcript's heading.
- Scan into the transcript any images you might have used in your questioning.

- Do not use ellipses (. . .) in transcribing oral history interviews because they suggest that material was omitted.
- Nonverbal sounds that occur on tape are noted and enclosed in parentheses. For such notations use no capital letters, unless for proper nouns or proper adjectives, and no ending punctuation. Reserve the use of parentheses for such activity notes. Descriptive terms: (laughs, winks, expression of sorrow). Other examples: (unintelligible); (telephone rings); (truck passing by). When these occur at the end of a sentence or a clause, position them after the punctuation. Avoid editorializing; just put (laughs), not (laughs rudely).
- Note the need for additional information, such as first names, dates, definitions of technical, obsolete, or slang terms. Add information in [square brackets] in the text or as information footnotes at the bottom of the page.
- Enclose in brackets explanations about why the interview was interrupted or why the tape recorder was turned off, for example, [Interview interrupted by a telephone call].
- Place a question mark before and after a word or phrase to indicate any uncertainty about it, e.g., (?destroyed?).
- Indicate the end of a side of the tape in capital letters, for example, END OF SIDE ONE, TAPE ONE; BEGIN SIDE TWO, TAPE ONE.
- Identify garbled or unintelligible portions of the tape. If one word is inaudible, indicate the gap with a ___??. When multiple words are inaudible, insert ___??+.
- Respect the interviewee's right to review and make changes to the transcript, but note such edits in the transcription heading.

Audio/Video Time Indexing Log

1. Interviewer: _____

2. Interviewee: _____

3. Date of interview: _____

4. Location of interview: _____

5. Recording format: _____

Audio Type: Video Type:

Cassette	_____	Cassette	_____
Microcassette	_____	Microcassette	_____
CD	_____	CD	_____
Digital (DAT)	_____	Digital (DAT)	_____

6. In roughly five-minute intervals, summarize interview topics in the order they appear in the recording. Also note the tape number and tape side beginning with Tape 1, Side A.

Minute mark   Topics presented in order of discussion in recording

_____   _____
_____   _____
_____   _____
_____   _____
_____   _____
_____   _____
_____   _____
_____   _____
_____   _____
_____   _____
_____   _____
_____   _____
_____   _____
_____   _____
_____   _____
_____   _____
_____   _____
_____   _____
_____   _____
_____   _____
_____   _____
_____   _____
_____   _____
_____   _____
_____   _____

Historical Contextualization Paper

THE PURPOSE OF THE HISTORICAL CONTEXTUALIZATION RESEARCH PAPER FOR THIS ORAL HISTORY PROJECT IS THREEFOLD: (1) to provide the context in which readers can understand the interview (i.e., what was happening during the time in which the interview covers); (2) to allow the interviewer to become an expert in the period or event their interview will be focusing on; (3) to provide context from which interview questions can be developed both prior to, and during, the interview. *The ability to "think on your feet" during the interview will be enhanced by your thorough understanding of the history.*

The success of any oral history interview depends on how much the interviewer knows about the person, period, or event that the interview focuses on. A failure to thoroughly research your interview period or event will result in an ineffectual interview; it is also disrespectful to the interviewee. Be mindful that your interview selection is sharing his or her life with you, and you have an obligation to come to the interview with a thorough understanding of the history your interview covers. As you research keep in mind Edward Hallet Carr, who once called history "an unending dialogue between the historian and his [or her] facts."

- Like any good historian, you must examine all aspects of a historical period or event. When appropriate, insert your interviewee into the contextualization.
- Considering the "professional" nature of this project, your research should draw from "sophisticated" primary and secondary sources that must include the *experts* in the area you are focusing on (e.g., Stephen Ambrose on World War II, David Halberstam on the 1950s, or John Hope Franklin on race). Make sure that their interpretations are reflected in your contextualization. Your textbook and general encyclopedias should only serve as reference sources.
- In order to understand the broad context of the history you are researching, you are responsible for examining "newspapers of the day" (i.e., *New York Times, Washington Post*) that highlight what was being covered during the period you are studying.
- While the Internet is a valuable resource, it should be used with caution. Make sure you interview each source, questioning its validity.
- As you research, begin to develop possible interview questions as well as collect artifacts that might be useful in your museum exhibition. Throughout your research consider what is missing from the historical record and create questions for your interviewee to help fill in the gaps.
- Any successful research paper requires revision. Keep in mind that you will be revising this historical contextualization following your interview in order to ensure that any new history that emerges out of your interview is reflected in the historical contextualization.

You must include the following sources: four secondary sources (no encyclopedias), two primary documents, and two newspapers or periodicals from the time.

Interview Analysis

AS HISTORIANS YOU ARE CONSTANTLY ANALYZING, INTERPRETING, AND EVALUATING PRIMARY AND SECONDARY SOURCES and what each says about a particular period, event, or individual. Through your oral history interview and transcription you have created a primary source. Your analysis paper focuses on determining the historical value of that interview.

As you prepare the analysis paper, keep in mind that historians must continually evaluate their sources. Thus you must examine the strength and weaknesses of your interview in conjunction with other sources you examined in your historical contextualization paper. Since history is a complex subject, historians must, as E. H. Carr pointed out, evaluate the person who created the source, as well as the sources.

REQUIREMENTS
- Length of paper must be 3–5 pages (double-spaced, typed, 12-point font).
- You are expected to directly quote from your interview to support examples you are trying to make. The proper parenthetical citation would be your interviewee's last name and page number. You also must include your interview in the final works consulted page you create for the entire project as follows:

> Whitman, Glenn. Interviewed by Grace Whitman. 5 January 2004.

- A clear thesis must be established at the end of the introductory paragraph that assesses the historical value of the interview and thus oral history. Like all historians, you must be selective in determining what excerpts from your transcript are most valuable to your analysis.
- Do not forget to address your own, and your interviewee's "unconscious preconceptions."
- You are also allowed to compare research from your historical contextualization with the interview transcript.
- The successful analysis paper is well organized and well structured . . . outline, outline, outline!

STRUCTURE OF THE ANALYSIS PAPER
I. Introductory/thesis paragraph (one page; make sure your interviewee is present by name).

II. What is oral history and how does it compare to more traditional sources of documenting the past (consider Ritchie, Shopes, Carr, Schlesinger, and suggestions for additional reading)?

III. What does your interview say? (Provide a brief summary and focus on those areas you selected as the most important, valuable, or revealing.) Carefully select the major points your interviewee makes (what was important to her) about the period or event you are examining.

IV. What is the historical value of what the interviewee said? How does the interview fit into the whole of history (i.e., the history of the period you examined for your historical contextualization paper)? You must quote from your transcription as well as the sources examined in the historical contextualization paper to support your interpretations.

Consider the following questions:
- What are the strengths of your interview (consider both the content generated by the interviewee and the technique of the interviewee)
- What are some of the weaknesses of your interview (consider both the content generated by the interviewee and the technique of the interviewer; if you made some errors, what would you do next time to ensure a better quality interview?)

V. What have you learned from this process?

QUESTIONS TO CONSIDER AS YOU ANALYZE THE HISTORICAL VALUE OF YOUR INTERVIEW

- How does the transcription reinforce, as well as challenge, the history researched in the historical contextualization paper?
- What does the transcription say about the particular period or event that the interview focuses on (what does the transcript *not* say as well)?
- What new information does the transcript provide about the period or event that was examined?
- What does the interview contribute to our larger understanding of the period or event that was examined?
- How does the individual (your interviewee) fit into the whole of history?
- What is valuable, especially for someone who doesn't read the whole interview?
- What was important to the interviewee and why?
- How much of the interview can be verified by my research? What is the value of that which cannot be verified (using the interview as evidence)?
- What would a paper/project on this period or event look like without this interview?
- Who would be next to interview and why, keeping in mind that one interview, such as this, is a only a snapshot?
- What questions remain and how can they be answered (consider calling the interviewee back)?
- What is the value of oral history and this oral history project (consider how memory is shaped)?
- What did you get out of this experience with oral history, and has it changed you as a historian in any way (identify challenges you faced . . . be honest)?
- Match text from the transcript to the text from a textbook or other source. What is the same and what is different and why?
- What is the value of the interview if it only confirms everything I read in preparing my historical contextualization paper?

Oral History Project
Assessment Rubric (Narrative)

BIOGRAPHY

A Provides a strong sense of the interviewee's background with extended use of dates, details, and anecdotes to provide context. Interviewee's past is clearly established in the context of the interview period and includes a picture of the interviewee. (10 percent)

B Provides a sense of the interviewee's background with limited use of dates, details, and anecdotes to provide context. Interviewee's past is partially established in the context of the interview period. May or may not include a picture of the interviewee. (10 percent)

C Provides an unclear sense of the interviewee's background and does not include dates, details, and anecdotes to provide context. Interviewee's past is not established in the context of the interview period. Does not include a picture of the interviewee. (10 percent)

D Provides no sense of the interviewee's background using dates, details, and anecdotes for context. Interviewee's past is not established in the context of the interview period. Does not include a picture of the interviewee. (10 percent)

HISTORICAL CONTEXTUALIZATION

A Establishes a strong historical background for understanding the interview, drawing evidence from a minimum of eight primary and secondary sources (including "newspapers of the day") and leading historians of the subject in seven to ten pages. Dates are effectively used to ensure historical context, and analysis considers both sides of the historical event or period that the interview covers. Historical contextualization uses limited information intelligently and provides a clear context for understanding the interview. The final draft reflects suggested revisions by the instructor and peer review. (25 percent)

B Historical background for understanding the interview uses some evidence from a minimum of eight primary and secondary sources (including "newspapers of the day") in seven to ten pages. Limited use of dates to ensure historical context and analysis. Considers only one side of the historical event or period that the interview covers. Areas of the contextualization might lack detail for clarity. Contextualization establishes a fairly clear context for understanding the interview. The final draft reflects some of the revisions suggested by the instructor and peer review. (25 percent)

C Establishes a weak background for understanding the interview, drawing little evidence from a minimum of eight sources in seven to ten pages. Dates are used ineffectively or inaccurately for historical context and analysis considers one aspect of the period or event in a general way or both aspects in a superficial way. History provides an ineffective context for understanding the interview. The final draft reflects a limited number of the revisions suggested by the instructor and peer review. (25 percent)

D No historical background for understanding the interview is established. Contextualization does not use any evidence from a minimum of eight sources and falls short of the seven- to ten-page requirement. Exhibits inadequate or inaccurate understanding of the period or event. The final draft reflects few or none of the revisions suggested by the instructor and peer review. (25 percent)

INTERVIEW TRANSCRIPTION

A Minimum of fifteen open-ended questions that reflect thoroughness of research and an ordered plan for conducting the interview. Follow-up questions are utilized to clarify points put forth by the interviewee's responses. Transcription is properly formatted, reflects the tone of response, and includes informational footnotes that clarify ambiguous statements or references. (25 percent)

B   Approximately fifteen open-ended questions that might not reflect thoroughness of research and an ordered plan for conducting the interview. Limited use of follow-up questions to clarify points put forth by the interviewee's response. Transcription has minor transcription errors, might reflect the tone of response, and contains some informational footnotes that clarify ambiguous statements or references. (25 percent)

C   Fewer than fifteen questions that are not open-ended and do not use research. Questions are unorganized and at times do not remain focused on the period or event in question. Follow-up questions to clarify points put forth by the interviewee's responses are inconsistent. Few informational footnotes that clarify ambiguous statements or references are provided and there are a significant number of transcription errors. (25 percent)

D   Fewer than fifteen questions are extended to the interviewee. Questions are not open-ended and not developed to clarify interviewee's response. Questions are posed in an unorganized manner and do not relate to the period or event being examined. Transcription does not reflect the tone of response and contains no informational footnotes that clarify ambiguous statements or references. Major errors in transcription. (25 percent)

ANALYSIS

A   Sophisticated thesis that clearly establishes historical value. Application of historical contextualization in order to assess where the interview fits into the history of the particular period of event. Use of the interview, through quotations, to support interviewer's interpretations. (25 percent)

B   Contains a thesis that establishes historical value. To varied degrees historical contextualization is used in order to assess where the interview fits into the history of the particular period of event. Limited use of the interview, through quotations, to support interviewer's interpretations. (25 percent)

C   Presents a limited, confused, and/or poorly developed thesis assessing historical value. Ineffective application of historical contextualization in order to assess where the interview fits into the history of the particular period of event. Interview, through quotations, is not effectively used to support interviewer's interpretations. (25 percent)

D   Contains no thesis or a thesis that does not address historical value. No or ineffective use of historical contextualization in order to assess where the interview fits into the history of the particular period of event. No or ineffective use of the interview, through quotations, to support interviewer's interpretations. (25 percent)

MECHANICS

A   Keeping in mind that persuasive historical writing requires clarity of prose, the entire project contains minor mechanical errors often limited to typing errors. The project is clearly organized and well written. Every three proofreading errors will result in a grade reduction. (10 percent)

B   Keeping in mind that persuasive historical writing requires clarity of prose, the entire project contains a few errors, such as spelling, punctuation, capitalization, pronoun usage, and word choice. Every three proofreading errors will result in a grade reduction. (10 percent)

C   Keeping in mind that persuasive historical writing requires clarity of prose, the entire project contains major mechanical errors. In varied aspects of the paper, weak organizational and/or writing skills interfere with comprehension. Every three proofreading errors will result in a grade reduction. (10 percent)

D   The entire project is so poorly organized or written that it inhibits understanding. Every three proofreading errors will result in a grade reduction. (10 percent)

TECHNICAL REQUIREMENTS

A   Project contains a title that reflects the subject of the interview and adherence to formatting requirements for project's ordering, page numbers, quotations, and works consulted as outlined by the MLA handbook. (5 percent)

B   Project contains a title that might reflect the subject of the interview. Minor errors adhering to formatting requirements for page numbers, quotations, and works consulted as outlined by the MLA handbook. (5 percent)

C   Project contains a title that does not reflect the subject of the interview. Major errors adhering to formatting requirements for page numbers, quotations, and works consulted as outlined by the MLA handbook. (5 percent)

D   Project contains a title that does not reflect the subject of the interview, major and minor errors adhering to formatting requirements for page numbers, quotations, and works consulted as outlined by the MLA handbook. (5 percent)

MUSEUM EXHIBITION ASSESSMENT

The exhibition can be in the form of one of the following unless otherwise approved by the instructor: poster board, PowerPoint, website, video documentary, one-act play (10 minute limit).

A   Exhibition effectively reflects both the interview and history surrounding a particular period or event. The presentation centers around the experiences of your interviewee and utilizes relevant parts of the interview, as well as selected primary and secondary sources—in addition to photographs or pictures to highlight the interviewee's place in America's past. The exhibition is well organized and clearly written and includes creative means and "artifacts" to convey both the history and interview of a particular period of event.

B   Exhibition reflects both the interview and history surrounding a particular period or event. The presentation is balanced between the experiences of the interviewee and the history of the period through varied use of excerpted parts of the interview and photographs or pictures. Might include the use of more traditional primary and secondary sources. The exhibition is organized but might contain minor mechanical errors.

C   The exhibition is imbalanced between the experiences of the interviewee and the history surrounding a particular period of event. Limited or ineffective use of excerpted portions of the interview. Does not include the use of more traditional primary and secondary sources. Exhibition emphasizes history, not the interviewee's place in history. The exhibition demonstrates little attention to organization or detail and contains mechanical errors that interfere with comprehension.

D   The exhibition does not reflect the subject of the interview and ineffectively examines a particular period or event. No use of excerpted portions of the interview. The exhibition appears done hastily, with no attention to organization and detail while containing major mechanical errors.

Oral History Project
Assessment Rubric (Checklist)

Student Interviewer: _____   Interviewee: _____

Title: _____   Date: _____

	A	B	C	D	F	Comments • Strengths • Areas for Improvement
Biography (10 percent)						
• Is historically accurate						
• Uses dates, details, and anecdotes						
• Places interviewee in historical context						
• Visual (photograph)						
• Maintains length requirements (1 page)						
• Revised final draft						
Historical Contextualization (25 percent)						
• Broad historical background established						
• Creates context for understanding the interview						
• Uses a wide range of primary sources						
• Uses a wide range of secondary sources						
• "Newspapers of the day"						
• Paper length						
• Research is balanced						
• Dates used to establish context						
• Research is historically accurate						
• Maintains length requirement (7–10 pages)						
• Revised final draft						
Interview Transcription (25 percent)						
• Minimum fifteen open-ended questions						
• Question organization						
• Follow-up questions						
• Transcription reflects tone of responses and includes parenthetical notes (smiles, cries, etc).						
• Informational footnotes, or [bracketed] information, to clarify references						
• "Thinking on feet" (ability to create questions based on interviewee's responses)						
• Formatting according to OHA standards						
• Revised final draft						

(continued on next page)

	A	B	C	D	F	Comments • Strengths • Areas for Improvement
Analysis (25 percent)						
• Thesis that establishes historical value of interview						
• In-depth analysis and interpretation						
• Draws conclusions						
• Application of historical contextualization and interview transcription through quotations						
• Revised final draft						
Mechanics (10 percent)						
• Text is clear, grammatical, and spelled correctly. Grade reduction for every three errors.						
• Text is carefully proofread						
Technical Requirements (5 percent)						
• Relevant title with interviewee present						
• Bibliography/works consulted (MLA formatting)						
• Pagination						
• Appendix (relevant materials)						
Museum Exhibition (100 percent)						
Poster board PowerPoint Website Video documentary One-act play (10 minute limit)						
• Exhibit is historically accurate						
• Shows analysis and interpretaztion						
• Places interview in historical context						
• Shows wide research						
• Uses primary sources, including interview						
• Uses secondary sources (where appropriate)						
• Exhibit is clear and organized and has visual impact						
• Text is clear, grammatical, and spelled correctly						
• Exhibit is neatly prepared						
• Includes bibliography or works consulted						

Overall Grade:

Source: Adapted from Teaching Rubrics Created for National History Day, www.nationalhistoryday.org.

Interview Portfolio

THE INTERVIEW PORTFOLIO ALLOWS FOR THE PRODUCTION OF AN ORAL HISTORY PRODUCT ALONG WITH A METHODOLOGY for assessment and grading. The interview portfolio is a suggested accumulation of activities that offer ways in which to assess student accomplishments by providing an alternative to the traditional forms of grading such as tests and quizzes, and so on. It is not expected that all of the suggested items be included in a final portfolio. Conversely, it is intended that the creative teacher will augment the portfolio with items that reflect their specific subject, teaching style, students, capabilities, and goals/outcomes. The interview portfolio is an excellent opportunity for students to select or contract certain sections of the portfolio, thus allowing for student-directed assessment.

In addition, a variety of activities and assignments have been suggested in the interview portfolio that address the strengths of the visual, auditory, and kinesthetic learner, as well as left- and right-brained thinking processes. The theories on multiple intelligence have also been considered.

Depending on your goals/outcomes, a point system and/or letter grade can be assigned to the portfolio areas and items that were agreed on in advance. The teacher should take advantage of every opportunity to have students complete self-assessments along with the process of peer review.

To complete the oral history experience, a final evaluation and assessment are necessary and will guide the teacher back to the planning stages for the next encounter with oral history as an educational methodology.

1. A creative cover reflecting the specific research and overall oral history experience
2. Title page
3. Background information on the research topic and interviewee. Background research notes, outlines, related assignments, and bibliographical references. Background information on the interviewee, including a brief biographical summary.
4. Interview data
   - A 250-word interview abstract (interview summary)
   - A timed index (each 5-minute section of tape summarized)
   - A name index
   - An interview timeline that graphically shows how the interview fits into the overall time period of study
5. An analysis of the research question/research hypothesis
   - State the research question/research hypothesis.
   - In what ways did the interview(s) address the research question?
   - In what ways did the interview(s) not address the interview question?
   - If more than one interview was completed, did the interviewees agree on the major issues? (Explain.)
   - Did the interviewee(s) agree with the other traditional primary and secondary research sources? (Explain.)
   - How does the research demonstrate the following:
   Change
   Cause and effect
   Stability
   Fact versus opinion
   Conflict
   Perceptions/biases

Source: Portfolio used with the permission of Dr. Barry A. Lanman, director, Martha Ross Center for Oral History at UMBC (userpages.umbc .edu/~tatarewi/mrc).

Note: This analysis can be directed toward one or more of the following areas, depending on the research question/research hypothesis.

>Political
>Philosophical
>Economic
>Esthetic
>Social

- What individual(s) had the most impact on the interviewee? (Explain.)
- List three documentary questions that were asked to determine factual reliability of the interviewee. List at least two sources that agree or disagree with the interviewee. What assessments can be made from this analysis?
- Write a short story answering the research question. This narrative should include knowledge gained from the interview as well as research gained from other primary and secondary sources. This document should also contain the overall research conclusions demonstrating original thought.

6. An analysis of the interview process
   - Describe the positive and negative personal dynamics between the interviewer and interviewee.
   - Assess the importance of eye contact, body language, building rapport between the interviewer and interviewee.
   - Assess your control of the interview.
   - Assess the sequence of the your questions. (Were they logical and sequential?)
   - Assess the effectiveness of the questions asked.
   - Assess the objectivity and basis of the interviewee.

7. Personal analysis
   - Keep and submit a journal describing your feelings about the interview process before, during, and after the interview.
   - Explain what you like best about the oral history experience.
   - If you could change one or more things about the oral history experience, what would it (they) be?
   - If you were talking with a student about to begin the oral history experience, what suggestions would you give to that person?
   - Evaluate the strengths and weaknesses of oral history as a research method.
   - Evaluate the importance of oral history as a research method and as a method of instruction.
   - What were the three main things you learned from the oral history experience? (Explain.)

8. Legal agreement and supporting documents
   - A signed legal agreement
   - A photograph of the interviewee
   - Photographs
   - Copies of supporting primary and secondary documents
   - Graphs
   - Maps
   - References

"Experiencing Oral History" Learning Module and Rubric

ORAL HISTORY LEARNING MODULE GOAL

EIGHTH GRADE STUDENTS WILL LEARN THE TECHNIQUES AND VALUE OF ORAL HISTORY THROUGH A SERIES OF ACTIVITIES and projects. Each of the skills involved in collecting and analyzing oral history is scaffolded over a series of 4–5 activities throughout the school year. Each student will begin by collecting and analyzing the personal historical memories of a parent or significant adult. The purpose of this activity is to introduce the student to the interview experience in a familiar environment. The next activity requires each student to interview a peer about a common experience they remember, September 11, 2001. In this activity the use of recording devices is introduced. The interview techniques used during the previous interview are reinforced. The students will also gain experience in transcribing information from the interview. The third activity requires the students to generate a questionnaire, conduct an interview, and write a reflective piece about the experience. The module will conclude with a culminating research activity that shows the student's mastery of how to collect oral history.

DESCRIPTION OF STUDENTS

- Eighth grade students from honors, heterogeneous, and inclusion classes in a predominately white suburban school district

LEARNING OUTCOMES

- Over the course of this learning module students will gain an introductory understanding of what oral history is. They will develop and refine their interviewing skills. Through the interview process they will enhance their communication skills while meeting Social Studies and English Language Arts Standards relevant to the learning module (see table 9.10).
- Through the use of this learning module students will recall, reflect, and share their experiences and memories of September 11, 2001. This module has been constructed so that students will build oral history techniques as the year progresses. Assignments have been scaffolded so that prior learning must always be recalled.
- The culminating project will involve WWII oral history. The students will have to complete a research component, conduct an interview/play the role of interviewee, analyze the transcript, and reflect on their experiences.
- A rubric will be used for the Veterans Day and culminating WWII project.

BACKGROUND

- Historical content and characteristics of groups interviewed in this learning module:
  Personal historical memories
  Students' memories of September 11, 2001
  Memories of veterans from the armed forces
  WWII history

LESSON PLANS

Lesson 1

ANTICIPATORY SET Students will watch a twenty-minute video titled *What Is History?*

ACTIVITY Students will engage in a discussion on what history is, why it is important, and the role of historians. Ask the question, *What is oral history?*

Introduce "What do you remember?" activity by having students interview the teacher.

ASSIGNMENT Students interview parent about their first historical memory.

Students share their findings during class discussion.

Lesson 2

ANTICIPATORY SET Place a poster commemorating the events of September 11, 2001, in the front of the room. Ask students to reflect in a two- to three-minute writing assignment.

ACTIVITY Students are given questionnaire.

Pair the students.

Each student interviews a peer and records the interview.

After the interviews are completed, the recording is played back and notes are taken on the responses.

ASSIGNMENT Put finishing touches on interview notes and be prepared to share findings the next day.

The following day, show a portion of the memorial service and share interview responses with the class.

Lesson 3

ANTICIPATORY SET Play a patriotic song for the students. Ask the students what the song means to them. Guide the discussion toward Veterans Day.

ACTIVITY/ASSIGNMENT Explain the project outline.

Allow students time to brainstorm in teams for potential interview questions.

Individually each student will create a questionnaire and interview a veteran. See project outline for details.

The day before Veterans Day, reflect on interview responses as a group.

Each student will submit the interview, responses, and reflective piece.

Lesson 4

ANTICIPATORY SET The students will watch a clip from the movie *Back to the Future*. This will help them get into the time machine mode.

ACTIVITY/ASSIGNMENT Explain the project outline.

Individually research the person, create a questionnaire, and be able to role-play that person during the Time Machine Day that is scheduled.

Remembering Those Who Have Served

Goal: Each student will collect the oral history of a veteran of the armed forces.

Steps:

1. Find a subject.
    a. Use a member of your family who has served or is currently serving in the armed forces.
    b. On October _____ visiting veterans will be available for interviews after school.
2. Create a questionnaire using previous oral history assignments and the brainstorm session held during class.
3. Conduct your interview.
    a. If possible, use a recording device during the interview.
    b. Follow the interview techniques practiced in the previous oral history assignments.
4. Notes should be taken after each question and brought to class on November 3 for sharing.
5. Write a reflection of the interview based on your notes and experience, using the guiding questions provided. This should be a minimum of one page.

Due Dates:
Friday, October 24: Assignment given during class.
Monday, October 27: Brainstorm questions for questionnaire in teams during class.
October 27–November 2: Conduct your interview.
Monday, November 3: Bring in interview questions with notes from interview.
Friday, November 7: Reflective writing assignment, questions, and notes due.
Tuesday, November 11: Observe Veterans Day.

Questions for the Questionnaire:

• Each questionnaire should contain at least ten questions.
• The first four or five questions can be basic background information (i.e., name, date of birth, branch of military, time they served, reasons for entering the military).

- The remaining five or six questions should focus on their experiences and feelings about their military service.
- Remember to use past oral history assignments for help in creating questions.
- A good oral history website to reference when creating questions is www.stg.brown.edu/projects/WWII_ Women/tocCS.html.
- Leave an appropriate amount of space after each question to record notes.

Guidelines for the Reflective Piece:

- It should be a minimum of one and a half pages.
- Preferably typed and double-spaced.
- Your reflective piece should read like a story.
- Please use the following guidelines for your reflective piece:
  One paragraph should include basic information such as who, what, when, where, and why.
  One paragraph should describe a personal experience given by the interviewee.
  One paragraph should include your thoughts on what it means to celebrate Veterans Day.

Format for the Final Copy:

- On the due date, November 8, 2003, you will be expected to turn in a copy of the questionnaire, notes on the interview, and the reflective piece.
- All of these should be placed in the manila folder provided.
- The cover of the folder should be decorated with drawings, magazine/newspaper clippings, and/or copies of pictures, which relate to the subject or Veterans Day.

Parent Signature: _____

Remembering Those Who Have Served: Rubric or Grading Sheet				
Category	1	2	3	4
Questionnaire	Ten questions, typed	Nine questions	Eight questions	Fewer than eight questions
Notes	❖ Legible ❖ Detailed as possible	❖ Legible ❖ Notes could have been more detailed	❖ Barely legible ❖ Notes were of poor quality	❖ Barely legible ❖ Notes were taken sporadically
Typed Reflection	❖ 1½ pages ❖ Typed ❖ Follows guidelines	❖ 1 page ❖ Typed ❖ Followed most of the guidelines, but lacked detail	❖ Less than one page ❖ Lacked details about the interview	❖ Less than one page ❖ Unorganized summary that did not follow guidelines
Deadline	Turned in on time	Submitted after class or one day late (Phone call home if late!)	Two days late	Three days late
Cover	Creative, colorful cover that reflects the goal of the project	Creative, colorful cover that vaguely follows goal of the project	Cover was submitted, without color or creativity and did not capture the goal of the project	Cover was submitted, but was barely legible and did not capture the goal of the project

Source: This material was used with permission from Elizabeth Hoffman and Michael Barker, Johanna Perrin Middle School, Fairport, New York.

Oral History Coffee House Invitation

The Student Oral Historian and the Democratization of History:
Preserving the Voices of the American Century

PARENTS AND FRIENDS OF THE SAINT ANDREW'S COMMUNITY ARE INVITED TO:
The 7th Annual Oral History Coffee House
Sponsored by the Advanced Placement United States
History & America in the Twentieth Century World Classes
Monday, March 1, 2004 @ 7:00pm
Saint Andrew's Episcopal School, MacDonald Hall
Guest Speaker: Donald A. Ritchie, author of *Doing Oral History*

Doing history at St. Andrew's has taken on an all-new meaning for students. Since November, students have been conducting an oral history project which breaks the mold of textbook-centered learning, as students go into the "field" and, as oral historian Studs Terkel once said, uncover the "living repositories of our past."

This coffee house will not only celebrate the work of each student, but also recognize the history they have uncovered. Students will read excerpted portions of their projects, while many of those interviewed will also be on hand to share their stories with you. Museum exhibitions and student work will be displayed throughout the evening including PowerPoint and website presentations. Gain a new perspective on the American Century from student interviews of World War II, Korean, Vietnam, and Cold War veterans, civil rights leaders, student protestors, survivors of the Great Depression and Holocaust, women who challenged the "feminine mystique," and immigrants who pursued the American Dream. Visit the project's website at www.americancenturyproject.org.

PLEASE JOIN US!
For further information contact Glenn Whitman at Saint Andrew's Episcopal School
301.983.5200 (x322) or gwhitman@saes.org
Saint Andrew's Episcopal School is located at 8804 Postoak Road, Potomac, Maryland

Oral History Coffee
House Newspaper Invitation

ST. ANDREW'S EPISCOPAL SCHOOL

Dear _____:

I am writing to invite you to a unique educational event that the *Potomac Gazette* should consider covering for the benefit of its readers. The Seventh Annual Oral History Coffee House is taking place at St. Andrew's Episcopal School in Potomac, Maryland, on Monday, March 1, 2004, beginning at 7:00 P.M. The keynote speaker for the evening will be Donald A. Ritchie, author of *Doing Oral History*.

Since November, students have been going into the surrounding area and, as oral historian Studs Terkel once said, "uncovering the living repositories of our past." Students have researched, analyzed, and interviewed individuals about a particular period or event in their past. Since the project's inception ten years ago, interviewees have included New Jersey Governor Christine Todd Whitman, former chairman of the Joint Chiefs of Staff John Shalikashvili, and civil rights activist Amiri Baraka. This year, students have interviewed congressman and civil rights leader John L. Lewis, adviser to Lyndon Johnson Jack Valenti, and Jack Steadman, an eyewitness to the attack on Pearl Harbor. A good portion of those interviewed come from the Potomac area. By disclosing the stories of these individuals, students gain a better understanding of the "American century" from those who are often omitted from the history texts.

This project is not only unique among high school students in this area, but throughout the country. The Oral History Association recognized this project with the Precollegiate Oral History Teaching Award.

At the coffee house, students will read excerpted portions of their projects while many of those interviewed will be on hand to share their stories with you. Museum-type exhibitions and student work will be on display throughout the evening. More information about the project and coffee house is available at the project's website, www.americancenturyproject.org.

I hope your paper will consider covering this event. The evening celebrates the experiences of those interviewed while providing a model for not only what students are capable of doing when challenged, but also what type of history work students throughout the area should be doing. In the end, I believe coverage of this event will encourage other educators to begin providing students with similar opportunities to "do history."

If you have any questions, feel free to contact me at St. Andrew's or at home. Covering this event is an important opportunity to share with the community what is possible when students are empowered with the responsibility to preserve history. Directions to the event are provided on the reverse. It would be wonderful to have a representative from the *Potomac Gazette* there.

Sincerely,
Glenn Whitman
Project Coordinator

Sources and Resources for Oral History

WHAT FOLLOWS ARE RESOURCES THAT EDUCATORS HAVE found most useful in addition to those listed throughout the book. Please note that URLs may change and material is sometimes removed from the World Wide Web.

ORAL HISTORY WORKSHOPS

Advanced Oral History Summer Institute, Regional Oral History Office, University of California, Berkeley. bancroft.berkeley.edu/ROHO.

Columbia University Oral History Research Office, Summer Institute on Oral History. www.columbia.edu/cu/lweb/indiv/oral/index.html. (212) 854-7083.

Foxfire Museum and Center. www.foxfire.org.

Oral History Training Institute. Sponsored by the Ohio Humanities Council, the Ohio Association of Historical Societies and Museums, the Ohio Historical Society, and the Rural Life Center at Kenyon College. www.ohiohumanities.org/his_institute/his_institute.htm. (800) 858-6878.

The Oral History Workshop led by Charles Morrissey, former president of the Oral History Association. (802) 828-8764. www.tui.edu/prospective/lifelong/conferences/oral/default.asp?strLink=Bb.6.4.5.

Oral History Workshop on the Web. Baylor University Institute for Oral History, P.O. Box 97271, Waco, TX 76798-7271. www3.baylor.edu/Oral_History/Workshop.htm9.

Portland State University Oral History Workshop led by Charles Morrisey. www.summer.pdx.edu.

Virginia Folklife Program. Oral History Workshop. www.virginia.edu/vfh/vfp/program_history.php.

WORKSHOPS AVAILABLE THROUGH NATIONAL, REGIONAL, AND STATE ORAL HISTORY AND RELATED ASSOCIATIONS

American Association for State and Local History. 1717 Church Street Nashville, TN 37203-2991. (615) 320-3203. www.aaslh.org.

American Folklife Center Library of Congress. 101 Independence Ave., SE, Washington, DC 20540. lcweb.loc.gov/folklife/.

Canadian Oral History Association. www.ncf.carleton.ca/oral-history.

Consortium of Oral History Educators (COHE). P.O. Box 24, Ellicott City, MD 21041. (410) 744-5565. COHELanman@aol.com. www.geocities.com/aohelanman.

International Oral History Association. Alexander Von Plato, secretary. Fernuniversität Hagen Leibigstr. 11 D-58511 Ludenscheid, Germany. www.ioha.fgv.br.

Martha Ross Center for Oral History at the University of Maryland, Baltimore County. userpages.umbc.edu/~tatarewi/mrc.

Michigan Oral History Association. 5580 West State Road, Lansing, Michigan, 48906. (517) 321-1746. www.h-net.msu.edu/~moha.

National Council on Public History. 327 Cavanaugh Hall-IUPUI, 425 University Boulevard, Indianapolis, IN 46202. (317) 274-2716. ncph.org.

New England Association for Oral History. www.ucc.uconn.edu/~cohadm01/neaoh.html.

Northwest Oral History Association. C/o Idaho State Historical Society, 450 North Fourth Road, Boise, ID 83702. www.ohs.org/collections/oralhistory/NOHA.cfm.

Oral History Association. Dickinson College, P.O. Box 1773, Carlisle, PA 17013. (717) 245-1036. OHA@dickinson.edu. omega.dickinson.edu/organizations/oha.

Oral History Association of Australia. cwpp.slq.qld.gov.au/ohaa.

Oral History Association of Minnesota. www.oham.org.

Oral History in the Mid-Atlantic Region (OHMAR). 4041 Fragile Sail Way, Ellicott City, MD 21042-5017.www.ohmar.org.

Oral History Society. c/o Department of History, Essex University, Colchester C04 3SQ, United Kingdom. Telephone 020 7412 7405. www.oralhistory.org.uk.

Southern Oral History Program. www.sohp.org/index.html.

Southwest Oral History Association. soha.fullerton.edu/Default.htm.

Texas Oral History Association. P.O. Box 97271, Waco, TX 76798-7271. (254) 710-3437. www3.baylor.edu/TOHA.

ORAL HISTORY AS AN EDUCATIONAL METHODOLOGY

Brooks, Michael. "'Long, Long Ago': Recipe for a Middle School Oral History Program." *OAH Magazine of History*, Spring 1997, 32.

Brown, Cynthia Stokes. *Like It Was: A Complete Guide to Writing Oral History*. New York: Teachers & Writers Collaborative, 1988.

Carter, Jeff. "History and Technology: Using Today's Tools to Help Students Access, Analyze, and Make History." *Cable in the Classroom*, November 2002, 13.

Clegg, Luther B., et al. "Creating Oral History Projects for the Social Studies Classroom." *Social Studies Review* 32 (1992): 53–60.

Dean, Pamela, Toby Daspit, and Petra Munro. *Talking Gumbo: An Oral History Manual for Secondary School Teachers.* Baton Rouge: Louisiana State University, 1996. A companion to *You've Got to Hear This Story*, a thirty-minute how-to video for conducting oral history interviews. Available through the Williams Center for Oral History.

Gillis, C. *The Community as a Classroom: Integrating School and Community through Language Arts.* Portsmouth, N.H.: Boynton/Cook. 1992.

Hamer, Lynne. "Oralized History: History Teachers as Oral History Tellers." *Oral History Review*, Summer–Fall 2000, 19–39.

Hill, Margaret. "Oral History Research: Internet Resources and Reports." *Social Education* 65, no. 1 (2001): 4–6.

Hoopes, James. *Oral History: An Introduction for Students.* Chapel Hill: University of North Carolina Press, 1979.

Hudson, Larry E., Jr., and Ellen Durrigan Santora. "Oral History: An Inclusive Highway to the Past. *History Teacher*, February 2003, 206–20.

Huerta, Grace C., and Leslie A. Flemmer. "Using Student-Generated Oral History Research in the Secondary Classroom." *Clearing House* 74, no. 2 (2000): 105–10.

Jennings, Judy. "My Mama Told Me: Reclaiming the Story in Oral History." *History Teacher* 30 (1996): 89–95.

K'Meyer, Tracey E. "'It's Not Just Common Sense': A Blueprint for Teaching Oral History." *Oral History Review*, Summer–Fall 1998, 37–38.

Lanman, Barry A. "Oral History as an Educational Tool for Teaching Immigration and Black History in American High Schools: Findings and Queries." *International Journal of Oral History*, June 1987, 122–35.

———."The Use of Oral History in the Classroom: A Comparative Analysis of the 1974 and 1987 Oral History Association Surveys." *Oral History Review*, Spring 1989, 215–26.

Lanman, Barry A., and George L. Mehaffy. *Oral History in the Secondary School Classroom.* Pamphlet no. 2. Los Angeles: Oral History Association, 1989.

Lee, Charles R., and Kathryn L. Nasstrom. "Practice and Pedagogy: Oral History in the Classroom." *Oral History Review*, Summer–Fall, 1998, 1–7.

Mehaffy, George L., Thad Sitton, and O. L. Davis, Jr. *Oral History in the Classroom. How to Do It.* Series 2, no. 8. Washington, D.C.: National Council for the Social Studies, 1979.

Neuenschwander, John A. *Oral History as a Teaching Approach.* Washington, D.C.: National Education Association, 1976.

Olmedo, Irma M. "Junior Historians: Doing Oral History with ESL and Bilingual Students." *TESOL Journal*, Summer 1993. www.ncela.gwu.edu/miscpubs/tesol/tesoljournal/juniorhi.htm.

"Oral History." *OAH Magazine of History*, Spring 1997.

Oral History Project for Adult Education Classes. New Bedford Division of Adult/Continuing Education, 455 County Street, New Bedford, MA 02740. literacytech.worlded.org/docs/oralhist/ma2a.htm.

Payne, Emily M., and Barbara G. Lyman. "Family and Community Oral History." *Reading Improvement* 31 (1994): 221–23.

Ritchie, Donald A. "Teaching the Cold War through Oral History." *Organization of American Historians Magazine of History*, Winter 1994. www.oah.org/pubs/magazine/coldwar/ritchie.html.

Roy, Loriene. "Planning an Oral History Project." *Journal of Youth Services in Libraries* 6 (1993): 409–13.

Sitton, Thad, et al. *Oral History: A Guide for Teachers (and Others).* Austin: University of Texas Press, 1983.

Steinberg, Stephen. "The World inside the Classroom: Using Oral History to Explore Racial and Ethnic Diversity." *Social Studies* 84 (1993): 71–73.

"Tell Us How It Was: Students Interview Their Elders." *What Kids Can Do: Student Work Oral Histories.* www.whatkidscando.org/oralhistories.html.

"Using Oral History: Lesson Overview." Library of Congress American Memory. memory.loc.gov/ammem/ndlpedu/lessons/oralhist/ohhome.html.

"Voices of Experience: Oral History in the Classroom." *Magazine of History*, Spring 1997, 23–31.

Whitman, Glenn. "Teaching Students How to Be Historians: An Oral History Project for the Pre-collegiate Classroom." *History Teacher*, Fall 2000, 469–81.

Wigginton, Eliot, ed. *The Foxfire Book.* Garden City, N.Y.: Doubleday, 1972.

———. *The Foxfire Book: Hog Dressing, Log Cabin Building, Mountain Crafts and Foods, Planting by the Signs, Snake Lore, Hunting Tales, Faith Healing, Moon* (Garden City, N.Y.: Anchor Books/Doubleday, 1972).

———. *Sometimes a Shining Moment: The Foxfire Experience.* Garden City, N.Y.: Doubleday, 1985.

Wigginton, Eliot, and Christopher Crawford. "Foxfire and the Educational Mainstream." In Rebecca Sharpless and David Stricklin, eds., *The Past Meets the Present: Essays on Oral History*, 101–18. Lanham, Md.: University Press of America, 1988. Available at Baylor University's Institute for Oral History's Workshop on the Web. www3.baylor.edu/Oral_History/Workshop.htm.

Wood, Linda. *Oral History Projects in the Classroom.* Pennsylvania: Oral History Association, 2001; and companion video *History from the Living: The Organization and Craft of Oral History.* Newport, R.I.: Grin Productions, 1998. 17 minutes. Available from J. Long Grin Productions, 6 Carey Street, Newport, RI 02804.

ORAL HISTORY AS A HISTORICAL METHODOLOGY

Allen, Barbara, and William L. Montell. *From Memory to History: Using Oral Sources in Local Historical Research.*

Nashville: American Association for State and Local History, 1981.

Baum, Willa K. *Oral History for the Local Historical Society.* Nashville: American Association for State and Local History, 1987.

———. *Transcribing and Editing Oral History.* Nashville: American Association for State and Local History, 1977.

Berliner, Alan. *Nobody's Business.* Directed by Alan Berliner. Milestone Films, 1996. 60 minutes.

Bogart, Barbara Allen. *Using Oral History in Museums.* American Association for State and Local History (AASLH) Technical Leaflet no. 191. *History News,* Autumn 1995.

Dunaway, David K., and Willa J. Baum, eds. *Oral History: An Interdisciplinary Anthology.* 2d ed. Nashville: American Association for State and Local History, 1997.

Everett, Stephen E. *Oral History: Techniques and Procedures.* Washington, D.C.: Center of Military History United States Army, 1992.

A Field Notebook for Oral History. Boise: Idaho Oral History Center, 1997.

Frank, Benis M. *A Do-It-Yourself Oral History Primer.* Washington, D.C.: History and Museums Division Headquarters, United States Marine Corps, 1982. www.au.af .mil/au/awc/awcgate/oralusmc.htm.

Frisch, Michael. *A Shared Authority: Essays on the Craft and Meaning of Oral History and Public History.* Albany: State University of New York Press, 1990.

Georges, Robert A., and Michael Owen Jones. *People Studying People: The Human Element in Fieldwork.* Berkeley: University of California Press, 1980.

Gluck, Sherna Berger, Donald A. Ritchie, and Bret Eynon. "Reflections on Oral History in the New Millennium: Roundtable Comments." *Oral History Review,* Summer–Fall, 1999, 1–27.

Green, Anna. "Returning History to the Community: Oral History in a Museum Setting." *Oral History Review,* Winter 1997, 53–67.

Grele, Ronald J., ed. *Envelopes of Sound: The Art of Oral History.* 2d ed. New York: Praeger, 1991.

Hardy, Charles, III, and Alessandro Portelli. "I Can Almost See the Lights of Home: A Field Trip to Harlan County, Kentucky." *Journal for MultiMedia History* 2 (1999). www .albany.edu/jmmh/vol2no1/lightsportelli.html.

Herstory: An Oral History Handbook for Collecting Military Women's Stories. Women's Memorial Foundation. www.womensmemorial.org/historyandcollections/ oralhistorysplash.html.

Hirsch, Jerrold. *A Cultural History of the Federal Writers' Project.* Chapel Hill: University of North Carolina Press, 2003.

Ives, Edward D. *An Oral Historian's Work: Oral History Instructional Videotape.* Blue Hill Falls, Maine: Northeast Historic Film, 1987. 33 minutes, color. Distributed by Northeast Historic Film, P.O. Box 900, Bucksport, ME 04416.

———. *The Tape Recorded Interview: A Manual for Fieldworkers in Folklore and Oral History.* Knoxville: University of Tennessee Press, 1995.

Kyvig, David, and Myron Marty. *Nearby History.* 3d ed. Walnut Creek, Calif.: AltaMira, 2000.

McMahan, Eva, and Kim Lacy Rogers, eds. *Interactive Oral History Interviewing.* Hillsdale, N.J.: Erlbaum, 1994.

Mercier, Laurie, and Madeline Buckendorf. *Using Oral History in Community History Projects.* Pamphlet no. 4. Los Angeles: Oral History Association, 1992.

Moyer, Judith. *A Step-by-Step Guide to Oral History.* 1993. www.dohistory.org/on_your_own/toolkit/oralHistory .html.

Neuenschwander, John N. *Oral History and the Law.* 3d ed. Carlisle, Pennsylvania: Oral History, 2002.

Oral History Association. *Evaluation Guidelines.* omega .dickinson.edu/organizations/oha.

Perdue, Thesda. *Nations Remembered: An Oral History of the Five Civilized Tribes, 1865–1907.* Westport, Conn.: Greenwood, 1980.

Perks, Robert, and Alistair Thomson, eds. *The Oral History Reader.* New York: Routledge, 1998.

Portelli, Alessandro. *The Battle of Valle Giulia: Oral History and the Art of Dialogue.* Madison: University of Wisconsin Press, 1997.

———. *The Death of Luigi Trastulli and Other Stories: Form and Meaning in Oral History.* Albany: State University of New York Press, 1991.

———. *The Order Has Been Carried Out: History, Memory, and Meaning of a Nazi Massacre in Rome.* New York: Palgrave Macmillan, 2003.

Ritchie, Donald A. *Doing Oral History.* 2d ed. London: Oxford University Press, 2003.

Rosenzweig, Roy, and David Thelen. *The Presence of the Past: Popular Uses of History in American Life.* New York: Columbia University Press, 1998.

Sheridan, Thomas E. "How to Tell the Story of a 'People without History.'" *Journal of the Southwest,* Summer 1988, 168–89.

Shopes, Linda. "Making Sense of Oral History." History Matters: The U.S. Survey on the Web. historymatters .gmu.edu/mse/oral.

Slim, Hugo, and Paul Thompson. *Listening for a Change: Oral Testimony and Community Development.* Philadelphia: New Society, 1995.

Sommer, Barbara W., and Mary Kay Quinlan. *The Oral History Manual.* Walnut Creek, Calif.: AltaMira, 2002.

Stricklin, David, and Rebecca Sharpless, eds. *The Past Meets the Present: Essays on Oral History.* Lanham, Md.: University Press of America, 1988.

Suquamish Oral History Project. *A Guide for Oral History in the Native American Community.* 3d ed. Suquamish: Suquamish Tribal Cultural Center, 2000.

Terkel, Studs. *My American Century.* New York: New Press, 1997.

"Thinking about Doing Oral History? Here's How." Women in Military Service for America Memorial Foundation, Inc. www.womensmemorial.org/historyandcollections/oralhistorysplash.html.

Thompson, Paul. *The Voice of the Past: Oral History*. 3d ed. London: Oxford University Press, 1988.

Truesdell, Barbara. "Oral History Techniques: How to Organize and Conduct Oral History Interviews." Indiana University Oral History Research Center. 1999. www.indiana.edu/~cshm/techniques.html.

United States Holocaust Museum. "Oral History Interview Guidelines." www.ushmm.org/archives/oralhist.pdf.

Woodward, C. Vann. "History from Slave Sources." *American Historical Review*, April 1974, 470–81.

Yow, Valerie. "'Do I Like Them Too Much?' Effects of the Oral History Interview on the Interviewer and Vice-Versa." *Oral History Review*, Summer 1997, 55–79.

———. *Recording Oral History: A Practical Guide for Social Scientists*. Beverly Hills, Calif.: Sage 1994.

PRECOLLEGIATE ORAL HISTORY PROJECTS

Anand, Bernadette, Michelle Fine, David S. Surrey, and Tiffany Perkins. *Keeping the Struggle Alive: Studying Desegregation in Our Town; A Guide to Doing Oral History*. New York: Teachers College Press, 2002.

Bland County History Archives. www.bland.k12.va.us/bland/rocky/gap.html. Maintained by the students of Rocky Gap High School (Rocky Gap, Virginia).

Brody, Barry, and Alan J. Singer. "Franklin K. Lane High School Oral History Project and History Magazine." *OAH Magazine of History* 4 (1990): 7–9.

Countdown to Millennium: An Oral History Collection Project. frognet.net/countdown.

D.C. Everest Area Schools: Oral History Program. www.dce.k12.wi.us/srhigh/socialstudies/histday.

Foxfire. www.foxfire.org.

Gulledge, Judy H., and Christine A. Capaci. *Pennywinkle: Oral Histories from Tylerton, Smith Island in the Chesapeake Bay*. Norfolk, Va.: Letto Gooch, 1999.

Hudson Falls High School World War II Living History Project. www.hfcsd.org/ww2.

Llanogrande Center's Oral History Project. www.llanogrande.org.

Loudoun Valley High School (Partners with Library of Congress) Veterans Oral History Project. www.loudoun.k12.va.us/schools/lvhs.

Montana Heritage Project. www.edheritage.org.

Mooresville High School (Mooresville, Indiana). We Made Do: Recalling the Great Depression. ipad.mcsc.k12.in.us/mhs/social/madedo.

North Coast California Rural Challenge Network Oral History Project. www.ncrn/org/projects/av/av_vov.html.

Reston Reflections Oral History Archive: The Langston Hughes Middle School Project (Reston, Virginia). www.gmu.edu/library/specialcollections/pcaoral.html.

Stones of Service. www.stones-of-service.org.

Tell Me Your Story: An Oral History Curriculum for High School and Middle Schools Involving Students with their Families and Community. tellmeyourstories.com/index.htm.

Telling Their Stories: Oral History of the Holocaust. www.tellingstories.org.

Wayland High School History Project. www.whshistoryproject.org.

The Whole World Was Watching: An Oral History of 1968. www.stg.brown.edu/projects/1968.

POSTSECONDARY AND PROFESSIONAL ORAL HISTORY PROGRAMS AND PROJECTS

ACTUP Oral History Project. www.actuporalhistory.org.

BRATS: Growing Up Military. www.tckworld.com/thebratsfilm/project.html.

Civil Rights Documentation Project: University of Southern Mississippi. www-dept.usm.edu/%7Emcrohb/index.html.

Civil Rights Oral History Interviews. Washington State University Manuscripts, Archives, and Special Collections. www.wsulibs.wsu.edu/holland/masc/xcivilrights.html.

The History Makers. www.thehistorymakers.com.

Indiana University Center for the Study of History and Memory. www.indiana.edu/~cshm.

Martha Ross Center for Oral History. userpages.umbc.edu/~tatarewi/mrc.

National Visionary Leadership Project. www.visionaryproject.com/home3.html.

Oral History Project: How Can You Help Preserve the Record of the Vietnam War? www.vietnam.ttu.edu/oralhistory/general/about.htm.

Oral History Project Online. alexanderstreet2.com/oralhist.

Oral History Project of the World War Two Years. people.csp.edu/saylor/OHP/OHPhomepage.htm.

Oral History on Space, Science, and Technology. www.nasm.si.edu/nasm/dsh/oralhistory.html.

Rosie the Riveter Project. www.ford.com/go/rosie.

Rutgers University World War II Oral History Archives. http://fas-history.rutgers.edu/oralhistory/orlhom.htm.

South Dakota Oral History Center: Institute of American Indian Studies. www.usd.edu/iais/oralhist.cfm.

Southern Oral History Program: UNC Chapel Hill. sohp.org.

Studs Terkel: Conversations with America. Chicago Historical Society. www.studsterkel.org/index.html.

Suffragists Oral History Project. sunsite.berkeley.edu:2020/dynaweb/teiproj/oh/suffragists.

T. Harry William Center for Oral History at Louisiana State University. www.lib.lsu.edu/special/williams.

Talking History: Aural History Productions. www.talkinghistory.org.

UCLA Oral History Program. www.library.ucla.edu/libraries/special/ohp/ohpindex.htm.

Unchained Memories: Readings from the Slave Narratives. www.time.com/time/classroom/unchained.

United States Senate Oral History Program. Conducted by Donald Ritchie. www.senate.gov/pagelayout/history/g_three_sections_with_teasers/oralhistory.htm.

University of New South Wales Archives. www.oralhistory.unsw.edu.au.

Utah State University: Theatre Arts Oral History Program. www.usu.edu/oralhist/oh.html.

Veterans History Project. A Project of the American Folklife Center at the Library of Congress. www.loc.gov/folklife/vets.

Vietnam: The Never Ending War. San Mateo Middle College. pages.prodigy.net/meng25/mchs.

Virtual Oral/Aural History Archive (VOAHA). www.csulb.edu/voaha.

Voices from the Thirties: Life Histories from the Federal Writers' Project. memory.loc.gov/ammem/wpaintro/exhome.html.

Washington Press Club Foundation Oral History Project: Women in Journalism. npc.press.org/wpforal/ohhome.htm.

Wieder, Alan. "White Teachers/White Schools: Oral Histories from the Struggle against Apartheid." *Multicultural Education*, Summer 2003, 26–31.

"Witness to a Jewish Century." Centropa: Jewish Heritage and Central and Eastern Europe. www.centropa.org/mainpage/main.asp.

EDUCATIONAL METHODOLOGY AND ASSESSMENT

Allan, E. Yarema. "A Decade of Debate: Improving Content and Interest in History Education." *History Teacher*, May 2002, 391.

Armstrong, Thomas. *Multiple Intelligences in the Classroom.* Arlington, Va.: Association for Supervision and Curriculum Development, 1994.

Becker, Carl. "Everyman His Own Historian." *American Historical Review* 37 (1931): 221–36.

Bloom, Benjamin S. *Taxonomy of Educational Objectives: The Classification of Educational Goals.* New York, 1956.

Combs, Barbara, and Christy Stevens with Linda Koch. *Considering Assessment and Evaluation: A Foxfire Teacher Reader.* 2d ed. Mountain City, Georgia: Foxfire Fund, 1999.

Drake, Frederick D. "Using Alternative Assessment to Improve the Teaching and Learning of History." *ERIC Digest,* June 1997. www.ericfacility.net/ericdigests/ed412170.html.

Drake, Frederick D., and Lawrence W. McBride. "Reinvigorating the Teaching of History through Alternative Assessment." *History Teacher,* February 1997, 145–73.

Expectations of Excellence: Curriculum Standards for Social Studies. National Council for the Social Studies. Maryland: National Council for the Social Studies, 1994.

Gagnon, Paul, ed., and the Bradley Commission on History in Schools. *Historical Literacy: The Case for History in American Education.* New York: Macmillan, 1989.

Gardner, Howard. *Multiple Intelligences: The Theory in Practice.* New York: Basic, 1993.

Goleman, Daniel. *Emotional Intelligence: Why It Can Matter More Than IQ.* New York: Bantam, 1997.

Hoerr, Thomas R. *Becoming a Multiple Intelligences School.* Alexandria, Va.: Association for Supervision and Curriculum Development, 2000.

Kennedy, David. "The Art of the Tale: Story-Telling and History Teaching." *History Teacher,* May 1998, 319–30.

Loewen, James. *Lies My History Teacher Told Me.* New York: Touchstone, 1996.

Nash, Gary, Charlotte Crabtree, and Ross E. Dunn. *History on Trial: Culture Wars and the Teaching of the Past.* New York: Knopf, 1997.

National Council for the Social Studies. *Expectations of Excellence: Curriculum Standards for Social Studies.* Maryland: National Council for the Social Studies, 1994.

National Standards for History: Basic Edition. National Center for History in the Schools, 1996. www.sscnet.ucla.edu/nchs/standards.

Nystrom, Elsa A. "Remembrance of Things Past: Service Leaning Opportunities in U.S. History." *Oral History Review,* Summer_Fall 2002, 61–62.

Shaw, Bruce. "Dickens and the Competency-Based School." *Education Week* on the Web, December 6, 2000. www.edweek.org.

Wiggins, Grant. *Educative Assessment: Designing Assessments to Inform and Improve Student Performance.* San Francisco: Jossey-Bass, 1998.

Wiggins, Grant, and Jay McTighe. *Understanding by Design.* Alexandria, Va.: Association for Supervision and Curriculum Development, 1998.

Wineburg, Sam. *Historical Thinking and Other Unnatural Acts: Charting the Future of Teaching the Past.* Philadelphia: Temple University Press, 2001.

Woodward, Katherine S., ed. *Alignment of National and State Standards: A Report by the GED Testing Service.* Washington, D.C.: GED Testing Service, 1999.

Index

Page numbers in *italics* refer to figures or tables.

About the Author

Glenn Whitman is currently History Department chairman at St. Andrew's Episcopal School in Potomac, Maryland. He has been using oral history as an educational methodology with students at three independent schools since 1991. In 1997 his work with students was recognized with the Oral History Association's Precollegiate Teaching Award. Whitman has been active in regional and national oral history activities for many years. He has served as an at-large board member for Oral History in the Mid-Atlantic Region and presented at the Oral History Association's annual conference. In addition to sharing his work with oral historians and educators through conferences and workshops, Whitman wrote "Teaching Students How to Be Historians: An Oral History Project for the Pre-collegiate Classroom," *History Teacher*, Fall 2000. Whitman currently resides in Potomac, Maryland, with his wife and daughter.